The Social Thought
of Erving Goffman

Social Thinkers Series

Series Editor
A. Javier Treviño
Wheaton College, Norton, MA

Published
The Social Thought of Georg Simmel
By Horst J. Helle

The Social Thought of Karl Marx
By Justin P. Holt

The Social Thought of Erving Goffman
By Michael Hviid Jacobsen and Søren Kristiansen

The Social Thought of Émile Durkheim
By Alexander Riley

The Social Thought of C. Wright Mills
By A. Javier Treviño

Forthcoming
The Social Thought of Talcott Parsons
By Helmut Staubmann

The Social Thought of Erving Goffman

Michael Hviid Jacobsen

Aalborg University

Søren Kristiansen

Aalborg University

Los Angeles | London | New Delhi
Singapore | Washington DC

Los Angeles | London | New Delhi
Singapore | Washington DC

FOR INFORMATION:

SAGE Publications, Inc.
2455 Teller Road
Thousand Oaks, California 91320
E-mail: order@sagepub.com

SAGE Publications Ltd.
1 Oliver's Yard
55 City Road
London EC1Y 1SP
United Kingdom

SAGE Publications India Pvt. Ltd.
B 1/I 1 Mohan Cooperative Industrial Area
Mathura Road, New Delhi 110 044
India

SAGE Publications Asia-Pacific Pte. Ltd.
3 Church Street
#10-04 Samsung Hub
Singapore 049483

Copyright © 2015 by SAGE Publications, Inc.

Printed in the United States of America.

Library of Congress Cataloging-in-Publication Data

Jacobsen, Michael Hviid, 1971–

The social thought of Erving Goffman / Michael Hviid Jacobsen, Aalborg University, Soren Kristiansen, Aalborg University.

pages cm.—(Social thinkers series)
Includes bibliographical references and index.

ISBN 978-1-4129-9803-1 (pbk. : alk. paper)

1. Goffman, Erving. 2. Sociology—Philosophy. I. Kristiansen, Søren, 1971– II. Title.

HM479.G64J33 2015
301.01—dc23   2014014577

This book is printed on acid-free paper.

Acquisitions Editor: Jeff Lasser
Editorial Assistant: Nick Pachelli
Production Editor: David C. Felts
Copy Editor: Kim Husband
Typesetter: C&M Digitals (P) Ltd.
Proofreader: Lawrence W. Baker
Indexer: Will Ragsdale
Cover Designer: Gail Buschman
Marketing Manager: Erica DeLuca

14 15 16 17 18 10 9 8 7 6 5 4 3 2 1

Contents

Series Editor's Foreword

The SAGE Social Thinkers series is dedicated to making available compact, reader-friendly paperbacks that examine the thought of major figures from within and beyond sociology. The books in this series provide concise introductions to the work, life, and influences of the most prominent social thinkers. Written in accessible and provocative prose, these books are designed for advanced undergraduate and graduate students of sociology, politics, economics, and social philosophy, as well as for scholars and socially curious general readers.

The first few volumes in the series are devoted to the "classical" thinkers—Karl Marx, Emile Durkheim, Max Weber, Georg Simmel, George Hebert Mead, Talcott Parsons, and C. Wright Mills—who, through their seminal writings, laid the foundation for much of current social thought. Subsequent books will feature more "contemporary" scholars as well as those not yet adequately represented in the canon: Jane Addams, Charlotte Perkins Gilman, Harold Garfinkel, Norbert Elias, Jean Baudrillard, and Pierre Bourdieu. Particular attention is paid to those aspects of the social thinker's personal background and intellectual influences that most impacted his or her approach in better understanding individuals and society.

Consistent with SAGE's distinguished track record of publishing high-quality textbooks in sociology, the carefully assembled volumes in the Social Thinkers series are authored by respected scholars committed to disseminating the discipline's rich heritage of social thought and to helping students comprehend key concepts. The information offered in these books will be invaluable for making sense of the complexities of contemporary social life and various issues that have become central concerns of the human condition: inequality, social order, social control, deviance, the social self, rationality, reflexivity, and so on.

These books in the series can be used as self-contained volumes or in conjunction with textbooks in sociological theory. Each volume concludes with a Further Readings chapter intended to facilitate additional study and research. As a collection, the Social Thinkers series will stand as a testament to the robustness of contemporary social thought. Our hope is that these books on the great social thinkers will give students a deeper understanding of modern and postmodern Western social thought and encourage them to engage in sociological dialogue.

Premised on Newton's aphorism, "If I have seen farther, it is by standing on the shoulders of giants" (an aphorism, incidentally, that was introduced into sociology by Robert K. Merton, himself a towering figure in the discipline), the Social Thinkers series aims to place its readers on the shoulders of the giants of 19th- and 20th-century social thought.

Acknowledgments

I n this volume of the SAGE Social Thinkers series, we are proud to present the work of one of the key sociologists of the 20th century, namely Erving Goffman. His work has intrigued and inspired new generations of sociologists and students within neighboring disciplines such as anthropology, psychology, criminology, media studies, behavioral sciences, and philosophy to take seriously what people say and do in ordinary, everyday encounters.

We want to extend our gratitude to A. Javier Treviño for inviting us along on this exciting project and for his competent suggestions for revisions of the manuscript. Some of the material used in this book is revised, expanded, and updated from a Danish introductory book to the work of Erving Goffman titled *Erving Goffman—sociologien om det elementære livs sociale former* [*Erving Goffman—The Sociology of the Social Forms of Elementary Life*] published by Hans Reitzels Publishing House of Copenhagen in 2002. We are grateful for their permission to publish revised and translated parts of this book in this volume, thereby making it accessible to an English-speaking audience. We also want to extend our gratitude to Kirsten Gammelgaard for assistance in translating some extracts from this Danish volume. Moreover, we are grateful to Routledge of London—the publisher of *The Contemporary Goffman* (edited by Michael Hviid Jacobsen in 2010)—in which an earlier version of Chapter 4 appeared and from which the introductions to certain ideas and points have been extracted.

Michael Hviid Jacobsen
Søren Kristiansen
Aalborg, autumn 2013

Introduction

This book serves as an invitation and introduction to the sociology of Erving Goffman. Because he is one of the most prominent social thinkers in postwar sociology, Goffman's work has continued to influence scholars in various fields and has also attracted many readers outside conventional academia. Goffman's overall research agenda was the exploration of what he termed "the interaction order"—that is, the microsocial order that regulates the comingling of people in each other's immediate presence. Throughout his career, Goffman coined several neologisms (face-work, impression management, role distance, civil inattention, etc.) with which to grasp and understand the complexities and basic social restructuring of everyday life, and many of these are now considered standard sociology vocabulary. This book gives a thorough and systematic account of the foundations of and core elements in Erving Goffman's unique approach to the study of face-to-face behavior in everyday life. Moreover, it demonstrates how his work has inspired the theory building of later generations of sociologists and social theorists as well as numerous empirical studies in various social domains.

Erving Goffman is a curious character in the discipline of sociology. On the one hand, his writings remain some of the most widely read, discussed, dissected, analyzed, and applied. On the other hand, Goffman's work still seems as if it never really became an integral part of the mainstream of the discipline, as he deliberately shunned any association with the major schools of thought of his time. Goffman thus never embraced the discipline of sociology as an elevated discipline deserving of any unreserved loyalty and despite his surprise election as president of the American Sociological Association—a position he, due to advanced illness, was unable to fulfill—he remained at the outskirts of the main theoretical concerns and methodological preoccupations of most of his contemporaries. Indeed, Erving Goffman *was* different. His research interests, his compelling way of writing, his unconventional methods, his teasing conceptual suggestions, and his playful yet shy persona all contribute to the strange aura around him as an outsider. Throughout his career, Goffman consciously sat astride the academic barriers intended to keep disciplines and modes of thought apart and, in his writing, bridged different domains.

Although this book is titled *The Social Thought of Erving Goffman*, Erving Goffman's contribution to "social thought" or "social theory" is a matter of some debate. In truth, the development of "social theory" as such was not his main concern. By "social theory" we often envision something approximating a comprehensive, systematic, abstract, unfolded, and detailed description of how a certain segment (or the whole) of society looks like with its own explanatory laws, iron-clad conceptual apparatus, methodological implications, critical diagnoses of the times, and so on. This was certainly not Goffman's ambition. Although he did in fact develop a comprehensive arsenal of useful and poignant concepts aimed at describing intricate details about microsociological aspects of social life, he never ventured into proposing a "grand theory" as such of society. He was much more content with and engaged in providing the discipline of sociology with a much-needed understanding of why the minutiae of social life deserved conceptual clarification and analytical attention.

Erving Goffman—as we shall show later in this book—is therefore difficult to label or pigeonhole. Lingering somewhere between empirical observations and theoretical exposé, his work remains at odds with most conventional social theory books. In fact, most of his books bore titles or subtitles (such as "microstudies," "reports," "essays," or "notes") indicating that they were more to be regarded as sketches or works in progress than as systematic or comprehensive accounts to be taken all too seriously. After his death, it has been discussed whether Goffman should be regarded as a major contributor to the discipline of sociology and whether his contribution in any way warrants a label as a systematic sociologist. Renowned sociologist Anthony Giddens insisted that "Goffman would not ordinarily be ranked among the major social theorists" (Giddens, 1988, p. 250). Although Goffman did perhaps not as such contribute to the systematic development of the discipline of sociology, his work, as Eliot Friedson contended, nevertheless "lives and will live not as a contribution to the development of systematic sociological theory but rather as a contribution to human consciousness" (Friedson, 1983, p. 361). At the end of the day, Goffman himself was probably also rather unconcerned with whether his contribution to the discipline was regarded as systematic or not, theory or otherwise. According to him, sociologists, like himself, were all in the last instance just "elegant bullshitters" (Lofland, 1984, p. 21).

Although Erving Goffman passed away much too early in 1982, his work lives on and very much remains alive and kicking in contemporary sociology and related disciplines. In fact, in recent years, there has been a torrential revival of interest in his work, at times almost amounting to "Goffmania" (see Jacobsen, 2010a). Several edited books dealing with Goffman's work have been published throughout the last decades; numerous academic articles keep using, discussing, and updating his ideas; his perspective is being taught in social science departments around the world; and a multitude of scholars and students are attracted to the continuous vitality and relevance of his work, which all testify to the fact that Goffman, in many ways, is still among us.

Outline of the Book

This book is intended as an introduction to the work of Erving Goffman—an introduction providing a comprehensive rather than detailed and exegetical account of Goffman's writings and locating these within a wider sociological context. The book is to some extent constructed in a chronological fashion through which we in the initial chapters look at the concerns of the early Goffman and locate him within the sociological tradition of his time. In later chapters, we concern ourselves with the later Goffman's writings and show how his work inspired new generations of sociologists.

Chapter 1 delineates the main contours of Goffman's personal and professional biography. It covers his early sociological training in the late 1930s and early 1940s, his fieldwork experiences at the Shetlands, through which he earned his PhD, and his appointments at the University of California, Berkeley, and later at the University of Pennsylvania and his presidency of the American Sociological Association. Along with a few details of Goffman's private biography, some of the well-known tales from academia are also reported in this chapter. The chapter concludes that Goffman's thinking was heavily influenced by the intellectual milieu at the University of Chicago, where he received the main part of his sociological training.

Besides being inspired by the academic environment at the University of Chicago, Goffman was also influenced by several classical thinkers. One way to understand a thinker is to contextualize and locate his writings within the tradition of sociology. In Chapter 2, we read, as it were, Goffman "backward," looking for sources of inspiration and discussing how his own ideas evolved and matured as a result of his debt to a range of sociological predecessors. The chapter shows Goffman's debt to earlier giants in sociology. From Georg Simmel he gathered his interest in social forms as well as the molecular processes of social life. From Émile Durkheim, Goffman adopted the concept of ritual, which he used to shed light on the affirmation of the self and the moral dimension in interactions of daily life. From George Herbert Mead, he gained an interest in the symbolic communication between people. Goffman also found stimulation in existentialism's conception of the absurd nature of modern life as well as in ethology (especially the idea of the development of personal territories).

In Chapter 3 we turn to Goffman's methodology and methods. Although Goffman is considered as one of the most important sociologists in the postwar era, his research methods were not always standard. Aside from practicing "traditional" ethnography and participant observation in various social settings, he also invented his own methodology, which has been termed "metaphorical spiraling" or "metaphorical redescription." In exploring the interaction order and how people, via face-to-face interactions, reconstruct the social structure, Goffman made use of various metaphors by which he analyzed everyday life behaviors. Goffman proposed that viewing face-to-face behavior as a ritual or as a theatrical performance allowed new understandings of our social life to emerge. This chapter provides an overview of the various methods and techniques that can be detected in Goffman's sociology.

Chapter 4 delineates and discusses Goffman in relation to the wide branch of sociology known as "everyday life sociology." It is demonstrated how Goffman shares certain features with the everyday life tradition and also how he practiced his own special type of everyday life sociology. The chapter shows how Goffman, through a series of studies of behavior in public places and the use of various interaction rituals, was concerned with the order and structure that permeates people's daily and mundane interaction.

Apart from studying the normality of everyday life interaction, Goffman also spearheaded an interest in understanding the social nature of deviance. Throughout parts of his writings, Goffman paid close attention to the intricate nature of labeling and stigmatization, and he conducted research into the social life of mental hospitals as a way to demonstrate how the so-called "deviants" are treated in society and how they make sense of an incarcerated life. Chapter 5 recaptures Goffman's view of the "underworld" of normality and his studies of deviance and institutionalization.

A core theme in Goffman's sociology is the social nature of the self. For Goffman, the self is the result of the negotiating process unfolding between a performer presenting a face and an audience receiving and reacting to this presentation of self. This conception of the self primarily unfolds throughout his dramaturgical analysis of face-to-face behavior and his use of ritual terminology. Chapter 6 concludes, along with several other interpretations, that Goffman's social or interactional understanding of the self may be seen as a precursor for the postmodern idea of the self.

Throughout the latter parts of his career, Goffman began to lay the groundwork for some new areas of interest, which are the focal point of Chapter 7. For example, Goffman developed the idea of "frame analysis" as a way to understand how people make sense of the world. Moreover, he analyzed not only nonverbal interaction but increasingly also took an interest in verbal communication and its specific rules and sequences. Finally, he took a keen interest in how gender was performed—how people "do" their gender. In many ways, Goffman's later work anticipated much of what later took place in phenomenology, ethnomethodology, and gender studies. This chapter provides an overview of Goffman's latest writings.

Just as Chapter 2 proposed to read Goffman "backward" in order to backtrack his own sources of inspiration and his intellectual heritage, Chapter 8 proposes to read Goffman "forward" in order to see who Goffman's work has inspired. In the chapter, we will look specifically at Goffman's influence on a host of international social thinkers, including Anthony Giddens, Michel Foucault, Nicklas Luhmann, Zygmunt Bauman, Pierre Bourdieu, the ethnomethodologists, the sociology of emotions, and the work of Randall Collins and Jonathan H. Turner.

Chapter 9 explores and recapitulates the wider impact and bearing of Goffman's thinking. Some examples from contemporary social research are presented that illustrate Goffman's continued relevance to social research. The chapter is concluded by a summary of Goffman's legacy and a prognosis of how Goffman's work may be used in the years to come.

The book ends with a chapter on suggested readings in which we demonstrate and discuss relevant material for those who wish to become further acquainted with the secondary literature on Erving Goffman.

Each chapter is concluded with a set of questions aimed at making the reader reflect upon the content of the chapter. However, the answer to each question might not be found directly within the individual chapters but will also require the reader to look elsewhere in the book or even consult Erving Goffman's own writings for answers. At the end of the book, we have also provided a glossary of some of the most central concepts from Goffman's writings. Moreover, we have compiled a complete bibliography of Goffman's own writings placed at the end of the book.

1

The Life and Times of Erving Goffman

E rving Goffman was undoubtedly one of the most significant, inspirational, and original sociologists on the post–World War II academic scene in the United States. Although at the beginning of his career it seemed unlikely that Goffman would succeed and eventually end up as an internationally renowned and recognized social thinker, he gradually—despite his continuous status as an outsider compared to the major paradigms of his time—grew into one of the finest stalwarts of postwar sociology whose ideas and perspective inspired ever new generations to take an interest in the microsociological aspects of social life. As one commentator once observed about the particular impact of Goffman's work: "Once you have been spellbound by his studies of the structure of events, you are never quite the same" (Ledger, 1982, p. 36). This was a sensation felt and shared by many, which has contributed to Erving Goffman's lasting relevance to and attraction within sociology.

Setting the Sociological Scene

At the time when Canadian sociologist and social anthropologist Erving Goffman (1922–1982) began to practice and publish sociology in the post–World War II years, American society and sociology increasingly found themselves in stagnant waters. It was a postwar period in which society was being rebuilt and during which sociology increasingly became Americanized.

It was also a time of self-complacency and social optimism due to booming industrial development, high employment rates, increased consumerism, and the export of American culture as symbolizing everything good in the world. Obviously, in such a society any detour from the norm was regarded with suspicion. The same was the situation for sociology—the "coming crisis of sociology," which Alvin W. Gouldner (1970) later anticipated, was still far away. The—at the time almost uncontested—work of American structural-functionalist sociologist Talcott Parsons on the American family—which, among other things, insisted on the functional necessity of separate gender roles and the socialization of children—may serve as a prime example of the 1950s reactionary American society and sociology (see, e.g., Parsons & Bales, 1955). Such self-complacent periods in time are normally not conducive for innovative or creative thinking. The academic waters were stale and the paradigms frozen. This is also why Goffman in many ways was an anachronism, a bombshell in a peaceful atmosphere, a wild cat among the pigeons. But we need to move a bit back in time to understand why Goffman's appearance on the sociology stage caused such a stir.

During the 1920s, sociology increasingly consolidated its presence on the American continent, although as early as the mid-19th century there were visible signs and indications of the development of an actual sociology department, which officially took place in 1892 when the University of Chicago established the first ever sociology department (Matthews, 1977). From around the early 1920s, sociology had become an integral part of the educational setup in several universities. Meanwhile, the discipline had gradually abandoned some of the most obvious political connotations that characterized the first pioneering period. For a considerable period of time, however, American sociology was divided between the so-called **Chicago School** and the Harvard School (Ritzer, 1992). Whereas the so-called Chicago School (particularly epitomized by the renowned Department of Social Science Research) served as the center of sociological research during the 1920s and 1930s, the Harvard School, especially after World War II, claimed the position as the powerhouse of sociology. Whereas the Harvard School (in close association with sociologists at Columbia University such as Robert S. Lynd, Robert MacIver, and most prominently Robert K. Merton) primarily nurtured the perspective of structural-functionalism with its focus on general social theory, causal argumentation, abstract model building, and a preference for quantitative methods, the Chicago School, on the contrary, nourished a much more inductive, qualitative and micro-oriented strand of sociology. As Ruth Shonle Cavan once observed, contrary to the large-scale survey research or theoretically abstract model building conducted by sociologists at Harvard and Columbia, the Chicago School sociologist "concentrated on collecting facts, grouping them under concepts, and/or identifying relationships among them. These facts, concepts, and relationships might be compared to building blocks; the construction of theories was to come later" (Cavan, 1983, p. 416). Names such as Robert E. Park, William I. Thomas, Florian Znaniecki, George Herbert Mead, and Everett C. Hughes all represented this type of sociological approach and mentality in which, for example, human ecology, urban studies, and research on immigration, deviance, and crime were trademarks (Jørgensen & Smith, 2008). Inspired by this intellectual environment, Goffman began to shape his own theoretical and methodological ideas. A key component in the Chicago School methodology toolbox was the use of "participant observation" techniques in order to get access particularly to hidden, shady, or inaccessible areas of social life as well as to observe in an unnoticed manner the multitude of everyday doings and dealings between people. This strategy also inspired Goffman's own empirical studies of an island community and casino gamblers as well as inmates in a mental hospital (Goffman, 1953a, 1961). The Chicago sociologists undertook conceptual development and theory construction, especially within specific areas of research in which available knowledge was either sparse or empirically unsubstantiated. Also, this trademark characterized many of Goffman's writings (Goffman, 1959, 1961, 1963), and he thus belonged to and was a significant figure in the so-called Second Chicago School or the New Chicagoans alongside, among others, Howard S. Becker and many of the symbolic interactionists (Ford, 1975, p. 157).

As mentioned, opposite the Chicago School—although it was more a strand of or perspective on sociological research than an actual paradigmatic school—stood the Harvard School and its structural-functionalism, which in almost any possible respect represented ideas that were theoretically and methodologically directly at odds with those of the Chicago sociologists. The "softer," qualitative, or more impressionistic perspective of the Chicago School was in postwar America increasingly coming under pressure due to the demand for advanced statistical analyses, formalized theoretical development, and more comprehensive and sophisticated sociological studies (Bulmer, 1984). Simultaneously, an envious attitude toward the agelong domination of the Chicago School gradually developed, which meant that some of the key representatives either retired or moved elsewhere, and their disappearance contributed to the downfall of the Chicago School. Coupled with the gradual rise of structural-functionalism at Harvard with prominent names such as Talcott Parsons, Robert K. Merton, Kingsley Davis, and Wilbert Moore (Coser, 1976), the domination of the Chicago School was thus, at least for a longer spell of time, broken, and its monopoly, in the apt words of Norbert Wiley, "came down like a giant oak tree" (Wiley, 1979, p. 63). It was in

Goffman's formative years as a sociologist that the Harvard School—together with Columbia University in New York and the Ivy League universities of New England—formed the so-called orthodox consensus in sociology privileging functional analysis, survey methods, positivistic methodology, behaviorist images of man, and modernization theories (Giddens, 1976). It was against this backdrop—the closest the preparadigmatic social sciences have perhaps ever come to an actual paradigmatic situation (Kjørup, 1985)—that Erving Goffman gradually began to make an impact.

Enter Goffman: Biography and Perspective

Erving Goffman was not an ordinary social scientist. His perspective was neither representative nor prototypical of the branch of science—sociology—within which he produced several notable pieces of work about different yet interrelated aspects of the social world. Although he specialized in studying the all-too-ordinary dimensions of social life, Goffman was by no means himself ordinary—he was, for all practical intents and purposes, atypical. At least on the surface, he was not a politically engaged scholar as so many others from his generation were but maintained a distanced perspective on his discipline as well as on the world he studied. Goffman's sociology, which according to himself could hardly be considered as proper sociology, could not be categorized as belonging to a particular school of thought, paradigm, or research tradition. It was rather a hybrid of various influences—scientific and nonscientific—that were otherwise often depicted as incommensurable and mutually excluding. Although he turned his back on time-honored traditions and schools of thought, Goffman gained widespread respect and recognition for his original perspective and his thought-provoking books, many of which were bestsellers in campus bookstores (Elkind, 1975, p. 25).

Contrary to many sociologists who were preoccupied with studying economic and productive forces, religion, historical transformation, social stratification, voting behavior, or other macrosocial phenomena, Goffman was interested in uncovering the mundane, often quite trivial and everyday character of society—the elementary forms of social life, as it were. By the time he started writing, studying such topics was largely unrecognized and definitely viewed as counterproductive in terms of positive career promotion. To Goffman, however, what to others seemed scientifically irrelevant deserved scientific scrutiny. He was neither an eminent methodologist nor a traditional theoretician, but he was successful in combining theory and method into a unique form of sociological practice with a unique focus that had not quite been seen before.

After these initial remarks on who and what Erving Goffman *was not*, let us turn to some facts and observations about Goffman's life and perspective. It is no secret that the development of intellectual ideas is not an activity that can easily be separated from the rest of a thinker's biographical background or life experiences. Ideas are necessarily surrounded and shaped by personal, historical, and social conditions. However, information regarding Goffman's biography is rather sparse, one of the main reasons being that he was not himself very informative about his childhood or early years. As French sociologist Yves Winkin—one of the few who have been able to excavate and gather material about Goffman's early life—once stated on the main reasons for this lack of biographical information:

> Goffman never wrote about his own life. . . . He did not reveal very much about his life, his youth, his family or his past experiences to either his colleagues or friends. Many of them had vague notions about him, but these were usually associated with the multiplicity of anecdotes about Goffman as a personage rather than with his actual social and intellectual trajectory. (Winkin, 1999, p. 19)

Paradoxically, Goffman—who made a career and reputation of teasing out intimate details about other people's deeds and doings—zealously guarded his own private life, as journalist Marshall Ledger (1982) concluded after his encounter with Goffman in the early 1980s. Goffman was in many respects a shy man. As Marshall Berman once observed:

> Wherever [Goffman] has been, he has been virtually anonymous. He has taken no part in political or cultural affairs. He does not speak at conferences or appear on talk shows. He almost never allows himself to be photographed. . . . In his books, as in his life, he projects a persona of utter impersonality. (Berman, 1972/2000, p. 267)

Goffman was, in Dmitri Shalin's (2010) apt words, "averse to self-revelation," and according to a feature article in *The Times Higher Education* from 1980, "the world's most widely read contemporary sociologist is a recluse who has shunned public interviews for seven years" (David, 1980, p. 7). Compared to the often highly detailed bibliographical material available about the lives of other key social thinkers, the information about Goffman's life can thus almost be boiled down to the mere essentials. But let us look at what is known.

Although frequently but nevertheless misleadingly referred to as an American sociologist, Erving Goffman was in fact Canadian—born in Manville, Alberta, into a Ukrainian Jewish family on June 11, 1922. Ian Hacking (2004, p. 289) informs us that Erving was the son of Max Goffman, who served as a Jewish conscript in the Russian Army, later to desert and immigrate from Novokrainka to Winnipeg together with almost a quarter of a million other Ukrainians who arrived in Canada in the early decades of the 20th century to seek out a new life. There is little mention of Erving's mother Anne in biographical descriptions, but together with Max she started a small tailoring business. Together with his sister Frances Bay—who later became a famous actress in film and television dramas—Erving grew up in the Winnipeg area, where he attended St. Johns Technical School and quickly showed his skills in gymnastics and chemistry (Winkin, 2010). Goffman's childhood was different from that of most of his classmates. Being part of an immigrant culture, he quickly found out how it felt to be different from the rest. As Goffman once recalled in one of his very few comments about his childhood: "You forget that I grew up (with Yiddish) in a town where to speak another language was to be suspect of being homosexual" (Hymes, 1984, p. 628).

After graduation in 1939, Goffman moved on to the University of Manitoba to do his major. Initially, Erving did not have any interest in sociology, his primary subject being chemistry. However, upon a chance meeting with sociologist Dennis Wrong during a stay in the early 1940s at the National Film Board in Ottawa, he switched his interest to sociology. This led him—without ever completing his science degree—to move to the University of Toronto to complete his undergraduate degree. Here he encountered social scientists encouraging especially an interest in cultural anthropology as well as bodily communication such as C. W. M. Hart and Ray L. Birdwhistell. Goffman graduated with a degree in sociology in 1945, and after an encounter with fellow Canadian sociologist Everett C. Hughes, he decided to move to the prestigious University of Chicago to write his PhD thesis under the supervision of W. Lloyd Warner, who was to become famous for his extensive studies spanning several years of "Yankee City." Goffman's master's thesis, which was directed by the work of Warner and William E. Henry, consisted of an exploration of the relationship between class and personality measured via visual influence (termed "depicted experience"; Goffman, 1949), although his focus shifted several times during the completion of the thesis due to problems with the intended research design (Smith, 2003, 2006, pp. 16–18). Apart from Hughes and Warner, Goffman in Chicago got in touch with some of the other stalwarts of sociology (and especially qualitative interactionist sociology) at that time such as Herbert Blumer, Anselm L. Strauss, and Louis Wirth and also got to know some of the up-and-coming names such as Howard S. Becker, Joseph A. Gusfield, Robert Habenstein, and Fred Davis. Apparently, Warner expected of Goffman that he would conduct fieldwork for his thesis (in a style similar to

Warner's own work) and recommended him to the University of Edinburgh. The fieldwork for Goffman's PhD thesis—which turned out differently than what Warner might have expected (Platt, 1995, p. 100)—was thus conducted in the small village of Baltasound at the Shetland Island of Unst, where he stayed for an extended period of one and a half years to do in-depth ethnographic observations of the everyday lives of the islanders. Goffman wrote up the thesis in Paris and received his PhD from the University of Chicago for his to this date still officially unpublished thesis *Communication Conduct in an Island Community* (Goffman, 1953b). His first published academic works during the period of completing his thesis were articles on class status, on how to "cool the mark out," and a report on the service station dealer.

After obtaining his PhD, Goffman enjoyed a brief spell as research assistant to famous sociologist Edward A. Shils before serving as an assistant to the athletic director at the National Institute of Mental Health in Bethesda, Maryland. During this three-year period Goffman began to establish himself as a sociologist and conducted his much-publicized fieldwork at the mental institution of St. Elizabeth's, later to be published in *Asylums* (1961). His first book to appear on the market, however, was *The Presentation of Self in Everyday Life* (1959; first edition published in 1956), which consisted of insights and ideas from his PhD thesis inscribed within a dramaturgical metaphorical imagery. Prior to the publication of the book, Goffman was in 1958 personally hired by Blumer to teach at the University of California, Berkeley, where he ended up staying for a decade, first serving as a visiting professor and from 1962 as a full professor. This proved to be a highly productive period and established Goffman as one of the most promising sociologists of his generation. In 1961, he received the American Sociological Association's MacIver Award for *The Presentation of Self in Everyday Life*, which was acknowledged as "a brilliant analytical essay on interaction among persons" (Oromaner, 1980, p. 288). From the early 1960s, a stream of books authored by Goffman began to appear dealing with everyday life encounters and the multitude of routines and rituals governing contacts between strangers in public and private spaces. After a short sabbatical stay at Harvard in the mid-1960s, Goffman resigned the position at Berkeley in 1968 and decided to take on a position at the—compared to Berkeley—less prestigious University of Pennsylvania, which proved to be his final academic destination. Here he was offered a well-paid position—according to himself the highest paid for any sociology professor in the United States—as the Benjamin Franklin Chair of Anthropology and Psychology. It was during these years that the general public also came to know a little of Goffman's work due to a feature article in *Time Magazine* that labeled him "one of the most illuminating—and disturbing—cartographers of that shadowy terrain where man plays at being a social animal without fully understanding exactly what he is doing" (*Time Magazine*, 1969, p. 50). In 1969, he became a fellow of the American Academy of Arts and Sciences. During this time, his last works also began to be published, usually with a few years of interval—*Strategic Interaction* in 1969, *Frame Analysis* in 1974, *Gender Advertisements* in 1979, and finally *Forms of Talk* in 1981. Goffman also received a Guggenheim Fellowship for 1977 through 1978. He was elected—apparently as a rather controversial and surprise candidate—to take up the prestigious position as the 17th president of the American Sociological Association in 1982, succeeding William Foote Whyte—another exquisite ethnographic observer of everyday life—but due to advanced illness, Goffman was unable to deliver his much-anticipated presidential address, which was published posthumously (Goffman, 1983a). Erving Goffman died after a brief spell of illness due to stomach cancer on November 19, 1982, in Philadelphia. At the time of his death, he was known to be one of the most read and inspirational sociologists in the world.

Despite zealously guarding his private life, a few "strips" (as Goffman himself called those arbitrarily cut slices from the ongoing stream of life) should be mentioned. Goffman's love life materialized in two marriages. His first wife, the psychologist Angelica Choate, to whom he was married from 1952 to 1964 and had a son, Thomas Edward, committed suicide at the age of 35, apparently due to mental illness. In 1981, he married the sociolinguist Gillian Sankoff in Philadelphia and had a daughter with her shortly before his death. Their daughter, Alice Goffman, followed in her father's footsteps and became a sociologist, and she was awarded the 2011 American Sociological Association Award for the best PhD thesis of that year. It is also a known fact that Goffman enjoyed gambling throughout his life and that he was trained as a certified dealer in a Las Vegas casino. Apart from this, very little information about Goffman's personal affairs has to this day been made public.

After these insights into some biographical information on Goffman, let us take a brief look at his sociological perspective, to be elaborated further later in this book. Goffman's contribution to sociology cannot be under-stated. He left a lasting impression on the discipline and on neighboring fields of study. In 2007 he was listed by *The Times Higher Education Guide* as the sixth-most-cited author in the humanities and social sciences, behind the likes of Anthony Giddens, Michel Foucault, and Pierre Bourdieu but ahead of prominent names such as Jürgen Habermas, Max Weber, and Sigmund Freud. Particularly, the original substance and unconventional style of writing seem to be some of the main reasons his work attracted such attention. Although Goffman did not invent **microsociology** (Georg Simmel and the early Chicago Sociologists as well as others studying small-group interaction and behavior clearly anticipated and indeed inspired some of his own ideas), he became one of the main proponents of microsociology, social psychology, and particularly **symbolic interactionism**. Goffman's extended stays in Chicago (from the late 1940s to the mid-1950s) and at Berkeley (from 1958 to 1968) clearly shaped his vision of the world—both places were known as breeding grounds for the emerging perspective of symbolic interactionism (Mullins, 1973)—just as his own presence there also consolidated the status of symbolic interactionism. However, Goffman did not see or parade himself as a representative of symbolic interactionism as a school of thought (we return to this point again in Chapter 9). As fellow Chicago sociologist Anselm L. Strauss once stated on how symbolic interactionism was perceived by the students at the University of Chicago: "We didn't think symbolic interaction was a perspective in sociology; we thought it was sociology" (Strauss in Gusfield, 1995, p. ix). Whether recognized or unperceived, the ideas of symbolic interactionism—the topics of interest, the creative uses of methodology, the exquisite ways of writing, and the playful and down-to-earth approach to sociology—strongly underpinned all aspects of Goffman's work. In his introduction to *Goffman's Legacy*, A. Javier Treviño (2003b) perceptively captured and summarized what he regarded as the four cornerstones of Goffman's sociological perspective:

1. His detailed attention to the routine and seemingly trivial matters of everyday life

2. His rich array of metaphors, rhetorical techniques, and conceptual schemes

3. His powerful yet unarticulated qualitative research methodology

4. His carving out an exquisite interaction order

These four focal points—and several others might have been mentioned—testify to the fact that Goffman's legacy to sociology consisted in shedding light on a substantial subject matter (interaction) as well as a specific way of researching and writing about his findings. Goffman was indeed an excellent communicator, as is evident in the sheer elegance with which he delivered—in writing as well as in oral presentation—his points and ideas (Turner, 2010). As one sociologist has suggested, Goffman was nothing less than "the waste of a good novelist" (Elkind, 1975, p. 30). All of these points will be explicated, illustrated, and discussed in detail later in this book. For instance, in Chapter 3 we describe Goffman's research methods, including his creative development and vivid use of a metaphorical imagery, and in Chapter 4 we substantially deal with Goffman's contribution to everyday-life sociology, including his development of the notion of the **interaction order**. Throughout his career, Goffman was very much oriented toward the North American continent. Looking at his work—his interests, notes, and references—one is struck by its resonance with American society and American sociology. As Albert Bergesen observed, "Goffman didn't write about European theory. He worked from American roots" (Bergesen, 1984, p. 52). So although Goffman was indeed not an American sociologist, as we mentioned before, he was very much—in a roundabout way—an obscure presence in and simultaneously a product of American society and American sociology in the mid-20th century.

Goffman's Intellectual Trajectory

There are many ways to try to systematize Erving Goffman's work. Although his work at times has been described as slippery and diffuse with little continuity between books, there are still some thematic anchoring points to make his overall work both accessible and coherent. For example, some have attempted to tease out Goffman's central and continued thematic and conceptual concerns throughout his career (see Chriss, 1995a; Manning, 1992), such as Philip Manning's SIAC schema that propose that Goffman's key concerns were "situational propriety," "involvement," "accessibility," and finally "civil inattention." Although this way of organizing Goffman's writings has its obvious merits, it fails to capture the dynamic character of Goffman's intellectual development and the fact that Goffman was also inspired by the work of others. Another and more processual way to decipher his work is therefore chronologically to excavate what themes and ideas occurred during which points in Goffman's career and discuss why they developed and how they relate to each other. This latter way of organizing and systematizing Goffman's work was proposed by Randall Collins (1981a), who argued that his work is characterized by three interrelated stages, each covering a relatively specific time period with a specific focus and content that is evident in specific publications.

The work of many key social thinkers has analytically been divided into phases such as "the Younger" and "the Older" (just think of the works of Karl Marx, Ludwig Wittgenstein, or Martin Heidegger). In the lives and ideas of these thinkers, certain distinctive ruptures have occurred—or been posthumously proposed—due to dramatic events in either their personal, historical, or intellectual lives. Such ruptures would entail that a social thinker at certain points in his or her life radically revise or downright reject their "youthful ideas" and instead give room for a more mature but less daring thinker to step into character and to systematize and summarize what has gone before. According to Collins, it is not possible to find such dramatic or significant ruptures in the work of Goffman; rather, one can detect some minor changes in perspective and some smooth transitions into new areas of interest. Collins thus believes that it is possible and useful to divide Goffman's intellectual trajectory into three distinct yet interrelated stages.

The first stage is defined as the Durkheimian stage and is characterized by Goffman's Durkheim-inspired interest in the multitude of mundane rituals and everyday life as a social and moral ceremony. Here Goffman is primarily interested in developing and refining his conceptual apparatus from his aforementioned PhD thesis. The main publication from this stage was obviously *The Presentation of Self in Everyday Life* (1959). The Durkheimian dimension is this book is evident in Goffman's interest in analyzing the preconditions and character of social order at a micro level of social analysis. Moreover, Goffman's interest in deviance, rule-breaking behavior, and anomic features of everyday life (such as stigma and mental illness) in his later books *Asylums* (1961) and *Stigma* (1964a) also bears a significant mark of Durkheimian inspiration.

The second stage is the empirical phase, which, as the title indicates, was characterized by Goffman's preoccupation with empirically studying a variety of everyday-life settings in order to buttress, develop, and expand his conceptual apparatus even further. The inspiration from game theory became increasingly apparent, and especially in books such as *Interaction Ritual* (1967) and *Strategic Interaction* (1969) is this influence particularly evident. Here the focus is on how to manipulate the situation in order to optimize one's own benefit and outcome. The interest in rituals from the preceding phase gradually moved into the background in favor of a focus on the functional requisites and rules regulating interaction. It is also in this phase that one clearly gets a glimpse of a conflict or stratification perspective in Goffman's work, which has otherwise been characterized by a consensual understanding of everyday life (Collins, 1981a, p. 226). However, by conflicts and stratification is not meant macro-scale social phenomena (such as class conflicts, social inequality, revolts, or upheavals) but rather potential microstruggles between different and competing interpretations of reality among participants in the actual interaction situation.

The third stage is according to Collins labeled the social-epistemological or social-phenomenological phase. This phase stretches from the early 1970s to the end of Goffman's writings a decade later and is characterized by being more formalized and philosophical than the preceding two stages. This phase is significantly less empirical and oriented toward the development of a more abstract and new approach: frame analysis. The last years of Goffman's life were thus marked by a growing interest in talk (and thus verbal behavior) as an important aspect of interaction that could be seen as a mediating and structuring tool that could be drawn upon and become part of one's self-presentation during social gatherings. Therefore, in later works such as *Frame Analysis* (1974) and *Forms of Talk* (1981a), we see a different Goffman than before—a much more theory-constructing researcher who attempts to systematize his previous findings and results into a formal and coherent theoretical frame or a *magnum opus* and who, to some extent, is less concerned with describing what people actually do during interaction but is rather interested in analyzing how they think and talk about it. Table 1.1 graphically recapitulates these three stages by delineating the period each of them covers, by showing the conceptual content and analytical and empirical focus of each phase, as well as by listing the works that were published during each of these stages.

Table 1.1   The Three Stages of Erving Goffman

Period	Focus/Content	Works
Stage 1: The Durkheimian Phase (approx. 1950s and early 1960s)	• Dramaturgy • Face-to-face interaction • Deviance • The social construction and maintenance of reality • Everyday rituals	*The Presentation of Self in Everyday Life* (1959) *Asylums* (1961) *Behavior in Public Places* (1963) *Stigma* (1964a)
Stage 2: The Empirical Phase (approx. late 1960s and early 1970s)	• Empirical studies of everyday-life situations • Inspiration from game theory • Potential conflicts in everyday life	*Interaction Ritual* (1967) *Strategic Interaction* (1970) *Relations in Public* (1971) *Encounters* (1972)
Stage 3: The Social-Epistemological/Social-Phenomenological Phase (approx. late 1970s and early 1980s)	• Analytical language theory • Returning to Durkheim • The frame metaphor • Ethnomethodological inspiration and critique	*Frame Analysis* (1974) *Gender Advertisements* (1979a) *Forms of Talk* (1981a)

Source: Inspired by Randall Collins (1981a). Table based on various writings by Randall Collins.

Among Goffman interpreters, there is a common consent that during the latter parts of his career, Goffman's work gradually developed into a more systematic and formalized position (Grimshaw, 1983, p. 147). However, when it came to focus and content, he—with only some minor shifts in perspective and conceptual preference—continuously stuck to the project he outlined in his PhD thesis (Smith, 1999b, p. 1), namely the detailed study and carving out of an "interaction order" in everyday life.

The "Tales of Goffman"

As we have already indicated, Erving Goffman was indeed a curious character—as a sociologist but also as a private person. According to John Lofland, one of Goffman's contemporaries who was also inspired by his ideas, Goffman particularly left four legacies when he died: (1) the substantive study of the interaction order and the explication of this order by way of numerous analytical concepts, (2) an intellectual stance toward or perspective on sociology—a stance privileging the micro, the mundane, and the overlooked dimensions of face-to-face interaction, (3) a spirit, attitude, or mood with which to go about scholarship—such as his sarcasm, irony, and alternative approach to methodology, and (4) a mode of being a scholar, a colleague, and a friend (Lofland, 1984, p. 8). The first three points will be dealt with throughout this book, but here we will briefly dwell on the fourth and more personal point.

Let us initially stress an important point: We never knew or met Goffman. When he passed away, we were on our way to becoming teenagers. Therefore, we must rely on what others who knew him have stated and recalled. The people who knew Goffman either intimately or more superficially often seemed to share a rather identical impression of him. Here we have attempted to collect some of the most illuminating observations of the man who himself made a career of observing others. Although one of his students recalled how there were two main impressions of Goffman—one as a warm, humorous, friendly, and accommodating teacher, the other as a controlled, insensitive, and indifferent teacher—he nevertheless summarized that "most of the 'Tales of Goffman' are negative. In many of his dealings with others he did not reflect the sensitivity and concern for the underdog shown in his early written work" (Marx, 1984, p. 657). These "Tales of Goffman" mentioned by Gary T. Marx were collected by John Lofland, who by way of wonderful examples illustrated how Goffman in his dealings with others—friends as well as strangers—always lingered somewhere between sincerity and cynicism. Here we reproduce from Lofland (1984, pp. 20–21) a few of the most characteristic of these tales:

> A line he used frequently: "In the time I'm talking to you, I could be writing a paper."

> At a sociology department party where he encountered an assistant professor who had just been denied tenure and who is angry and bitter about it: "After all, all of us aren't good enough to teach here."

> Passing a group of old friends in a hotel lobby at a sociologists' convention, he was heard saying loud and clear: "If I can't find anybody more important to talk with, I'll come back and talk with you."

> Replying to a student who is suggesting that the dignity and integrity of the self are moral concerns that permeate his work: "I only put in all that self stuff because people like to read about it."

Irony mixed with playful insult was thus part and parcel of Goffman's personal self-presentation. However, Goffman also joked about more academic matters. It is no great secret that politics and the critique of macrostructural and social arrangements—even at a time during the 1960s and 1970s when such issues concerned many academics—were not featured anywhere in Goffman's work. In fact, he seemed sarcastically distanced toward politics, as an encounter with another scholar revealed:

> Once a scholar declared to Goffman: "All the world will eventually be Marxist." Goffman reportedly replied: "I'm not denying that. But tell me one thing: Do Marxists brush their teeth in the morning?" (Ledger, 1982, p. 42)

As these anecdotes all reveal, Goffman was a prankster—someone who was amused by and found pleasure in teasing, at times even insulting, his colleagues and students and who supposedly also used these private observations in his own theorizing on shame, embarrassment, and rituals used to save face.

The "Tales of Goffman" show how Goffman's relationship with his surroundings was rather ambivalent. They either saluted or distanced themselves from him (as he distanced himself from them), apparently with an overweight of the latter experience. Goffman was, as so many throughout the years have expressed, a gifted and excellent lecturer, who, according to some, never really engaged or immersed himself in the teaching situation. According to others, Goffman not just in writing but also in person was a mercurial entertainer, a sublime performer, and Gary T. Marx recalls how

Goffman in the opening remarks to a class with a wry smile would say: "We will try and keep you entertained" (Marx, 1984, p. 652). As was obvious, however, he was the protector of the clever students but lacked the empathy and sensitivity that made him popular among the students at large. Apparently, Goffman was also close-fisted when it came to his marking of student assignments and did not hold high thoughts for students in general. One of Goffman's students, Bennett M. Berger, once overheard Goffman say that he only gave top marks to those students who actually taught him something (Berger, 1973). Besides this, irony was not just something Goffman used to keep his surroundings at bay, he also used it as a way to present his own oddity and make fun of his own academic position. For example, he once stated that "a university is a place to pick up your mail" (Marx, 1984, p. 658).

Goffman made his own everyday life an integral part of his sociological experimentation. In one of the more curious anecdotes of Goffman's whims, Roger Abrahams recollected how he would use any kind of social event as a miniature scientific experiment:

> Goffman brought an amused enthusiasm to personal encounters. He enjoyed organizing groups to have a "great meal" at meetings and conferences, but going out with him in public was not always an unqualified pleasure. He knew how to play social games with great decorousness, but he often couldn't resist breaking their rules to see what would happen. In fact, he was often abruptly rude. He liked to give the impression that he would not suffer fools gladly, but one never knew whom he would cast in such a role, nor how seriously he meant the scenes that he staged. (Abrahams, 1984, p. 76)

Goffman was thus a constant observer, and, as a colleague recalled, "he's always observing and never not observing. He's never anything but professionally involved. Therefore, he's difficult to deal with because he's a critic of the least moment—which he is also a student of" (Ledger, 1982, p. 40). Such constant observation obviously placed a strain on social relationships and estranged Goffman from certain colleagues and students who saw him as eccentric. Humor, irony, and sarcasm—or what might perhaps more appropriately be termed a playful and experimental approach to social life—was thus a characteristic of Goffman's persona in his academic writing, as we shall see later, as well as in his personal affairs.

In the literature on Goffman, it is also mentioned that he was a relatively short man, and this combined with his Jewish descent and a background as immigrant from Canada to the United States apparently influenced and shaped his self-conception. According to Randall Collins (personal communication), he was about 5'4" and very self-conscious about it. He was annoyed with colleagues who teased him with his moderate height, but, as Collins has informed us, this also made him capable of—especially during his fieldwork at St. Elizabeth's Hospital—moving around relatively unnoticed among patients and staff. Apparently, nobody paid any attention to this short, quiet man. Conversely, and especially after he became a famous character, Goffman could be very aggressive in his confrontation with others, particularly with large and "rowdy" people such as Alvin W. Gouldner. On the other hand, Collins questions whether Goffman's Jewish background had in fact any profound effect on his self-conception. Goffman was, as Collins in personal communication expressed it, "in his innermost being a man from the mid-century, which means before the rebirth of ethnical identities towards the end of the 20th century."

Goffman's Interdisciplinary Outlook

Even though Goffman's concepts and ideas were very capable of capturing the intricate details and minutiae of social reality, he himself was a sociologist who resisted and evaded any attempt at classification. In general, he upheld an ambivalent and self-critical attitude toward intellectual classifications and categories, as this snippet from a conversation reveals: "I'm getting very tired of slogans and flags and kinship acknowledgements and membership badges, no doubt because I have employed so many myself" (Goffman in Hymes, 1984, p. 626). Goffman was a true master in classifying, naming, and labeling, but he detested the numerous attempts made by others to include him and his work within the existing narrow social scientific communities and traditions.

Besides his desire to evade association with any one specific tradition or school of thought, Goffman also excelled in sitting astride disciplinary boundaries aimed at keeping the distinct sciences apart. Although Goffman by training was a sociologist, he also willingly drew on and benevolently contributed to other scientific cultures. He was truly an interdisciplinarian. Goffman's work was and still is known and read by sociologists, anthropologists, psychiatrists, linguists, philosophers, social workers, and students of literature, medicine, and media studies as well as by scholars working within almost any social scientific discipline. He reached far beyond his own discipline of sociology and stimulated discussions, studies, and conceptual development within other scientific disciplines.

The social sciences, like any other scientific discipline, are classificatory and analytical scientific practices. From the onset, the social sciences—and perhaps particularly sociology—have maintained an almost compulsory urge to construct and impose categories on reality, those who inhabit it, and those who study it. Eleanor Rosch has thus described how "the purpose of category systems is to provide maximum information with the least cognitive effort. . . . Maximum information with least cognitive effort is achieved if categories map the perceived world structure as closely as possible" (Rosch, 1978, p. 30). The purpose of categories is to mirror and reflect reality as closely as possible. To categorize Goffman based on this premise thus poses both an internal and external social scientific problem. It is possible neither to monopolize Goffman within any distinct school of thought nor exclusively to contain his work within any one scientific discipline. Even though we primarily focus on Goffman as a sociologist, in parts of his work he was simultaneously a cultural anthropologist and a social psychologist. He is frequently quoted in studies of communication in different forms of media and he is used as an analytical framework when studying medical professions, disability, ecology, politics, childcare, and policing, just to mention a few examples of the versatility and utility of his work, to which we return more substantially later. Despite Goffman's chameleon quality, his work, however, was solidly placed within the classical sociological tradition. As we shall show later, his two main sources of inspiration were French sociologist Émile Durkheim and German sociologist Georg Simmel. Moreover, his work has also inspired a number of contemporary key sociologists and social thinkers, perhaps most notably Anthony Giddens, Pierre Bourdieu, Jürgen Habermas, Thomas J. Scheff, Arlie Hochschild, and Randall Collins. So despite his interdisciplinary potentials, Goffman was a sociologist par excellence.

When such classificatory problems have been explicated, what remains to be said is that there is hardly another sociologist of Goffman's generation who has been read and respected by so many nonacademics and scholars from other disciplines than him (Giddens, 1988, p. 250). Apart from being respected within his own discipline of sociology, Goffman has thus also appealed to researchers and readers from other disciplines (Leeds-Hurwitz, 1986). Many readers have in his work discovered an engagement with and understanding of the not-always-unproblematic nature of social life, which requires careful attention as well as detailed study. Moreover, people outside the academic realm have also in Goffman's work been able to recognize themselves and their lives in his detailed descriptions of the often unnoticed everyday events such as using the lift, sociable (and often trivial) conversations at the dinner table, chance encounters with the stigmatized, and interactions with strangers in public places, as well as institutional practices. Goffman was truly a "sociologist of the of course" because ordinary people were able to recognize themselves and their behavioral whims in his writings on the world of the mundane. Goffman's language, however, was far from mundane and accessible (something many translators have struggled with over the years) but had a touch of sophisticated elitism and metaphorical mystique about it. However, his most famous terminological trick was neither elitist nor inaccessible. Goffman's development and use of the dramaturgical metaphor (see Chapters 3 and 4) from his bestselling book *The Presentation of Self in Everyday Life* (1959) was immediately understandable—though not necessarily incontestable—to most, which was one of the main reasons this metaphor for decades has inspired scholars across conventional disciplinary boundaries.

Conclusion

As we have shown in this chapter, Erving Goffman rose to prominence at a time in postwar America when sociology to a large extent was dominated and shaped by macrosociological schools of thought such as structural-functionalism and later also conflict theory and Marxism. This was also a time when the methodological preferences of positivism and behaviorism were setting the research agenda. It was therefore surprising that someone like Goffman, with his unmistakable predilection for microsociological studies and a rather impressionistic approach to research methods (see Chapter 3), would succeed and make a lasting impression on the discipline.

In many ways, Goffman was and remained an outsider. Biographically, his early life as a child in an immigrant Jewish family that had moved from Ukraine to Canada undoubtedly, as the chapter has shown, shaped his perspective on the world. Later in life, Goffman moved from Canada to the United States, where he also in many respects remained at the outskirts of social and disciplinary inner circles, keenly observing the behavioral antics of the inhabitants of his new habitat. Intellectually, he was also an outsider, who throughout his career preferred and privileged subject matters and methods that by many others were looked upon with skepticism and suspicion. Perhaps it is thus no surprise that Goffman also began to study outsiders. Goffman's intellectual trajectory, as the chapter has outlined, is marked by a remarkable continuity and consistency, with only some minor shifts in empirical attention and conceptual development. Looked upon from afar, Goffman throughout his career—via some detours and excursions—continued to move on the same track and gradually developed and refined his study of patterns of human interaction. At times, he was influenced by new theoretical developments or discovered new areas of interest, but apart from minor concessions to critics and conceptual clarifications, Goffman over the years stayed loyal to his own perspective and insisted that his findings were in fact of importance to his discipline as well as to others interested in observing, describing, and analyzing social interaction.

Already from early childhood, Goffman was different (Winkin, 2010, p. 56). As a private person, as friend, colleague, and teacher, Goffman was a complex character who was apparently difficult to work with and to be around—perhaps one of the main reasons his work is exclusively one-author productions. As John Lofland stated, "Goffman was a complicated man who grew ever more Gordian as he matured" (Lofland, 1984, p. 7). On the one hand, Goffman was liked by some of his students and colleagues who saw in him a magisterial communicator and mercurial observer of the minutiae of social life. On the other hand, Goffman apparently also alienated himself from others because of his playful—some would say cynical or mean—attitude toward participating in social events and his elitist tendencies in the class-room. The "Tales of Goffman" illustrate this duality of his personality and how others responded to him as well as attest to the fact that Goffman was far from a one-dimensional man.

During his lifetime and after his death, Erving Goffman inspired new generations of sociologists as well as students and colleagues from other disciplines to take the study of the "interaction order" seriously as a realm in its own right and to undertake empirical studies and devote their efforts to tease out new, overlooked, and characteristic dimensions and patterns of social interaction from the myriad of human meetings and encounters in everyday life. After his death, as we shall see later in this book, several schools of thought attempted to appropriate or lay claim to the intellectual legacy of Goffman, undoubtedly because his ideas proved so innovative, useful, and of lasting importance to so many of his predecessors.

Questions

- What were the dominant theoretical paradigms and methodological perspectives in sociology in postwar America at the time when Erving Goffman gradually began to publish his work, and how did his work relate to these paradigms and perspectives?
- What were the main stages in Erving Goffman's intellectual trajectory, and how and why did he change perspective throughout his career?
- What were the main legacies Erving Goffman left behind?
- Why did Erving Goffman's work attract such attention?

2

Reading Goffman "Backward"

In this chapter, we address Erving Goffman's theoretical roots and sources of inspiration. The primary aim is to illustrate the theoretical sources of Goffman's works and the influence of these in the construction of his own position. We begin by introducing the theorists and traditions to whom Goffman refers explicitly and directly, and afterward we turn to perspectives and theories that are not so explicitly elaborated in Goffman's works but nonetheless seem to have had an impact on his sociological thinking. We have permitted ourselves to be selective and have chosen the traditions we believe have had the greatest influence on or display the most significant similarities to his work.

Émile Durkheim

Although French sociologist Émile Durkheim is often associated with the tradition of positivism or "variables sociology" (Snell, 2010), he was in fact one of Goffman's most important theoretical sources of inspiration (see, e.g., Chriss, 1993; Collins, 1988b, 2004; Giglioli, 1984; MacCannell, 1990). Randall Collins (2004, p. 22) has suggested Goffman's Durkheimianism is one constant point of anchorage and that his works may be viewed as a continuation of the Durkheimian sociology that proposes that social reality

> is at its core a moral reality. Society is held together by feelings of right and wrong, emotional sentiments that impel people towards certain actions, and into righteous revulsion against certain others. Durkheim also proposed ... a mechanism by which these moral sentiments are produced and shaped into

specific social forms. That mechanism is *ritual*. Its nature is easiest to understand by examining explicit rituals with very strong moral sentiments. . . . In its various modifications, it is found in all societies, and in forms which are merely implicit rather than explicit. (Collins, 1988b, p. 44)

One of the obvious reasons Goffman may be placed in Durkheim's footprints is his "discovery" of and his preoccupation with the so-called interaction rituals permeating everyday social interaction (Collins, 1988b). In *The Elementary Forms of Religious Life*, Durkheim (1943) highlighted it as a fundamental feature of religions that they are based on a worldview in which everything may be divided into the categories of sacred and profane. Moreover, Durkheim's analysis indicates that religious ceremonies constitute the ways in which people socialize, make contact with, pay tribute to, and respect the sacred. According to Durkheim, rituals prescribe the ways in which the members of a religious community are supposed to act in relation to the sacred, and this insight Goffman brought down to micro level in his analyses of the interaction rituals through which people confirm their relations with each other (Smith, 1988, p. 120).

Goffman's Durkheimian heritage, then, is evident in his conceptualization of everyday life social interaction as a highly ritualized practice. Obviously, he did not attempt to describe an overall macroritual inclusive of all members of society and in which these are subsequently ritualized or forced into an all-encompassing conformity. On the contrary, in the numerous social encounters of everyday life, Goffman suggested, rituals may be identified that impose restraints on individual behavior and thus reflects the moral and normative foundation of society. As noted by Collins, Goffman's Durkheimian imprints are also seen in his focus on the sacredness of the self. In his essay *The Nature of Deference and Demeanor* (1956a), Goffman began his analysis by referring to Durkheim's theory of the human soul, conceptualizing it as a superindividual, moral, and social entity incorporated in individuals. Thus, referring to Durkheim, Goffman (1967, p. 47) stated that "the individual's personality can be seen as one apportionment of the collective *mana*, and that (as he implies in later chapters) the rites performed to representations of the social collectivity will sometimes be performed to the individual himself." Durkheim considered the human soul to be animated by *mana* and thus to be a sacred thing. This conception is evident in Goffman's analyses of how people avoid violating each others' selves and thus ultimately avoid violating the moral order of society.

So, whereas Durkheim explored and identified a stable and all-pervading moral order that acted as a stable "backdrop" for the behavior of individuals, Goffman saw a more fragile order in constant need of repair (Burns, 1992,

p. 26). Society (in the form of the prevailing moral order) is installed in our consciousness and hence also in our selves. Therefore, Goffman claims, the self must be protected, and individuals do this by complying with a number of different and seemingly "insignificant" interaction rituals that assist in mutual self-preservation and, secondly, in the preservation of societies' moral order. By treating each other with respect and dignity, by turning our attention away when others who are about to lose face, in short, by practicing "face work," we protect each other's selves and hence the social order installed in all of us. Goffman's sociology may then indeed be read as a continuation of Durkheim's idea that the individual has, so to speak, replaced the gods. Goffman did, however, take this analysis much further than Durkheim did, as he investigated the ways in which the sacred nature of the individual is created and maintained in everyday social interaction (Hall, 1977, p. 540). Similarly, on the question of social order, Goffman also differs from Durkheim. Whereas Durkheim conceptualized social order, society, as a compelling outer fact, Goffman was far more interested in the micropractices maintaining social order. Durkheim and Goffman shared the view that individuals interact, as do types of particles, within a larger structural framework, but whereas Durkheim considered *society* to be a determining reality in itself, Goffman viewed the *social encounter* as a reality in itself, as an order that is preserved through the participation of individuals in various interaction practices (Ølgaard, 1975, p. 65). Goffman, thus, invented his own level of functional ritual analysis, focusing not on institutional integration but on the functional requirements of the situation (Collins, 2004, p. 16).

Georg Simmel

Goffman's professors, Robert Park and Ernest Burgess, and his mentor, Everett C. Hughes, were instrumental in bringing the ideas of German sociologist Georg Simmel to the University of Chicago, and these early Chicago scholars were all inspired by Simmel's sociology. Thus, at quite an early stage in his academic career (during his studies at the University of Chicago), Goffman became acquainted with the works of Georg Simmel, and in the introduction to his doctoral dissertation he quoted a passage from Simmel's (1909) essay "The Problem of Sociology." This passage served as a kind of manifesto for his doctoral work as well as for much of his subsequent works. In the rather lengthy quote, Simmel suggested that society should be understood as an entity crystallizing from the reciprocal effects (*Wechselwirkungen*) that take place between individuals and thus as an entity that is evoked by individual motives, intentions, and interests. In Simmel's view, society is the total sum of these relational forms, and it is therefore created by the reciprocal effects of individuals. According to Simmel, sociology had focused exclusively on observable societal phenomena (forms of reciprocal effects) that have been "disengaged" from their immediate bearers (e.g., the state, professional organizations, clergy, and family structures). However, Simmel (1992, pp. 32–35; 1998, p. 38) suggested that, in addition to these "clearly visible phenomena," an immense number of minor relational forms and reciprocal effects exist between humans, which constitute the "unnamed or unknown tissue" or fragile threads that constitute and create society.

Simmel's methodological specifications were relatively unconventional. Since it is not possible, according to Simmel, for sociology to reach underlying social regularities, sociological research should deal with the mapping and description of the numerous everyday actions that contribute to maintaining and regulating the distinguishing organization of social life. Goffman's *sociological microscopy* and his reluctance to deal with larger societal types of reciprocal effects bear witness to the influence of Simmel. Further, Goffman was influenced by Simmel's so-called *formal method*. In the essay "The Problem of Sociology," Simmel expounds the fundamental view that runs like a thread through all his analyses of social types, social life, and culture, namely that "the world consists of innumerable contents which are given determinate identity, structure and meaning through the imposition of forms which man has created in the course of his experience" (Simmel, 1971, p. xxxii). According to Simmel, society is constituted by reciprocal effects between impulse-, motive-, and purpose-controlled individuals who have a reciprocal effect on one another. Simmel conceptualized this process of unity-creation as "sociation" (*Vergesellshaftung*). In Simmel's view, the task of sociologists is to understand and conceptualize this process of sociation. Methodologically, Simmel urged sociologists to think through abstraction, to separate content (impulses, instincts, motives) from form and thus to identify the purely social forms.

In the same way as Simmel attempted to abstract the multiple forms of sociation, Goffman's ambition was to abstract and identify interactional forms (e.g., the dramaturgical techniques and the idiom of ritual expression forms that render behavior socially meaningful) behind the infinite number of social appearances (Cahill, Fine, & Grant, 1995, p. 611). Goffman practiced the formal method by concentrating on ways in which the mental energies, instincts, motives, intentions, and feelings of individuals (content) manifest themselves in such forms. Peter K. Manning (1976, p. 22) identified the different steps in Goffman's formal analysis: (1) the identification of the form of a given social activity ("situations" or "meetings" where individuals interact and/or communicate face to face with others); (2) the outlining of different subtypes or adjacent types; (3) a focus is on tensions and the different combinations and tactics involved in the maintenance of equilibrium in the situation, and finally; (4) the listing of the social consequences of the social forms.

Goffman's use of analytical analogies may also be viewed as one of his Simmelian inspirations. Stating, in the introduction to "Interaction Ritual," that his project is not concerned with studying the individual and his psychology (content) but rather "the syntactical relations among the acts of different persons mutually present to one another" (Goffman, 1967, p. 2), thus seems to be an echo of Simmel's formulations (in "The Problem of Sociology") regarding society as the product of mutually influencing, reciprocally effecting individuals. Compare, for instance, the following wording from Goffman: "I assume that the proper study of interaction is not the individual and his psychology, but rather the syntactical relations among the acts of different persons mutually present to one another" (Goffman, 1967, p. 2) to that of Simmel: "We are not interested in the psychological processes that occur in each of the two individuals but in their subsumption under the categories of union and discord" (Simmel, 1971, p. 34). Goffman's indebtedness to Simmel is thus evident in Goffman's substantial interest in microsociological themes, his methodological considerations as well as in his understanding of what sociology should focus on.

George Herbert Mead

Whereas Simmel primarily inspired Goffman's method and sociological *style*, and where Durkheim became important for his understanding of social interaction as a moral and socially ritualized order, American social psychologist George Herbert Mead became important primarily for Goffman's theory of the self (we shall return to this in more detail in Chapter 6). Mead (1967) argued in favor of the idea that the self is not a natural given entity but to a large extent a social construct. By way of the concepts of "significant others" and "the generalized other," Mead described how individuals, through a process of (symbolic) interaction, (1) learn that we are social beings and (2) internalize the normative foundation of society. One of Mead's fundamental ideas was that the human self is created through social interactions with others. According to Mead, the self is a processual entity that is constantly shaped and reshaped through the social interplay with the environment. Concerning human learning, Mead pointed to the fact that learning presupposes a special ability to assume the perspective of others. This capacity for "perspective taking" is, in other words, essential to social communication, to the creation of the self, and to the sustaining of social order. Essential elements of this line of thinking are observable in Goffman's conceptualization of the human self. Thus, Mead's thoughts about the significance of perspective taking and the generalized other correspond with Goffman's concept of **impression management,** which concerns the individual's capacity to manage the impression he makes on others by placing himself in their position in order to build an impression as to which behavior will be the most appropriate in the situation (Abels, 1998, p. 163). Goffman did not, however, perceive social participants as passive mirror images reflecting the image provided or projected by the individual. In "The Nature of Deference and Demeanor," he stated this very clearly:

> The Meadian notion that the individual takes toward himself the attitude others take to him seems very much an oversimplification. Rather the individual must rely on others to complete the picture of him of which he himself is allowed to paint only certain parts. Each individual is responsible for the demeanor image of himself and the deference image of others, so that for a complete man to be expressed, individuals must hold hands in a chain of ceremony, each giving deferentially with proper demeanor to the one on the right what will be received deferentially from the one on the left (Goffman, 1967, pp. 84–85).

Goffman pointed out that individuals do attempt to view themselves through the eyes of others, but at the same time he suggested that there is much more to this than mere role taking. The individual receives **deference** in response to his **demeanor,** and in this way we are inextricably linked to our social surroundings in a chain of ceremonies (or interaction rituals) that to a large extent is concerned with the maintenance and celebration of the self. Goffman states that even if individuals claim to possess a unique and personal self, evidence of this possession is thoroughly a product of joint ceremonial labor (Goffman, 1967, p. 85). Thus, as to the perception of the human self as a largely social product, Goffman is decidedly inspired by and in line with Mead. However, by combining this thinking with a Durkheimian-inspired conception of socially ritualized behavior, Goffman did, however, move substantially beyond the Meadian notion of role taking. Goffman also differed from Mead with regard to the formation of the self. Whereas Mead saw the formation of the self as a process of *internalization* in which the individual, so to speak, turns significant and generalized expectations of others into his own, Goffman viewed the creation of the self as a continuous process of *externalization* in which individuals, through manipulative and strategic "projection techniques" and information control, attempt to build a certain picture of who they are (Laursen, 1997, pp. 1–2).

Many sociology textbooks (see, e.g., Wallace & Wolf, 1999; Zeitlin, 1973), scientific articles (Posner, 1978; Stein, 1991), and monographs on Goffman (Manning, 1992) often categorize and discuss Goffman's work within the framework of symbolic interactionism. Goffman did not, however, see himself as a symbolic interactionist. Thus, in an interview with Jef Verhoeven (1993, p. 318) he stated, "I don't believe the label really covers anything." However, such denials must not be accepted at face value (Scheff, 2005, p. 148), and there are obvious parallels between Goffman's sociology and essential symbolic interactionist thinking. According to Herbert Blumer, who sociologicalized Mead's ideas and coined the term "symbolic interactionism," symbolic interaction means that social actions are mediated by symbols (e.g., language) that individuals convey and interpret:

> The term "symbolic interaction" refers, of course, to the peculiar and distinctive character of interaction as it takes place between human beings. The peculiarity consists in the fact that human beings interpret or "define" each other's actions instead of merely reacting to each other's actions. Their "response" is not made directly to the actions of one another but instead is based on the meaning which they attach to such actions. Thus, human interaction is mediated by the use of symbols, by interpretation, or by ascertaining the meaning of one another's actions. This mediation is equivalent to inserting a process of interpretation between stimulus and response in the case of human behavior. (Blumer, 1969, pp. 78–79)

Symbolic interactionists, in other words, study symbolically mediated interaction and thus how personality and identities are shaped through interactions with such collectively shared symbols (Nisbet, 1970, p. 59). The most obvious overlap between Goffman and symbolic interactionism is the shared assumption that social beings communicate with each other by means of symbols involving meaning and significance. When individuals interact, they send and interpret symbols and social actions that are, in other words, based on the meaning allocated to them by individuals, or, to put it more directly, the meanings that are negotiated through social interaction. In this respect, Goffman did not stand out from symbolic interactionism, and obviously his dramaturgical analysis incorporated basic elements from Meadian thinking. Furthermore, Goffman's dramaturgy is connected to the works of another early symbolic interactionist, Charles Horton Cooley. Cooley (1902) invented the notion of the "looking-glass self" suggesting that individuals build their selves by interpreting the judgments others make of them and their appearance. According to Cooley, individuals *mirror* themselves in their social surroundings and form their selves and self-feelings on the basis of their appearances that are *reflected* in the responses of others. This line of thinking is evident in much of Goffman's work. He analyzed, especially in *The Presentation of Self in Everyday Life*, how individuals mirror their appearances and projected self-images in the response from audiences and how they build a sense of self from the stream of continuous feedbacks. And what is more, Goffman showed how these mirroring processes involve quite distinctive forms of emotion management. Some of Goffman's works (at least up until *Frame Analysis*) may thus be read as an expansion of Cooley's conception of the looking-glass self with a special focus on the emotions of shame and embarrassment (Manning, 2005; Scheff, 2005). However, suggesting symbolic interactionism as the overall theoretical structure in Goffman's works, does, of course, obstruct a more nuanced understanding of Goffman's later works. Whereas symbolic interactionism stresses the ability of individuals to collaborate in the construction of situations and social rules, Goffman argued—perhaps most explicitly in *Frame Analysis* (1974)—that even though a definition of a situation is always identifiable, this is not always "created" or "constructed" by participating individuals (Gonos, 1977). Frames, in Goffman's view, serve as mechanisms that organize human experience, and thus they constrain the individual's social behavior. Further, it seems that Goffman's Durheimianism contradicts the somewhat voluntaristic view of symbolic interactionism. Goffman emphasized the existence of social structure, which imposes on and restrains individual thinking and behavior, and in many of his works (especially those dealing with interaction rituals) there are explicit examples of his distance from the optimistic individualism and voluntarism characterizing many American interactionists (McGregor, 1986). One way of describing Goffman's relationship with symbolic interactionism, then, might be that by analyzing social action from a dramaturgical perspective, he emphasized how individuals collaborate in maintaining each other's selves by way of conveying, controlling, and interpreting information, whereas, in his later writings, he focused more on the microstructures constraining individual's behavior in situations of copresence.

Ethology

Even though it is rarely reflected in textbooks and interpretations of Goffman's sociology, it remains a fact that Goffman was clearly inspired by ethology, the study of animal behavior. Thus, in *Behaviour in Public Places* (1963), he draws on ethological studies of the development of the concept of "spacing." According to Goffman, spacing is indicative of the way in which individuals in an unengaged gathering distribute themselves in the available physical space with a view not to "disturb" small engaged encounters among certain participants. Goffman refers to ethological studies by describing the tendency of certain birds on a fence or railing to stay at a particular distance from each other (Goffman, 1963, p. 161fn). Further, in the preface to *Relations in Public*, Goffman claimed that ethology ought to be considered as a source of inspiration for studies of interaction patterns among humans in situations of copresence since they have developed a field discipline that

> leads them to study animal conduct in very close detail and with a measure of control on preconception. In consequence, they have developed the ability to cut into the flow of apparently haphazard animal activity at its articulations and to isolate natural patterns. (Goffman, 1971, p. xvii)

Clearly then, Goffman was inspired by ethology, which is evident in his claims (presented in *Asylums* and *Relations in Public*) that humans, like animals, in interaction with each other make claims to "personal territories" (Burns, 1992, p. 78). Methodologically, Goffman also adopted ethological strategies as "he followed whatever human bands he could gain access to in their natural habitat—stores, hospitals, casinos, orchards, schools, theatres, and so on—anywhere he could, without disturbing them, watch what they actually do from moment to moment" (Erwin, 1992, p. 331). Thus, by applying a human ethological approach, Goffman prepared the ground for looking for the unexpected behind the appearances of what is immediately visible and audible, and those who followed his methodological lead have found, among other things, intimidating studies of women behind seemingly innocuous public encounters and moral education behind adults' unremarkable responses to children's public misbehavior (Cahill, House, & Grant, 1995, p. 611). By applying a human ethological perspective, Goffman enabled an understanding of how individuals in situations of copresence act in accordance with a particular or general "schedule" and how parts of their social interaction are, in fact, concerned with creating, maintaining, and respecting personal territories.

Existentialism

Even though, in the main, Goffman viewed individuals as secondary in relation to the social forms and the order of society, a clear existential element can be identified in several of his publications. As a theoretical school, existentialism has many faces and special strands (Albert Camus, Karl Jaspers,

Jean-Paul Sartre, and Søren Kierkegaard), sharing, however, the view that human beings are free individuals in a continuously progressive "formation process"; that a close connection exists between reality "out there" and the human being who thinks and perceives "within" himself; and a wider and more integrated view of the individual as a being constituted not only by thoughts (cogito) but also by feelings, senses, and insights (Lyman & Scott, 1970, p. 2). Conceptualizing a special strand of Goffmanian existentialism may be somewhat exaggerated, but it is evident (perhaps most obvious in *The Presentation of Self in Everyday Life*) that Goffman had an eye for *the human individual* behind its many dramatized facades, roles, and characters. Indeed, many passages bear clear witness to Goffman's attempts to combine a structuralist focus on social forms, situational requirements, and social order with the free, nondetermined, and sentient human being of existentialism. Towards the end of *The Presentation of Self in Everyday Life*, Goffman states:

> Whether the character that is being presented is sober or carefree, of high station or low, the individual who performs the character will be seen for what he largely is, a solitary player involved in a harried concern for his production. Behind many masks and many characters, each performer tends to wear a single look, a naked unsocialized look, a look of concentration, a look of one who is privately engaged in a difficult, treacherous task. (Goffman, 1959, p. 228)

Such juxtapositions of human "nature" on the one hand and "social order" on the other connect Goffman to existentialists such as Sartre (Manning, 1976, p. 15). In other words, Goffman made attempts to combine his structural perspective and his interest in a public interaction order with his existentialist interest in the individual "inside." The idea that the self is represented and projected toward others in social situations was a prominent theme in Sartre's writings, and in building his own theory of self-presentations, Goffman obviously was inspired by this line of existentialist thought (Rawls, 1984, p. 223). We may argue, then, that Goffman actually attempted to combine structuralist and existentialist perspectives in an overall analysis of social interaction (Manning, 1976). Also, there are certain existentialist undertones in Goffman's analyses of the human self as they are expressed in *Asylums* (1961) and *Encounters* (1972). As we shall see in Chapter 6, Goffman claimed that the self comes into being by simultaneously accepting and distancing itself from official identity attributions and practicing role distance. Finally, and in addition to these parallels between Goffman and existentialism, another but not less important type of existentialism is evident in Goffman's works, namely the relatively "cold" and prosaic aura characterizing the description of the social order. The world that Goffman describes is meaningless if the individual does not take the matter in hand and actively adds weight and meaning to his actions. In Goffman's works, human life appears to be empty; it is nothing in itself but that which actors make of it. Evidently Goffman was influenced by the spirit of the 1950s, which was impacted by existentialism, and which is found in many of the authors of the Beat Generation (e.g., Jack Kerouac and Allen Ginsberg), and in many ways, the figures in his texts resemble the main character in Samuel Beckett's *Happy Days*, who cheerfully accepts the meaninglessness of being (see, e.g., O'Mealy, 2013, p. xviii).

Norbert Elias

One of Goffman's main pursuits was his preoccupation with rituals and rules regulating human behavior in face-to-face situations. These rules and rituals of interaction or "etiquette" are the outcome of a long historical development process, and one of the sociologists who investigated this phenomenon with persistent commitment was German sociologist Norbert Elias. Even though the main part of Elias's writings was only available in German at Goffman's time (van Krieken, 1998, p. 2), the parallel between Goffman and Elias is nonetheless quite apparent.

In *The History of Manners*, Elias (1994) analyzed how different forms of behavior gradually were perceived as abominable and replaced by more polite and civilized ones. From the "court society" they spread like ripples in water to ever larger parts of social life. Thus, Elias's focus is on the origins of manners and on the way in which certain external impacts result in psychological self-control, causing humans not to commit a breach of etiquette but to live in accordance with existing conventions as regards manners and socializing. In other words, a "civilization process" took place in which a breach of etiquette and moral conventions results in either psychological pressure or social sanctioning. But decline of respectability has often been lamented, and the loss of etiquette in social life has caused vehement contributions even in sociology, yet Elias does the very opposite when, against the background of a comprehensive historical analysis, he claims that on the threshold of modernity, a completely new type of societal staging and support for etiquette is emerging:

> What is important is that in this change, in the inventions and fashions of courtly behavior, which are at first sight perhaps chaotic and accidental, over extended time spans certain directions or lines of development emerge.

These include, for example, what may be described as an advance of the threshold of embarrassment and shame, as "refinement" or as "civilization." A particular social dynamism triggers a particular psychological one, which has its own regularities. (Elias, 1994, p. 82)

In many ways, this may be considered a forerunner of Goffman's works. Both Goffman and Elias studied shame and embarrassment as social phenomena and conceptualizing shame related to either historical context or social situations (Heath, 1988). So whereas Elias analyzed the historical forerunner of a modern etiquette, Goffman directed his attention toward the virtues of situational intercourse as they are actually expressed in the concrete interaction between individuals. Even though he did not conclude such an analysis himself, there is no doubt that Goffman found it important to examine the emergence of virtues in social etiquette (see Goffman, 1971, pp. 184–185).

Further, both Elias and Goffman considered the role of self-restraints. However, whereas Elias perceived this type of internal self-imposed conduct to be a psychological side effect of external societal control as a historically emerging phenomenon, Goffman saw individual self-discipline and self-restraint as situationally determined mechanisms by which individuals confine selfish impulses and cooperate to make and facilitate performances and smooth social interaction (Kuzmics, 1991). Although Goffman only did refer to Elias's work sporadically, there might be essential realization involved in combining historical studies of the civilization process with microanalyses of social interaction. Not only has Elias's work placed Goffman's analysis of embarrassment in a certain historical era, other historical studies, such as those of Richard Sennett, have also demonstrated that what Goffman described as a "persona" oriented toward external conduct is not a limited modern construction applying exclusively to the end of the 20th century, as this was also extremely alive in 18th-century Europe (Lofland, 1995, p. 187).

Conclusion

Concluding this chapter, it may be said that the notion of perspectivism constitutes an essential key concerning the understanding of Goffman's way of contemplating and practicing sociology. Goffman found inspiration in widely differing thinkers and approaches. Partly due to this, some commentators have claimed that his work falls short of a consistent, organized theoretical core (Psathas, 1996, p. 383). On the face of it, such criticism may seem legitimate, but on second thought, it will become evident that, to a large extent, the eclectic element was the decisive reason for the indisputable success of Goffman's sociology. The fact that this strategy also enabled Goffman to avoid calling himself to account for a particular established theory of science and thus declined numerous labeling attempts is but a side effect of which he was undoubtedly aware. Finally, it should be noted that Goffman's aversion to being labeled, coupled with his pronounced eclecticism, may be considered a natural consequence of his unerring eye for the complexities of social reality (Lofland, 1984, p. 11). Allegedly, Goffman opposed the view that one single perspective may capture the nuances and depths of human social interaction. We conclude this chapter with a few questions for further consideration.

Questions

- What were the most prominent intellectual influences on Erving Goffman's work, and particularly where and how can their impact be seen in his work?
- In which way can Erving Goffman's eclecticism inspire cross-disciplinary thinking in contemporary sociology?
- To what extent does Erving Goffman's inspirational eclecticism differ from other social thinkers' approaches?

3

Goffman's "Mixed Methods"

N obody ever worked or wrote quite like Erving Goffman. The research topics he chose for attention, the way he presented them, and his approach to conducting sociological research in general were at the time of his writing quite exceptional. One of the main qualities of Goffman's writings was their sophisticated commonsensical character, which was evident in his unique ability to defamiliarize the apparently trivial nature of everyday life while at the same time making his readers sensitive toward the nuances, depths, and hidden dimensions of quite ordinary events. Alasdair MacIntyre once thus described Goffman's ability to capture this familiar and trivial world as a special way of seeing "the familiar with the eyes of a stranger, while at the same time retaining his familiarity with what is being viewed" (MacIntyre, 1969, p. 447). Although Goffman was trained as a sociologist, compared to most of his predecessors, contemporaries, and successors within the discipline of sociology, he seemed surprisingly unconcerned with matters of method. Sociology has not only always taken pride in its privileged object of analysis—society—but the discipline has also been keen to develop and refine a set of methods aimed at capturing this particular object. Goffman, however, never wrote a book about methodology, nor do any of his books contain much information of an epistemological or methodological character, telling the reader about how Goffman obtained his material, how he sampled and coded it, how his analytical strategy proceeded, or how his analyses or conclusions could be subjected to conventional criteria of validation and replication.

In their analysis of Goffman's methods, Jack Bynum and Charles Pranter therefore rightly commented:

> Goffman is not concerned with formal method, and his theoretical development and validation often veer toward the ungrounded pole. He does not rely on elaborate measurement or structured questionnaires or interviews. He does not hesitate to use literary examples if they help to illustrate a concept or idea. He relies heavily on case studies, gleanings of "expert opinion" from other sociological or psychological studies, as well as novels and casual conversations. His work is mainly of a descriptive, qualitative nature which seems to blend well with his own profound insights. (Bynum & Pranter, 1984, p. 96)

As is obvious, Goffman worked in a rather unconventional fashion. His studies did not follow any mainstream methodology and in many respects resembled as much literature as research. Many were critical of this unconventional approach. Pierre Bourdieu once observed how "the guardians of positivist dogmatism assigned Goffman to the 'lunatic fringe' of sociology, among the eccentrics who shunned the rigours of science and preferred the soft option of philosophical mediation or literary description" (Bourdieu, 1983, p. 112). However, as sociologist Wilhelm Baldamus once stated, we must "presume that side by side with the official methodology that one finds in the textbooks on systematic theory, formal logics, statistical methods, survey design or interviewing procedure, there exists a reservoir of *unofficial*, non-formalized techniques of inquiry" (Baldamus, 1972, p. 281, original emphasis). In this chapter, we want to delineate and discuss Goffman's official as well as unofficial "methods" (consciously put in quotation marks emphasizing the unconventional character of most parts of his methodology). We want to illustrate and discuss Goffman's unmistakable qualitative orientation, his ethnographic and participant observation studies, his conceptual development "from below," his creatively and abductively invoked metaphors, his particular writing style, and finally his methodology of violation.

A "Freewheeling" Qualitative Sociologist

That Goffman was indeed a peculiar sociologist should by now come as no surprise. His way of writing and practicing sociology differed in almost every respect from the mainstream sociology of his contemporaries—this was evident in his surprising perspectives on that which was largely taken for granted, his unauthorized sources of data, and his development and shifting use of concepts and metaphors that gradually uncovered the new and heretofore neglected sociological terrain he wanted to explore. One of the main qualities of Goffman's work was his gift of writing in a way that made room for recognition and identification—in his texts, we recognize things about ourselves and our social intercourse with others that simultaneously stimulate and provoke, creating equal amounts of empathy and embarrassment. As Allen Grimshaw stressed, "Goffman's gift was a facility to point out things about social life *at once* completely new *and* instantly recognizable" (Grimshaw, 1983, p. 147, original emphasis), while Charles Lemert stated that Goffman's work created a "shudder of recognition" (Lemert, 1997, p. ix). Without exaggerating, one may say that this peculiar style won him fame and readership among the general public but at the same time made him infamous and open to criticism among many colleagues. For example, when *Asylums* was first published in 1961, William Caudill (1962, p. 368) criticized it for being filled with endless provoking and descriptive comparisons of psychiatric hospitals with prisons, dilapidated boarding schools, badly run ships, and so on. Others were more positive. For instance, Stanford M. Lyman (1973) believed that one could reasonably say the same about Goffman as Max Weber once wrote about Georg Simmel:

> Nearly every one of his books abounds in important new theoretical ideas and the most subtle observations. Almost every one of them belongs to those books in which not only the valid findings, but even the false ones, contain a wealth of stimulation for one's own further thought. (Weber, 1972, p. 158)

One of the main reasons Goffman was and remains enigmatic and an outsider in sociology is not due only to his substantial topic of interest—the trivial matters of ordinary social life—but also to the way he decided to investigate and describe it. His metaphors, as we shall see later, were merely one part of his rather unconventional and diversified methodological toolbox. In general, Goffman remained critical of the ability of so-called traditional research designs to capture the essence of encounters, interaction, and social situations, and throughout the years he several times pointed to the severe limitations of such methods. At a time when large-scale quantitative studies loomed large in sociology (just think of the surveys of attitudes and voting behavior conducted by the likes of Samuel Stouffer and Paul F. Lazarsfeld or the collective research teams studying unemployment in the Austrian town of Marienthal or the (in)famous Kinsey studies reporting on sexual preferences and experiences in supposedly sexually puritan America), Goffman's one-man show was decidedly of a qualitative orientation, and today he is frequently counted among the major exponents of qualitative research (Brinkmann, Jacobsen, & Kristiansen, 2014). In fact, Goffman never officially worked with quantitative material and even seemed to find quantitative studies tedious and contentious.

In *Relations in Public*, he thus stated on the status of the knowledge generated by traditional research designs dominating social science (e.g., experimental laboratory research or statistical variable analysis) at the time of his writing:

> The variables that emerge tend to be creatures of research designs that have no substance outside the room in which the apparatus and subjects are located, except perhaps briefly when a replication or a continuity is performed under sympathetic auspices and a full moon. Concepts are designed on the run in order to get on with setting things up so that trials can be performed and the effects of controlled variation of some kind or another measured. The work begins with the sentence "we hypothesize that . . . ," goes on from there to a full discussion of the biases and limits of the proposed design, reasons why these aren't nullifying, and culminates in an appreciable number of satisfyingly significant correlations tending to confirm some of the hypotheses. As though the uncovering of social life were that simple. Fields of naturalistic study have not been uncovered through these methods. Concepts have not emerged that re-ordered our view of social activity. Understanding of ordinary behavior has not accumulated; distance has. (Goffman, 1971, pp. 20–21)

In addition to critiquing these conventional positivistic research designs with a focus on variables, correlations, and hypotheses, one of Goffman's gimmicks also consisted in understating the importance of his own creative methods and apparently dubious findings when in *Behavior in Public Places* insisting:

> Obviously, many of these data are of doubtful worth, and my interpretations— especially some of them—may certainly be questionable, but I assume that a loose speculative approach to a fundamental area of conduct is better than a rigorous blindness to it. (Goffman, 1963, p. 4)

Later, in *Frame Analysis,* he revealed even more of the nature of his own sporadic, impressionistic, or anecdotal research approach and of the data material involved in his analyses:

> By and large, I do not present these anecdotes, therefore, as evidence or proof, but as clarifying depictions, as frame fantasies which manage, through the hundred liberties taken by their tellers, to celebrate our beliefs about the work- ings of the world. What was put into these tales is thus what I would like to get out of them. These data have another weakness. I have culled them over the years on a hit-or-miss basis using principles of selection mysterious to me which, furthermore, changed from year to year and which I could not recover if I wanted to. Here, too, *a caricature of systematic sampling is involved.* (Goffman, 1974, p. 15, emphasis added)

So despite his multiple theoretical sources of inspiration (such as primarily Durkheim, Simmel, Mead, and Sartre) mentioned in Chapter 2, and despite his intensive periods of naturalistic fieldwork and data collection, Goffman was neither an armchair/theoretical sociologist nor a naturalistic/empirical researcher. He was a hybrid, a man with the ability to mix traditions, techniques, and ideas into his own unique and eclectic methodological position. His humorous disdain for those engaged only in airy or abstract theorizing—what C. Wright Mills (1959) in Goffman's own lifetime famously termed "grand theory"—is well known and he, according to Robin Williams, once described such theorizing as "two thirds corn flakes, one third taffy" (Williams, 1998, p. 157). In the Preface to *The Presentation of Self in Everyday Life*, he even warned his readers that "the introduction is necessarily abstract and may be skipped" (Goffman, 1959, p. vi). This humorous disdain for abstract theorizing was counterbalanced by an equal amount of dissatisfaction with statistical or empirical fetishism—what Mills labeled "abstracted empiricism"—without anchoring in anything but numbers, scorecards, and diagrams. These were types of information and reporting hardly ever resorted to or deployed by Goffman himself.

The proposal that Goffman to a large degree was a qualitatively oriented sociologist perhaps requires some qualification. His preference for participant observation is well known and celebrated and pertains both to the formally conducted fieldwork sessions in the Shetland Islands and in a mental asylum—as we shall present in what follows—as well as to a generally observant and curious attitude to everything that by happenstance went on around him, which was then strategically used as evidence or examples in most of his books. Goffman obviously enjoyed submerging into and subjecting himself to the microecological universe of everyday life, and he believed that the direct observation of events was indeed important to understanding. Despite or perhaps because of this, he was careful to provide any methodological recipes or analytical prophylaxes for others to follow. Therefore, his books never contained lengthy methodological discussions or descriptions of what he actually did, how, when, why, and to whom. Howard S. Becker commented on this reluctance to provide or reveal methodological guidelines by stating:

> [Goffman] felt very strongly that you could not elaborate any useful rules of procedure for doing field research and that, if you attempted to do that, people would misinterpret what you had written, do it (whatever it was) wrong, and then blame you for the resulting mess. He refused to accept responsibility for such unfortunate possibilities. (Becker, 2003, p. 660)

Direct interviewing—another favorite method among most qualitative sociologists—was not a technique practiced by Goffman (perhaps apart from in his master's thesis); neither was focus group interviewing or other means to extract meaning from people by way of their own accounts and explanations. One can ponder that this was perhaps due to his suspicion that people would refrain from telling the truth if interviewed or would hide their actual opinions behind a variety of impression-management maneuvers. Instead of trusting whatever people say they do or think, Goffman preferred to watch them. As he stated: "I don't give hardly any weight to what people say, but I try to triangulate what they're saying with events" (Goffman, 1989, p. 131). Goffman thus once, clearly sarcastically, called himself a "positivist" (Verhoeven, 1993, p. 325), which is, after all, not an entirely erroneous label, as he particularly excelled in the distanced observation of people's antics often also described in a somewhat distanced way. Although far from the experimental designs of behaviorists or interactionist social psychologists such as Robert Freed Bales, systematically studying group behavior, there is little doubt that Goffman, just like the more positivistic-oriented researchers at his time, wanted his work to be "objective" and "value free" when stating, "I suppose one can work towards a value-free social science. Or that's a realistic ideal to have" (Goffman in Verhoeven, 1993, p. 326).

Goffman apparently found it difficult to narrow down or summarize his own particular approach to research. As he said in interview, "It can be done well, and it can be done badly, and I can't provide the rules for doing it well. It isn't necessarily an art; it's a method of some sort" (Goffman in Verhoeven, 1993, p. 341). In many ways, Goffman's preferred research strategy—or perhaps rather his antistrategy—embodied Ken Plummer's notion of the AHFA principle—the "ad hoc fumbling around" with its emphasis on the impressionistic, pragmatic, tentative, and explorative as compared to more systematic sampling procedures and coherent research designs. Moreover, most of his books consciously bear subtitles containing notions such as "essays," "notes," or "studies" (see Goffman, 1961, 1963, 1964a, 1967, 1971, 1972, 1974) signaling something merely tentative, preliminary, or suggestive rather than systematic theoretical treatises. Due to Goffman's gifted ability to play with words on the covers of books as well as inside them, perhaps more than anything else he was a stylist (Atkinson, 1989; Hillyard, 1999). Just compare his texts—primarily consisting of a number of extended essays—with those of most of his contemporaries: the way he writes, discusses his approach, and reports findings is all very different from conventional sociology, and this difference was breeding both a lack of comprehension as well as downright hostility among some readers. Thus, his somewhat alternative, creative, and relaxed—some would perhaps even say arbitrary—attitude to research procedures meant that critical voices were raised every now and then making a mockery of Goffman's methods, his style, and his research interest and questioning the validity of his research findings.

As mentioned, Goffman's work was different from theoretically contemplative or armchair scholars who excelled in abstract and philosophical reasoning. This was not his ball game. However, rather than seeing his own work as "research," Goffman stated that it perhaps came closer to "scholarship." Commenting on his own later work, perhaps particularly *Frame Analysis* (1974) and *Gender Advertisements* (1979a), Goffman thus stated:

> What I have been doing recently is not what you would call research, it's more scholarship. It's taking some concepts or variables which I think have some relevance, significance, and reviewing various kinds of findings, of research, novels, all that sort of thing, in terms of them. So it is *a sort of freewheeling, literary kind of thing.* . . . I usually collect a larger number of illustrations and think about those maybe in a more systematic way, I hope, than would characterize persons who are merely scholars. (Goffman in Verhoeven, 1993, pp. 338–339; emphasis added).

Goffman here specifically—and very occasionally—commented on how his approach differed from that of "analytical induction" as advocated at the time by, among others, Alfred Lindesmith, Donald Cressey, and Howard S. Becker. His work, as we shall see later in this chapter, perhaps came closer to the so-called **creative abduction**, because it mixed empirical insights with theoretical guesswork in order to shed new light on overlooked or neglected social phenomena.

Ethnography and Participant Observation

Even though Goffman was a professor in both sociology and anthropology, and even though he conducted fieldwork based on systematic procedures of **participant observation**, these were hardly the primary methodological competences that won him international recognition. His way of conducting fieldwork and his methodological reflections about this part of his work did not differ substantially from the prevailing ideas at the time. In fact, throughout his career, Goffman conducted only a limited amount of fieldwork research, which we shall here illustrate and discuss.

As we mentioned in Chapter 1, Goffman's PhD thesis *Communication Conduct in an Island Community* (1953b) builds on extensive and in-depth participant observation in a relatively secluded island community in the largest settlement of Baltasound on the small Shetland Island of Unst located somewhere between the northern coast of Scotland and the Faeroe Islands. According to his PhD thesis, his aspiration was to be an "observant participant, rather than a participating observer" (Goffman, 1953b, p. 2). Goffman stayed in Unst for almost one and a half years, during which he presented himself to the islanders as an American college student who was interested in gaining firsthand experience in the economics of island farming. As Goffman stated: "Within these limits, I tried to play an unexceptional and acceptable role in community life" (Goffman, 1953b, p. 2), his goal being "to observe people off their guard" (Goffman, 1953b, p. 5). The actual participation followed two partly overlapping tracks. First, Goffman attempted to participate in as many different social situations as possible in which the local population were involved in face-to-face interaction with each other. For example, this would include during meals and work, at weddings and funerals, parties, or shopping. He wanted to make sure that his participation in events would involve as many different participants as possible, thereby providing him with as many nuances and variations in his material as possible. Second, Goffman throughout a period of time during his stay in Unst participated in specific social situations with the same group of participants. The purpose of this latter part of his "observant participant" strategy was to minimize the effect of the presence of a stranger upon social interaction and to obtain knowledge about interaction crises that regularly occur and that contain important information about behavioral forms, norms, and rules. This extensive and intensive fieldwork experience in Unst formed the background for many of Goffman's later conceptual developments such as the "interaction order," "information management," and "team performances" and throughout his career served as an almost inexhaustible pool of data and illustrative examples. Based on Goffman's continuous and extensive use of illustrative examples—and indeed extrapolations of these—of social interaction from the settlement of Baltasound in Unst, Yves Winkin (2000) aptly named this town "the symbolic capital of social interaction."

As we shall show in Chapter 5, Goffman also conducted extensive participant observation studies at a psychiatric hospital in Washington, D.C., which was later published in the book *Asylums* (1961). This fieldwork lasted almost a full year, during which Goffman on a regular basis was present among the patients in different wards. To the patients, he gave the impression that he was an assistant for the athletic instructor (Goffman, 1961, p. ix), which made it possible for him to move freely among them. According to his own statements, he refrained from becoming involved and kept at a safe distance from events. Besides Goffman's claim that he wanted to obtain knowledge about the social world of the patients as they themselves subjectively experienced it, we do not learn much about his actual research procedures or methodological considerations in this study.

When it came to commenting on the actual nature of his method and data collection strategy during these rounds of extensive participant observation, Goffman remained surprisingly silent. He was not particularly interested in detailing how he arrived at his specific conclusions or in showing the relationship between his empirical work and theoretical and conceptual developments. In only two places in Goffman's writings will one discover more elaborated reflections on method. One place is in Goffman's PhD thesis, in which he was still subjected to the institutionalized requirements to explicate his methodological considerations. The other place is in an article with the title "On Fieldwork" (Goffman, 1989) published seven years after his death in *Journal of Contemporary Ethnography*. The article is a transcribed version of a presentation Goffman gave in 1974 at a conference on fieldwork. In such an article, one might have expected that Goffman would finally have revealed some of the techniques that made his publications so famous. However, in the article Goffman primarily argues for already well-established principles of fieldwork methodology, for example, that the researcher ought to stay in the field for an extended period of time and that he or she should take elaborate field notes and try to compare participants' verbally expressed convictions and beliefs with their actual behavior. Despite the already established and commonsensical character of such ideas, it must be admitted that in between such conventional recommendations, one will also find some more original considerations of how to do fieldwork:

> [Participant observation is a technique] of getting data, it seems to me, by subjecting yourself, your own body, and your own personality, and your own social situation, to a set of contingencies that play upon a set of individuals, so that you can physically and ecologically penetrate their circle of response to their social situation, or their work situation, or ethnic situation, or whatever. So that you are close to them while they are responding to what life does to them. (Goffman, 1989, p. 125)

Despite such stimulating recommendations, the overall methodological principles of this article do not principally differ from what would be found elsewhere in anthropological and sociological textbooks on research methodology. The article is primarily interesting because Goffman here— contrary to his common practice—explicitly comments on questions of methodology. Apart from the formal fieldwork conducted by Goffman during his work with the PhD thesis and as the empirical groundwork for *Asylums* (1961), there is also the informal and sporadically conducted fieldwork in a Las Vegas casino—apparently he served as a pit boss for some time—as well as Goffman's constant utilization of impressionistic insights gained from his everyday encounters with colleagues, students, friends, and strangers, which also served to buttress his coining of neologisms and continuous refinement of his conceptual apparatus. In many ways, as Michael Pettit (2011) has recently suggested, Goffman's approach to fieldwork and observational studies clearly resembled the image of the confident man that Goffman often wrote about elsewhere in his writings, the image of the researcher as "a cool, detached observer who navigates the social by practicing small interpersonal hustles" (Pettit, 2011, p. 150).

Grounded Theory and Generating Concepts "From Below"

Goffman's procedure in the aforementioned ethnographic studies of social interaction patterns of Shetland Island inhabitants, mental patients, and card dealers in Las Vegas can initially be characterized as inductive and as having close affinities with the so-called constant comparative methodology advanced by the two American sociologists Barney G. Glaser and Anselm L. Strauss (1967) under the heading of "**grounded theory**." They advocated a progressive (and partly intuitive) procedure in which the researcher starts out with a relatively loose concept that is gradually substantiated and "filled out" through the continuous collection of and confrontation with new data, whereby new concepts and categories appear, relations and connections between existing concepts and categories are established, and the emerging theory is saturated through collecting and analyzing theoretically relevant data.

The Presentation of Self in Everyday Life (1959) partly gives the reader the impression that Goffman aimed at developing such an empirically grounded conceptual framework. Here Goffman, already from the onset of the book, introduces a concept or a model (namely the dramaturgical metaphor), which he continuously developed and expanded by introducing its different categories in one elongated movement at the same time as he illustrated and grounded the concepts by importing and incorporating a multitude of different empirical examples. For example, Goffman used a book about domestic life in Scotland in the 18th century to illustrate the concept of "idealization" with a story about a financially troubled noble family, which when they invited guests for dinner had five or six waiters at the table to remove attention from the fact that what was served was in fact nothing but oatmeal and pickled herring in various different disguises (Goffman, 1959, p. 47). Goffman also came up with his own examples. A few illustrations of this point:

Goffman substantiated his claim that the members of a performing "team" must often present themselves in an individually different and distinguishable manner in order to make the entire collective endeavor appear as successful as possible by way of the personal observation that when a middle-class couple presents itself at sociable events to new friends, the wife will appear to be more respectful and subordinate to her husband than she would otherwise be when they are all alone (Goffman, 1959, p. 84). In a similar vein, his concept of "role distance" was exemplified by the quotidian example of the maturing adolescent forced into riding a merry-go-round and throughout the ride flaunting a playful yet distanced and disdainful attitude toward this childlike preoccupation (Goffman, 1972).

There are thus certain unmistakable elements of grounded theory evident in Goffman's methodology (although it was used already prior to the development of grounded theory methodology throughout the 1960s) in the way he attempted to develop theory by way of a comparative procedure in which he made comparisons across different social situations. Goffman developed a system of concepts by more or less systematically saturating his concepts with empirical data. He gradually expanded his model construction by adding new concepts that are highlighted, confronted, and discussed through introducing every new empirical material. This procedure is very much in accordance with Glaser and Strauss's (1967, p. 32) understanding of theory as a "process" and as "an ever-developing entity, not as a perfected product."

Obviously, one can criticize Goffman's method of gathering data material. It is—so he admits—to a large degree eclectic. One often gets the impression that he used whatever he haphazardly or coincidentally came across. For example, there are 282 references in *The Presentation of Self in Everyday Life* and, based on a superficial and quickly conducted content analysis, one will discover that approximately two out of three references are made to scientific publications, whereas the last third consists of references to novels, short stories, autobiographies, etiquette manuals, conversations, or sources not relying on scientific methods. In *Stigma* (1964a), the distribution of references is even more significant. Here we know from a more systematic analysis that out of 292 references, 42% stem from scientific work, while 58% belong to the category of novels, short stories, autobiographies, and personal conversations (Bynum & Pranter, 1984, p. 98). Two interpretations are available here depending on whether one is a supporter of so-called hard or soft sociology. "Hardliners" will reject Goffman's mixing of theory with impressionistic data and claim that theoretical ideas must necessarily be grounded in systematically sampled and substantial amounts of quantitative data as well as consist of documented connections between variables. According to them, Goffman's analyses should most of all be classified as loose talk and hypothetical relations between concepts and data. Others, and usually more qualitatively oriented sociologists, will instead insist that Goffman elegantly combined his unique sense for observing the microscopic dimensions of social life with the ability to track down and weave together scattered examples into a comprehensive and fine network of concepts about social interaction. Notwithstanding one's position in this discussion, one must recognize the fact that this admittedly peculiar kind of research practice gives Goffman's studies a certain aura of coincidence. But what is perhaps even worse: if one remains within the confines of grounded theory methodology, Goffman's concepts are not sufficiently or systematically nuanced. The inventors of grounded theory stressed that if a theory is used to explain and understand social phenomena, then it must systematically integrate a very varied selection of data obtained from different situations. In Goffman's work, this integration seems to happen almost incidentally (Glaser & Strauss, 1967, p. 138). As mentioned, Goffman takes whatever he comes across but apparently only incorporated that which corroborated his concepts. Glaser and Strauss actually claimed that Goffman's theory is not sufficiently saturated, because he did not systematically confront his concepts with data until the point when new data could no longer nuance the concepts. Peter K. Manning seemed to suggest a similar critique when claiming about Goffman's many lists of examples and constant development of concepts:

> [Goffman] does not infer or induce from them, does not claim that these types are exhaustive, explicate the degree of kinds of possible logical interconnections between them, nor does he always relate his current efforts to previous ideas of himself or others. (Manning, 1980, p. 270)

But can Goffman's alternative version of grounded theory—for example, generating concepts from below—be used for anything at all? To a certain degree it can. One the one hand, one can learn a lot from Goffman's comparative approach, in which he analyzed various fundamentally different examples, phenomena, and situations and across these different inputs developed useful and poignant theoretical concepts. On the other hand, however, a certain element of coincidence in his data selection comes to stand in the way of a more systematic theoretical integration, which must not only be the purpose of an analysis grounded in data but also more generally of sociological research as such. As is a well-known fact, theories (at least sociological theories) consist of concepts, but if these concepts are not systematically saturated by data from different social situations, then it becomes difficult if not downright problematic to integrate them into a coherent theory.

Double Fitting, Creative Abduction, and Conceptual Development Through Metaphors

As is evident from the discussion of Goffman's work procedure, he was neither a clear-cut inductivist nor a definitive deductivist sociologist. He rather worked in a peculiar abductive manner, at times closer to the inductive or theory-generating pole, at other times closer to the deductive or theory-testing pole in what has been called "the qualitative continuum" (Kristiansen, 2002). In this qualitative continuum, one end is occupied by the radical induction of, for example, grounded theory, the middle section is occupied by more hybrid methodological approaches such as analytical induction, adaptive theory, and the extended case method, whereas the other end is reserved for more abductive-deductive approaches, such as Goffman's metaphorical perspectives, to which we return in what follows.

Greg Smith (1999b, p. 7) has suggested that Goffman regarded his concepts merely as temporary concepts or sketches, which necessarily had to be revised, rejected, substantiated, or supplemented in the course of further research. One need not read many books by Goffman before this distinctive conceptual understanding becomes evident. Concepts are continuously introduced, defined, used, revised, rejected, or developed further. New concepts are proposed, whereas others suddenly disappear again. It is therefore unsurprising that critics of Goffman have talked about certain conceptual inconsistencies and a lack of conceptual coherence. But might there be some meaning to this conceptual madness? Indeed so—at least according to Robin Williams (1988), who advanced an interesting analysis of Goffman's "method." In Williams's view, Goffman's method is far from slapdash or arbitrary, but is rather a highly reflexive and deliberate knowledge-creating process. Williams points to the common conceptual thread and thematic continuities between Goffman's PhD thesis from 1953 and his undelivered Presidential Address three decades later. In both publications, Goffman explicitly mentioned the concept of the "interaction order," and what is particularly interesting is that Goffman in his Presidential Address openly described his continuous endeavor to create coherence in his studies of this specific social order. So although Goffman clearly shunned the development of a rigorous and systematic research procedure, he nevertheless followed the same track throughout most of his career. Williams (1988, p. 77) points out that when Goffman continuously returned to old concepts in new ways, it was part and parcel of a doubled-tracked process through which he constantly subjected his conceptual apparatus to new tests (e.g., confronted it with new data and new problems). It is Williams's contention that Goffman consciously shifted back and forth between empirical observation and immersion and theoretical and conceptual development, among contexts of discovery, testing, and invention. According to Williams, there is an intimate connection among discovering new knowledge, testing existing knowledge, and putting the newly acquired knowledge together in new and innovative ways. Goffman's work procedure can be illustrated by Figure 3.1, which graphically captures his constantly shifting back and forth between incoming data and an emerging model.

Figure 3.1   The Data–Model Relationship

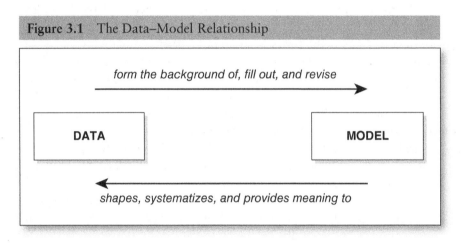

As is clear from this figure, Goffman worked in a dialectical and double-tracked manner. In many ways, he innovatively mixed surprising conceptual/theoretical/metaphorical preconceptions with various sources of empirical material, and via this methodological *unio mystico*, produced an expansive and powerful conceptual apparatus. Goffman's methodological approach therefore seems quite similar to the so-called double fitting described by Wilhelm Baldamus (1972, p. 295) as a kind of "informal theorizing [which] involves a continuous restructuring of conceptual frameworks," in which "the investigator simultaneously manipulates the thing he wants to explain as well as his explanatory framework." Goffman's insightful descriptions and conceptual delineation of face-to-face interaction were surely such a double-fitting interplay of informal and flexible metaphorical ideas with a constant inflow of impressions from everyday life events. Thus, the "model" referred to in the figure in Goffman's case was primarily *the metaphor*.

An enigmatic feature of Goffman's methodological perspective was his preferred way of dealing with and describing his favorite research focus: the study of face-to-face interaction in ordinary, everyday settings through metaphorical lenses. One of the most frequently discussed dimensions of

Goffman's methodology is therefore his extensive and elaborate use of metaphors—conventionally a literary device—to provide meaning to his data (Smith and Jacobsen, 2010). Gary Alan Fine once suggested that "to understand social science is to understand the metaphors that social scientists use" (Fine, 1984, p. 239). To understand important parts of Goffman's methodology is therefore to understand his metaphors. As many interpreters throughout the years have pointed out, Goffman described the grammar of social life through three or perhaps four main metaphorical frameworks— the theatre, the ritual, the game, and the frame (see, e.g., Branaman, 1997; Corradi, 1990; Jacobsen & Kristiansen, 2006; Kalekin-Fishman, 1988; Treviño, 2003b). Metaphors have had a longstanding use and appeal in literature and—particularly due to the so-called rhetorical, linguistic, or poetic turn in the latter part of the 20th century—now increasingly also in the humanities and social sciences. Looking at the history of sociology, one will in fact discover the deep-seated metaphorical roots of many central concepts, theories, and research areas (Brown, 1977; Nisbet, 1976/2002; Richardson, 1990; Rigney, 2001). The magic, promise, and allure of metaphors consist in the fact that they by their invocation *transfer* meaning from one (and often quite different) realm of language to another; they creatively *transform* our quotidian or common sense conception of reality; they *transcend* commonly held and ingrained assumptions within a discipline; they *transgress* strictly upheld boundaries between the real and the imagined; they *transmute* our ideas and notions about the world and its fundamental workings; and they—momentarily—*transport* the reader into a wonderful world of make-believe. Thus, there is a certain inherent "as if" quality to metaphors—they, as matters of linguistic circumscription and mental pretension, present selective aspects of reality as if they were something else (Jacobsen, 2014).

In all these facets of metaphorical reasoning, Goffman's application of metaphors was quite exceptional. His use of metaphors was not only highly original—it was also relatively systematic and consistent. We thus regard Goffman's metaphors as instances of Umberto Eco's idea of "creative abduction," which he defined as abductive thinking "in which the rule acting as an explanation has to be invented *ex novo*" (Eco, 1984, p. 42). Creative abduction is thus a way of applying a rule (e.g., a metaphor) to explain or understand phenomena (e.g., everyday interaction) in which the rule itself has been invented by its user. The metaphor helps us to see phenomena as if they were something else and thereby stimulate our imagination. However, despite their obvious originality, Goffman's metaphors were not entirely invented *ex novo*, from scratch—they, at least to a certain degree, relied on his reading of the work and ideas of others. So whereas his theatrical or dramaturgical metaphor was in part inspired by his devouring of novels, etiquette books, and crime stories with dramatic plots and in part shaped by Kenneth Burke's (1936/1984) idea of "dramatism," his ritual metaphor was clearly informed by the writings of Émile Durkheim and functional anthropologists. And whereas the development of the game metaphor was to a large degree inspired by personal experiences as a dealer in a Las Vegas casino as well as his reading of the game-theoretical work of Thomas C. Schelling, his last frame metaphor (although perhaps not really a metaphor) was clearly informed by Gregory Bateson and the cognitive turn in the social sciences.

In Goffman's work, the metaphors thus served as "idiosyncratic maps" (Manning, 1992), shedding light on and providing a roadmap for a heretofore unknown or unchartered territory. Another purpose of Goffman's many metaphors was to dress dull, trivial, and taken-for-granted social reality in new, powerful, colorful, and recontextualized conceptual garments, which— at one and the same time—simultaneously obscure as well as sharpen (perhaps sharpen through obscuration) our comprehension of what is going on there. Through such redescriptive metaphorical lenses, social life is suddenly made more transparent as well as more tangible to social researchers and their readership. Each metaphor—theatre, ritual, game, and frame—thus pictures the world in a novel and surprising light in which each concept provided meaning to other concepts, and in this way an intricate "metaphorical network" was constructed around the scattered empirical observations. Consuelo Corradi testifies to how the metaphor in Goffman's work was thus constitutive

> in the sense that it creates the analogy by offering, through the metaphorizer, a set of rules of usage, a dictionary of expressions with which to describe a given social phenomenon that explores the latter from a new perspective: the individual is conceptualized as an actor, and those who observe him/her as an audience, his/her behavior as a performance or masquerade, the place where it occurs as a setting or stage, and so on. (Corradi, 1990, pp. 166–167)

Moreover, the different metaphorical networks or frameworks served as an illustration of Goffman's methodological multiperspectivism—the fact that the same phenomenon, the interaction order, can be approached and bombarded with impressions and ideas from a variety of different directions, each shedding some light on what is actually going on. As George Psathas (1996, p. 383) recalls, Goffman once stated on his own perspective, "I snipe at a target from many different positions." His many metaphors, his shift in the use of the term "definition of the situation" to "frame" later in life, and his "freewheeling" mixing of methods—from covert participant observation in the Shetlands and in St. Elizabeth's Hospital via metaphorical frameworks to textual readings and listening to radio programs—all testify to the fact that Goffman all the time was aiming at an all-out approach to capture the self-same target from a multitude of different angles. In this way, his metaphors showed that you can enter the same room from many different doors. As a consequence of this, Goffman remained careful not to reify his metaphorical imagery and, in *The Presentation of Self in Everyday Life*, in which he introduced and deployed the dramaturgical metaphor, he—metaphorically—concluded that "scaffolds, after all, are to build other things with, and should be erected with a keen eye to taking them down" (Goffman, 1959, p. 246). So Goffman's many metaphors were only make-shift methodological devices aimed at setting a sluggish sociological imagination in motion. We will deal more substantially with the content of Goffman's metaphors in Chapter 4.

Goffman's Style—Textual Persuasion, Essayism, and Sophisticated Irony

Any kind of research methodology also implies a certain style of reporting findings and communicating with one's intended readership. Also in this respect, Goffman was indeed different. Paul Atkinson thus emphasized that "Goffman was a *stylist*" (Atkinson, 1989, p. 59, original emphasis), while Lawrence Hazelrigg (1992, p. 245) commented that Goffman deployed an unmistakable "playful style," and more recently, Richard Handel insisted that "Goffman was not only a great social theorist, he was a great writer. He thus needs to be read critically and carefully not only as a theorist, but as an author" (Handler, 2012, p. 179). Despite its conventional connotations, presentational style is not merely a shallow, superficial, or ornamental aspect of writing—it can, as in Goffman's case, constitute an integral part of a researcher's analytical strategy. Goffman's style was far from frivolous—it was a systematically pursued and well-orchestrated part of his overall research strategy. Throughout his career, Goffman was very much inspired by literary writers, just as he himself often referred to or even imitated the poetic sensibility of literary writers. In every sense of the term, Goffman was a literary sociologist—the aforementioned metaphors testify to this. As Arnold Birenbaum and Edward Sagarin once stated, Goffman "reminds us of no other social thinker so much as he does of great men of letters, perhaps Marcel Proust or Franz Kafka" (Birenbaum & Sagarin, 1973, pp. 3–4). Working consciously with writing style was a trademark of many of those working within the tradition of the Chicago School of sociology, and Goffman was far from the only Chicago-trained sociologist who took style seriously—just think of the likes of Robert E. Park, Everett C. Hughes, or Howard S. Becker (Cappetti, 1993; Jacobsen, Antoft, & Jørgensen, 2013). However, Goffman took the literary style to new lengths in his playful mixing of systematic or scant empirical observations with imaginative metaphors, and Adam Philips thus stated that "no sociologist has written with the mischievous wit and fervent logic of Goffman. Like William Empson, or Mary Douglas, or Roland Barthes, Goffman always seemed to have his own unique sentences, a sensibility and a style rather than a method" (Philips, 2010). Goffman was indeed a textually persuasive and rhetorically convincing writer (Smith & Jacobsen, 2010). He was a man of words. In Goffman's books, there are no graphics, statistics, models, cross-tabulations, or flow charts. By way of a dense and deep-layered network of interrelated concepts, examples, and illustrations, the reader is gradually persuaded that what Goffman is stating is in fact true—he is not presenting an open argument or a mere suggestion but rather, in a roundabout and downplayed way, proclamatory statements of fact. Ricca Edmondson aptly summarized Goffman's stylistic strategy as follows:

> Goffman differs from other sociologists chiefly in the *degree* to which he concerns himself with sensitizing the reader to his arguments, and in a sense this strategy is forced upon the reader. The "common-sense" views Goffman wants to dispute are deeply embedded in people's social consciousness, and are unlikely to be abandoned without considerable persuasion. Once the reader's viewpoint has been changed, he or she is able to complete Goffman's enthymematical explanations without any need for the text to make them explicit. (Edmondson, 1984, p. 148)

Moreover, Goffman—like Georg Simmel, with whom Goffman is often compared (Davis, 1997), and like Everett C. Hughes, whom Goffman later cast as his most significant teacher (Jaworski, 2000)—used the literary form of the essay as the overarching device with which to organize many of his texts. One of the many lessons Goffman might have learned from Simmel (via Hughes) is the enormous utility of the essay as a mode of sociological expression. In the essay, a topic is discussed in a formal or (more usually) an informal manner in a composition that is frequently shorter than book length. It is a flexible and accommodating literary form that allows wide scope for the expression of its author's individuality. As Robert Musil once observed, an essay is an "attempt," but it is an attempt that is qualified and determined. For Musil, the essay eschews conventional notions of "true" and "false," "wise" and "unwise," but it is "nevertheless subject to laws that are no less strict than they appear to be delicate and ineffable"

(Musil, 1953/1995, p. 301). The essay, still according to Musil, therefore lingers somewhere "between *amor intellectualis* and poetry." Sociology as a discipline has systematic and scientific ambitions, which means that the sociological essay will depart from the literary type in order to sustain these ambitions. The sociological essay must apply or contribute to the conceptual vocabulary and theoretical discourse of the discipline. It must guard against the excessively whimsical statement and have regard for some conception of objectivity if it is to be taken seriously. Thus, a logical and deliberate style of exposition is required. At the same time, however, it is an intensely personal and flexible mode of expression that allows fuller expression of an author's particular insights than more conventional academic textual modes.

Goffman embraced the essay as his preferred textual format. At best only 5 of Goffman's 11 books (*The Presentation of Self in Everyday Life, Stigma, Behavior in Public Places, Frame Analysis,* and *Gender Advertisements*) resemble monographs. The remainder are collections of essays on related themes. The essay mode is particularly well adapted to Goffman's socio-logical purposes. This is clearly shown in his memorable legitimating com-ment opening *Asylums.* Each of the four essays there collected together was originally designed to be freestanding:

> This method of presenting material may be irksome to the reader, but it allows me to pursue the main theme of each paper analytically and com-paratively past the point that would be allowable in chapters of an inte-grated book. I plead the state of the discipline. I think that at present, if sociological concepts are to be treated with affection, each must be traced back to where it best applies, followed on from there wherever it seems to lead, and pressed to disclose the rest of its family. Better, perhaps, different coats to clothe the children well than a single splendid tent in which they all shiver. (Goffman, 1961, pp. xiii–xiv)

Here Goffman adopted the "conscious essayism" that David Frisby (1981, pp. 70–72) identifies with Simmel, and Goffman not only admitted to this conscious essayism, he wallowed in it. Thus, in the introduction to *Forms of Talk,* he asked the reader "that these papers be taken for what they merely are: exercises, trials, try-outs, a means of displaying possibilities, not establishing facts" (Goffman, 1981a, p. 1). There is an ill-concealed element of sarcasm, staged modesty, and professional self-presentation embedded within these lines. Goffman was never apologetic about his "method," but he always seemed consciously aware that others might regard his preferred way of working with suspicion and ridicule, and, as Randall Collins (1986) remarked, Goffman was a virtuoso at using modesty as a weapon of attack.

Goffman's use of the essay mode contributed to the perception of a "modest" authorial voice. A common observation is that he writes in an "accessible" way. His analyses start from conceptual scratch, making few demands upon the reader's prior, specialized sociological knowledge. His writing is generally clear and peppered with vernacular expressions that give it a further appeal to the nonspecialized readership. It has a seductive quality, drawing the reader in to view the world in the way Goffman analyzes it. The primary justification for Goffman's conscious essayism is that the essay is well suited to his avowedly exploratory enterprise to develop the sociology of the "interaction order." In particular, the essay for Goffman facilitates the ongoing process of conceptual articulation that Robin Williams (1988) sees as the key to understanding Goffman's project as a whole, for it allows piecemeal modification and development to be readily carried out (the downside being that the essay mode does not facilitate assessment of the current state of development of that process of conceptual articulation).

Apart from the invocation of a vast metaphorical cornucopia, the deployment of an exquisite literary style and the essay as a form of expression, Goffman's stylistic antics also contained a decidedly humorous side. As was once observed, "reading Goffman can be fun" (Grimshaw, 1983, p. 148). One of the main reasons reading Goffman is fun is because he—in a sophisticated manner—often teased his reader. However, just as Goffman's style was not plain, neither were his sarcasm and irony. Alan Dawe (1973, p. 248) once described Goffman as "a sociological jester," and as we know from historical evidence, apart from the role of the court jester as affected entertainer, he was also known to be one of the few capable of saying the unsaid and of stating that which was otherwise unacknowledged, repressed, or silenced in social life. Anyone having read books by Goffman—or perhaps rather *most* books by him—will be struck by his ability to utilize a template of varied tricks of the trade to persuade the reader of his arguments and suggestions. Some of the most prominent of these "tricks" were irony, sarcasm, and humor (Fine & Martin, 1990). As Ricca Edmondson rightly observed, "Goffman's techniques of humour and irony have sensitising effects to support his reorganisations of perceived 'natural sequences' in everyday reality" (Edmondson, 1984, p. 155).

Conventionally, sociology is not appreciated for its humor or wittiness. However, Peter L. Berger once mused how "it is quite possible that the total absence of any sense of humor actually interferes with the attempt to give an intellectually adequate picture of society" (Berger, 1963, p. 67). Therefore, irony, sarcasm, and humor may in fact contribute positively and creatively to sociological thinking and theorizing. Supposedly, Goffman sensed this, and in his work, irony, sarcasm, and humor are permanent presences. In fact, in the majority—if not all—of his books, a **sophisticated irony** can substantially be detected. His pictorial presentation of women in commercial ads in *Gender Advertisements* (1979a) ironizes how they are routinely portrayed in absentminded states, cuddly situations, or inferior postures in consumer society. His musings over the carefully orchestrated verbal and nonverbal maneuvers involved in academic lectures or attempts to correct or downplay errors in radio talk shows in *Forms of Talk* (1981a) ironize pretentious academic self-presentations and public slips of the tongue and subsequent corrective efforts. His observant descriptions of social labeling processes and sophisticated passing strategies in *Stigma* (1964a) are by and large ironic accounts of how people try to wriggle their way into having their purported selves validated in a society obsessed with identity. His ironic stance in *Asylums* (1961) materialized in a subtle yet relentless antipsychiatric critique of the conditions offered to inmates, of the hypocrisy of the medical profession, and of the daily indignities of total institutions. In general, as Geoffrey Nunberg proposed in his review of *Forms of Talk* in the *New York Times*, Goffman gave "a mordant irony to the pretensions and theatricality of everyday interaction" (Nunberg, 1981).

Without ever stating the obvious or explicating his basic assumptions, Goffman in his books managed to hammer home hundreds of ironic points about contemporary social arrangements. We regard his ironic stance primarily as a strategically employed instrument or means of communicating with his readership, academic as well as nonacademic—alongside his metaphors, literary sources, and style as well as his essayism. On a personal level, there may have been a certain conscious role distance from more academic or technical sociology involved in his irony, or it can be seen as a defense mechanism or even as part of a presentation of self as a master of trope and prose. On the analytical level, Goffman's irony can be appreciated as a way of allowing him to say things contrary to truistic, commonly accepted, or commonsensical conceptions in order to highlight ambiguities, discrepancies, and fallacies.

Toward a Methodology of Violation

As mentioned, Goffman's project consisted in defining and constituting a special domain of sociological analysis. He termed this domain the "interaction order." According to Goffman, this notion covers, among other things, the fact that behind or beneath the apparently whimsical, trivial, scattered, and apparently disorganized character of the myriad of everyday encounters and situations, one can discern a certain regulated order and a structure that one enters and participates—knowingly or unknowingly—in maintaining. But how is such an "invisible" and "transparent" domain constituted, and how can one document its existence and nature? How does Goffman persuade us that this particular "interaction order" in fact exists, that it is at work in even the most insignificant of encounters, and that there apparently is an element of normative constraint and regulation in our presumably voluntary and unbounded social intercourse with each other? In a vein similar to that of Émile Durkheim—and later more systematically pursued in the work of ethnomethodologists Harold Garfinkel (2002)—Goffman proposed that in order to discover what actually constitutes microsocial order, we need to break, encroach on, or violate it. By observing these violations and rule breaches—and not least their consequences—Goffman seemed to claim that we, in a roundabout way, can learn about the actual theme: the regulated "interaction order."

In several of Goffman's writings, this **methodology of violation** or crisis becomes evident, perhaps particularly in the three essays "Alienation From Interaction," "Mental Symptoms and the Public Order," and "Embarrassment and Social Organization," all included in *Interaction Ritual* (1967). In the essay on becoming alienated from interaction, Goffman starts out by proposing that when people engage themselves in a social meeting, one may realize that the involvement in the interaction or conversation takes place and is gradually intensified almost without one taking notice of it. In other words, we become engaged almost in a self-forgetful way. Hereby a commonly shared microworld is constituted, making the situation into a small and overarching cosmos in itself, something—in Durkheimian fashion— amounting to more than the sum of the actual participants involved. Goffman (1967, p. 113) used the term *unio mystico* to describe this peculiar experience of social trance or commonly shared spontaneous involvement among participants. What he is then interested in are the situations in which this experience fails to materialize or is blocked and not least the social consequences of this absence of spontaneous involvement. He wants to show how the maintenance of a commonly shared spontaneous involvement is in fact a rather fragile arrangement. In his own words, Goffman wants to look at "conversational alienation" (Goffman, 1967, p. 114). Goffman thus proposes four ways—external preoccupation, self-consciousness, interaction-consciousness, and other-consciousness—in which interactants may refrain from becoming spontaneously involved in a situation as required. Although Goffman's approach to "alienation" differs radically from the macrosocial and class-based variant of the term as used by Marxist scholars or critical thinkers, we are nevertheless not dealing with trifles. It is, in short, the very foundation of normative social order that is at stake.

If we as participants in social situations—at the right moment—betray the obligation to show spontaneous involvement in the commonly shared microuniverse of mutual attention, then we simply jeopardize our individual and collective sense of reality.

In the second essay on mental symptoms and the public order, Goffman analyzes psychiatric symptoms as violations of public—that is social, normative, and moral—microorder. Goffman points out that psychiatric symptoms are not necessarily only medical, but that psychiatry regards them as expressions of medical disorders and that laypeople do the same when the diagnosis is given (Goffman, 1967, p. 142). When the psychotic person's behavior is described as "out of touch with the real world" or as "socially receding," this, according to Goffman, bears witness to the fact that these originally social violations by way of psychiatry are suddenly transformed into psychiatric and medical symptoms based on a morally derived obligation stating that participants in social life must always be in good, open, and direct communication and contact with each other (Goffman, 1967, p. 138). In other words, the symptoms are basically violations of socially sanctioned conventions, meaning that the symptoms—already from the onset—are constructed by the prevailing social order. Goffman claims that in the same way as theft relates to the legal order of private property and homosexuality relates to the (heteronormative) order of gender roles, psychiatric symptoms relate to so-called situational improprieties and therefore tell us something important about the organization of social life. When a person is defined as "psychotic," it is therefore often in relation to the unwritten rules of the "interaction order." These are rules, as we shall see in Chapter 4, that—for example—are concerned with how to show civil inattention, how to maintain an appropriate distance in public, how to practice deference and demeanor, how to present oneself, how to respect each other's territories, how to maintain an appropriate balance between the main focus of the encounter and situational "asides," and how to show an appropriate amount of involvement in the situation. Offenses against these rules are situational improprieties, threats to the microsocial order, and violations of the rights of coparticipants in the social situation. According to Goffman, it is by painting a systematic picture of the publicly accepted forms of behavior and their encroachment that we can establish a language by way of which we can discuss psychiatric symptoms. When psychiatric symptoms can be seen as destroying or threatening or be deemed deviant, it is because there is *something* that can be destroyed, threatened, and regarded as normal. This *something* is the "interaction order." Psychiatric symptoms are then suddenly seen as violations of the ceremonial order of everyday life, in which individuals worship each other's "sacredness" through tactful, peaceful, and respectful social intercourse.

Also in the third essay, titled "Embarrassment and Social Organization," Goffman hints at his methodology of violation. The essay highlights how confusion, fluster, and embarrassment are not necessarily unwanted or unfortunate deviations from successful interaction but may rather assist in enabling the smooth sequence of often conflicting expectations and thus securing the continued coherence of the social organization of encounters. To recapitulate Goffman's methodology of violation and crisis: his trick consists in, as he formulated it, listening to the dissonance in social meetings. By listening to this dissonance, "the sociologist can generalize about the ways in which interaction can go awry and, by implication, the conditions necessary for the interaction to be right" (Goffman, 1967, p. 99). Or, put differently: Goffman concludes from the negative to the positive, from the breaching of the rule to the nature of the rule itself (Boeskov, 1975, p. 143). By looking at alienation from interaction, one learns about the interaction rule that an individual is supposed to abide by. By considering mental illness as a breach of social rules, one learns about situational and territorial boundaries that must not be violated. And by focusing on embarrassment and flustering, one becomes familiar with how one is expected to present oneself during social meetings (Sylvest, 1975). Goffman thus methodologically penetrated the existing (situational) social order by looking at deviances, breaches, violations, and crises in people's engagements with each other.

Conclusion

As this chapter has illustrated and discussed, Erving Goffman approached sociology and the study of microsociological topics in an unmistakable Goffmanesque and somewhat peculiar methodological way. It is interesting how much can in fact be said and presumed about Goffman's "methods," particularly because he himself remained enigmatically quiet about them. As once observed by Jack Bynum and Charles Pranter, "Goffman's methodology is an adroit synthesis of differently derived data" (Bynum & Pranter, 1984, p. 99). However, not only Goffman's data material was of a diversified character; his overall approach to studying social interaction was also characterized by mixing and synthesizing. As is evident from this chapter, Goffman's perspective was a mixture of a qualitative sociologist using all of his senses—perhaps more impressionistically than systematically—to capture face-to-face interaction and a literary-poetic sociologist using metaphors, novels, short stories, newspaper clippings, and movies as creative sources of inspiration to concoct a sociological storyline about his research topic.

Perhaps unsurprisingly, Goffman's studies of the trivial and mundane aspects of the microsocial universe generated ambivalent responses among colleagues who regarded his findings either as unscientific, unsubstantiated, and indeed uninteresting or, on the other hand, as the epitome of the sociological imagination at work. As Greg Smith noted:

> For some, Goffman's writings represent the sociological imagination at its finest: his analyses are innovative, informative, even entertaining. For others, his work is merely descriptive, not genuinely explanatory, and ignorant of the press, of institutions and the social realities of power and exploitation (Smith, 1988, p. 118).

Whether one supports this or that view, it is difficult to deny that Goffman's work did have an immense impact on sociology. As we have shown in this chapter, Goffman—armed with his rather alternative methodology—succeeded in making the study of the heretofore largely neglected domain of everyday interaction, as we shall see in the next chapter, not only a trademark of his own persona but also a legitimate area of study for others to undertake. We thus propose four important methodological legacies Goffman left for sociology: (1) With his sociology, Goffman stressed the necessity to secure a constant dialectical process between inductive and deductive research strategies; (2) that Goffman, with his searching and impatient conceptual testing, development, and refining, emphasized that the end goal of sociology is not necessarily ironclad or tightly integrated theories but innovative, imaginative, and useful concepts; (3), that Goffman pinpointed the impossibility of a direct mirroring of nuanced, complex, and multilayered social reality in sociological descriptions, making, for example, metaphorical redescription necessary; and finally (4) that Goffman's peculiar writing style and his sophisticated ironic sense of communicating with his readers show the utmost importance of style if one's sociological message is to be received, understood, and appreciated. Sociology need not be dull in order to be either interesting, powerful, provocative, or useful.

Questions

- What were the main methods used by Erving Goffman in his studies?
- How would you describe and evaluate Erving Goffman's methodology?
- What were the main merits and strengths of Erving Goffman's methodology?
- What were the main weaknesses and problems with Erving Goffman's methodology?

4

Goffman's Sociology
of Everyday Life Interaction

This chapter endeavors to draw a rough picture of the most important themes and concepts in Goffman's analyses of everyday life face-to-face interaction. The chapter will illustrate how Goffman's various studies of everyday face-to-face interaction all add to the same overarching theme: the **interaction order**. Goffman's investigations of the theatrical, ritual, strategic elements of social interaction as well as his identification of the various interactional elements in everyday-life social interaction all contributed to outlining the contours of a "substantive domain in its own right" (Goffman, 1983a, p. 2). The chapter is laid out in four parts. The first part presents the dramaturgical perspective that unfolds in *The Presentation of Self in Everyday Life*; the second part introduces Goffman's analyses of social interaction based on game theory; the third part outlines Goffman's use of Durkheim's concept of **ritual**. We conclude the chapter by returning to Goffman's concept of the interaction order.

Theatrical Performances

Shortly before his death, in his 1982 presidential address to the American Sociological Association, Goffman (1983a) recapitulated his overall academic concern for promoting acceptance of the study of face-to-face interaction, such as the interaction that transpires in social situations in which two or more individuals are physically copresent. The investigation and promotion of this social domain involved various studies, each of which explored different types of social gatherings in different contexts with different equipment and among parties with different levels of acquaintanceship. In exploring the processes, structures, and elements of the interaction order, Goffman made use of conceptual metaphors (theater, game, and ritual). In Chapter 3 we went into detail with the methodological issues concerning Goffman's metaphorical redescription, while in this chapter we explore how each metaphor uncovers substantive processes and elements of the interaction order.

We start with the perhaps most well known of Goffman's conceptual metaphors: the theatrical metaphor that is presented in detail in *The Presentation of Self in Everyday Life* (1959). This book, which is considered his most influential, is based on experiences garnered from field study in the Shetland Islands, which formed the empirical basis for his PhD dissertation, and as such the monograph can be seen as a theoretical expansion of many of the concepts (impression management, performance, discrepant roles, etc.) that were first expounded in his doctoral work. In Goffman's own words, *The Presentation of Self in Everyday Life* may be considered a handbook presenting a sociological perspective that may be used to study the social lives of human beings. Specifically, he is interested in the type of mutual influencing that takes place between people who are physically copresent. Offering, then, a dramaturgical perspective, Goffman intends to explore certain fundamental principles underlying face-to-face interaction. Employing the dramaturgical perspective, Goffman throughout the book analyzed how a human being in "ordinary work situations presents himself and his activity to others, the ways in which he guides and controls the impression they form of him, and the kinds of things he may and may not do while sustaining his performance before them" (Goffman, 1959, p. 8). Introducing the dramaturgical framework, Goffman suggested that when an individual is in the immediate physical presence of other people, he or she will unavoidably seek to control the impression that others form of him or her in order to achieve individual or social goals. The actor will engage in impression management. On the other side, the other participants in the social encounter will attempt to form an impression of who and what this particular individual is. They will try to form a picture of his or her identity, and for that purpose they use a number of different types of **sign vehicles**, each saying something about the person in question. Unfolding the concept of impression management, Goffman differentiates between the information that actors "give" and the information they "give off." The first type of information concerns the verbal or nonverbal symbols we consciously use in order to convey a specific meaning (e.g., traditional, explicit communication). The other type of information consists of the signs and expressions that actors unwittingly and unconsciously emit, signs the surroundings perceive as characteristic for that person (Goffman, 1959, p. 14). In everyday face-to-face interactions, then, people are involved in two streams of communication. In Goffman's view, actors reciprocally form impressions of each other by noting the many bits of consciously emitted information, as well as through inference from appearances and nonintended information. Impression management, then, may take intentional as well as unintentional forms. When an audience member in a workshop session continually tries to make a speech instead of asking a question, he or she may be intentionally involved in forming a certain impression of him/herself as a highly dedicated scholar who rightly should have been on the presenting panel. Unintentional impression management may be illustrated by the fact that although we often feel that we behave authentically whenever together with our friends and colleagues, we may present different sides of ourselves to our friends and colleagues respectively, accommodating the specific expectations presented by our friends and colleagues.

A key concept in Goffman's dramaturgical analysis is that of **performances**. Goffman explores how everyday-life actors, by way of dramaturgical practices and the various props at hand, influence how the other actors perceive or define the situation at hand. An important part of performance is a person's "front." The front consists of the attitudes, presence and expressions actors—consciously or unconsciously—use in order to construct a certain image of who we are (Fine & Manning, 2003, p. 46). Thus, as Goffman's analysis points out, a person's chances of being taken seriously, say, as a university teacher, not only depend on the clarity and logic of his or her presentation but also eminently rely on that person's presence and comportment. With regard to the distinction between the signs and expression that are "given" and those "given off," respectively, the university teacher's work consists in an effort to control the audience's access to and perception of information so the signs consciously emitted will be interpreted by the audience as signs that are (unconsciously) revealed and therefore are an expression of that person's "true" identity (Fine & Manning, 2003, p. 46).

Goffman's dramaturgical analysis is concerned with situations of face-to-face interaction, and thus the core analytical unit is the social encounter. In everyday-life encounters, people are faced with various interactional tasks, and the most crucial task for participants in interaction, is to express and maintain a **definition of the situation**. By way of actions and gestures, participants unavoidably make suggestions as to how the situation is to be defined and thus as to how others are to perceive and treat them. As Goffman points out, usually the various situation definitions suggested by copresent participants will to a certain degree be in accord. However, this is not to say that a total and complete consensus prevails but that the parties may repress sincere emotions and present a view of the situation the others are presumed to be willing to accept. Most everyday-life encounters, Goffman argues, involve a "modus vivendi" allowing each of the participants to make his or her own contribution to a common definition of the situation while at the same time agreeing to avoid open conflict (Goffman, 1959, p. 21). Thus, a fundamental interactional goal is to sustain a collectively shared definition of the situation enabling participants to decode normative expectations and to adjust behavior accordingly. As we shall see in Chapter 7, in his later works Goffman employed the concept of "frame" to describe the fact that actors automatically interpret social situations within significance-providing frames that guide their understanding and definition of what is going on as well as the identities of those participants present. According to Goffman (1974, p. 11), frames, thus, constitute "the principles of organization which govern events—at least social ones—and our subjective involvement in them."

The definition of situations, thus, contains a moral component in the sense that individuals have a morally founded right to expect to be treated according to the social markers they implicitly or explicitly present. As Goffman contends,

> When an individual projects a definition of the situation and thereby makes an implicit or explicit claim to be a person of a particular kind, he automatically exerts a moral demand upon the others, obliging them to value and treat him in the manner that persons of his kind have a right to expect. (Goffman, 1959, p. 24)

With the dramaturgical framework outlined in *The Presentation of Self in Everyday Life*, Goffman analyzed how individuals cooperate in an effort to sustain definitions of situations that preserve the "faces" of those participating. A person's face, in Goffman's terminology, is, as it may appear, not a question of mere physiognomy but a social and emotional construct. In the dramaturgical perspective, a person's face comprises the image the person conjures up of himself and others (usually) help him maintain. Among other things, the book describes the preventative measures taken in order to avoid embarrassing breakdowns—the "defensive practices" employed to protect one's own definitions and the "protective practices" used to save other people's definition of the situation—as well as the dramaturgical problems encountered by people when the actors of daily life engage in their craft in the presence of others (Goffman, 1959, pp. 24–26).

Unfolding the dramaturgical model, Goffman considers six fundamental dramaturgical elements: performances, teams, regions and region behavior, discrepant roles, communication out of character, and the art of impression management. Let's take a look at each of them in turn.

A "performance" is about making an impression on those present and notably about asserting (to oneself and to the other parties present) that we are who we pretend to be. In staging his performance, a person uses his expressive equipment (clothes, gender, position, etc.) in expressing his messages or situational claims. According to Goffman, performances may be subject to "idealization," suggesting that performers may be prone to provide the audience with an impression superior to what reality will verify. Goffman illustrated such idealization with tales of domestic Scottish performances, where "the average laird and his family lived far more frugally in the ordinary way than they did when they were entertaining visitors," this including situations where dinner served by five or six servants and all the adherent pomp and circumstance consisted of nothing but oatmeal and pickled herring in different guises (Goffman, 1959, p. 47). According to Goffman, performances are not always rendered by individual actors but sometimes collectively by several people together, by "teams" of actors. According to Goffman, (1959, p. 85), a team is "any set of individuals who cooperate in staging a single routine." Thus, as we will explore in more detail in Chapter 5, the staff at a psychiatric hospital ward may be thought of as a team cooperating to sustain a medical-service definition of the situation that involves the idea of so-called rational-empirical treatment.

Everyday-life interaction is performed in various types of dramaturgical "**regions**," and in exploring the characteristics of these regions, Goffman presents his well-known distinction between the "scene" or the "front region" and the "back region." In much Goffman-inspired literature, these concepts are also referred to as **frontstage** and **backstage**. In the front region, Goffman contends, specific performances take place before an audience. Here, the performers play their roles and adjust their performances according to the prevailing normative structure. The back region is the area to which the performer can withdraw, providing the opportunity to relax, rehearse, and recharge. Particularly interesting situations are the transitions from the front region to the back region. By studying these transitions, Goffman argues, students may observe "a wonderful putting on and taking off character." Goffman provided an illustrative example from the works of British novelist George Orwell, who described how waiters change character by moving from the hotel kitchen to the dining room: "As he passes the door sudden change comes over him. The set of his shoulders alters; all the dirt and hurry irritation have dropped off in an instant. He glides over the carpet, with a solemn priest-like air" (Goffman, 1959, p. 123).

The fourth dramaturgical element, "discrepant roles," is concerned with how certain persons may "learn about the secrets of the team" and therefore may constitute "threats to their privileged position" (Goffman, 1959, p. 143). Gumshoes, snitches, or undercover field researchers are all immersed in discrepant roles, and therefore they constitute a potential risk for the entire team, which no longer is in full control of its own secrets. "Communication out of character" refers to those parts of the participants' expressions that are somehow incompatible with the impression that maintained during the course of interaction but that nonetheless always may be found in human encounters. Goffman uses this term to describe the fact that the performance of the moment does not constitute the only reality of the team members. They may, for instance, step aside from this reality and malign the audience ("treatment of the absent") or make use of secret and implied communication ("team collusion") even as the official performance unfolds. These discrepancies thus serve certain situational functions as they

> demonstrate that while a performer may act as if his response in a situation were immediate, unthinking and spontaneous, and while he himself may think this to be the case, still it will always be possible for situations to arise in which he will convey to one or two persons present the understanding that the show he is maintaining is only and merely a show. (Goffman, 1959, p. 168)

The final dramaturgical element, "impression management," designates the participants' efforts to control the impressions made during the course of interaction. The paramount aim of these efforts is to prevent embarrassing episodes or, eventually, situational breakdowns. The art of impression management involves, among other things, dramaturgical loyalty, dramaturgical discipline, and dramaturgical circumspection. Impression management, then, signifies how actors—through their utterances, body language, attire, and so forth—seek to gain control of the impression formed by the audience but also intimates the collaboration expected on the part of the audience, say, by ignoring or forgetting about a performer's slips, contradictions, and the like.

Viewed through the metaphor of **dramaturgy**, everyday-life face-to-face interactions emerge as continuous series of staged negotiations or exchanges. In Goffman's dramaturgical analysis, everyday-life performers must offer something fellow interactants will appreciate or reward. In other words, our presentations of self must be adapted to the situationally specific expectations formed by the participants and audiences present at any given time. Different situations have different adherent audiences and thus different expectations, which is why the self-images presented by everyday-life performers need constantly to be adapted to the changing social situations. Thus, by interpreting everyday-life face-to-face encounters through the prism of dramaturgy, Goffman demonstrates how the social interactions of everyday life should not only be construed as a game of masks in which we deliberately seek to hoodwink each other but also as a functional process in which individuality and social order are united in an endless process of dramatization (Münch, 1986, p. 53).

Strategic Games

As it appears, Goffman's dramaturgical analysis touches upon the game-like character of everyday-life behavior. The staged performances and the elements of information and impression control all point to the strategic and calculating elements of face-to-face social interaction, and in his later writings, Goffman explored these strategic interactional issues in detail. His interest in the strategic elements of social behavior was influenced by the works of the game theoretician Thomas Schelling, with whom he spent a sabbatical year cultivating and integrating game-theory elements in his microsociological perspective. The strategic-game perspective is especially evident in the monographs *Encounters* (Goffman, 1961) and *Strategic Interaction* (Goffman, 1969) and in the essay "Where the Action Is" (Goffman, 1967). The first part of *Strategic Interaction* is concerned with "expression games." This particular type of game involves situations in which individuals, or players, as Goffman calls them, reciprocally seek to decode and manipulate the information about themselves available in the microsocial world of the encounter:

> There will be situations where an observer is dependent on what he can learn from a subject, there being no sufficient alternate sources of information, and the subject will be orientated to frustrate this assessment or facilitate it under difficult circumstances. Under these conditions gamelike considerations develop even though very serious matters may be at stake. (Goffman, 1969, p. 10)

In order to maximize individual gain and advantage, the players in these microworlds make use of certain interactional moves, of which the basic ones are: "the unwitting move," "the naïve move," "the control move," "the uncovering move," and the "counter-uncovering move" (Goffman, 1969, pp. 11–28). Players in situated activity systems are thus involved in various types of strategic behavior (planning moves and teasing out and assessing information) within the constraints of a situational normative or moral structure. Stressing the importance of rules, Goffman indicates that however strategic or manipulative players may seem, they act within a set of norms that influences their moves. Players may thus act strategically to enhance the perception of them as rule-following individuals. Engaging in expression games, however, individuals may appear as everyday-life agents:

> In every social situation we can find a sense in which one participant will be an observer with something to gain from assessing expressions, and another will be a subject with something to gain from manipulating this process. A single structure of contingencies can be found in this regard which renders agents a little like us all and all of us a little like agents. (Goffman, 1969, p. 81)

In the second essay, titled *Strategic Interaction*, Goffman is seemingly not as interested in how we reveal, expose, or manipulate information but is more concerned with how we strategically plan and execute our actions in the most rational manner. Here he seeks to identify the different aspects the strategic player must take into consideration when he or she wants to plan actions in the most rational way, involving the situational counterpart and the situation itself. In this context, the most rational behavior means behavioral moves that lead to the highest degree of personal gain meaning maximizing social recognition. First, players may evaluate "the other's moves." Here, the objective is to analyze the counterpart's potential motives and possible alternate moves. Next, the player should observe "the operational code," that is, the counterpart's way of playing the game: his or her style of playing and goals. Third, actors must assess "the opponent's resolve" meaning an assessment of the counterpart's determination and ability to continue the game despite personal costs. Further, the actors need to take "the other's information state" into account. Any potential move must be built up around the counterpart's thoughts/knowledge. Finally, interacting parties need to take into account "the opponent's resources." It is important to know about the possible aids the counterpart (and the actor him/herself) have at their disposal when making the next move (Goffman, 1969, pp. 94–96). Phrased differently, the individual player must take several things into consideration when planning and executing the most rational actions. The player must make the necessary calculations concerning the other players in the game and, based on these calculations, must make the requisite moves. However, the characteristic feature of this game is that while player A tries to see through player B's motives, intentions, resources, and stockpile of information, player B is all the while simultaneously attempting to discern A's motives, intentions, and so on. Based on this, Goffman claims that strategic interaction is when persons find themselves in a well-structured situation of mutual impingement where each party must make a move and where every possible move carries fateful implications for all of the parties. In this situation, each player must influence his own decision by his knowing that the other players are likely to try to dope out his decision in advance. . . . An exchange of moves made on the basis of this kind of orientation to self and others can be called strategic interaction. (Goffman, 1969, pp. 100–101)

In other words, as participants in the game, we are at the mercy of the same game based on our *mutual assessment*. This ongoing surveillance is recipro-cal, and thus the power being exerted in people's interaction is in a certain sense democratic, since the surveillance is a two-way street, so to speak. Goffman stresses that we enter into a type of shared destiny during every-day interactions in which our "moves" entail consequences not only for ourselves but for the other players as well. Our ability to act rationally and thus strategically maximize our own gains pointedly depends on our ability to assess and predict the thoughts and actions of the other persons involved. But following George Herbert Mead, strategic interaction also comprises gaining influence on the situation by putting ourselves in the others' place and making use of this knowledge in planning our own moves.

In the essay "Where the Action Is," included in *Interaction Ritual* (1967), Goffman similarly analyzes social interaction through the game metaphor. His point of departure is the concept of "action," referring here to the often problematic chance- or risk-involving activities initiated for the sake of entertainment or excitement. Goffman's concept of action refers to those moments in which people, similar to casino gamblers, throw themselves into the game, place their bets, and reap their rewards or suffer their losses. Although modern everyday life does not present the same obvious physical elements of danger or risk as in earlier, precivilized ages, this life is not, in Goffman's view, totally devoid of risk. Human encounters and social situa-tions may be momentous and dangerous games in the sense that we may both win (receive praise, recognition, dignity) and lose (become embar-rassed, lose face or composure). Hence Goffman is not interested in the situ-ations, activities, and contexts that directly and quite patently appeal to the human thirst for excitement and taking risks, such as the aforementioned casino, racetracks, parachuting, mountaineering, and the like. His interest lies in the action revolving around human nature or the human ability to display self-control and dignity, often in the face of stress and momentous "fatal" situations. As Goffman sees it, our studies of situations of everyday interaction can lead us to pinpoint the so-called **character contests**—for example, the little social games, battles, or disputes we now and then "fight out" with each other and that are about demonstrating self-control and a strong character at the other's expense. Everyday life provides many opportunities for fighting such battles:

> Whenever individuals ask for or give excuses, proffer or receive compliments, slight another or are slighted, a contest of self-control can result. Similarly, the tacit little flirtations occurring between friends and between strangers produce a contest of unavailability. (Goffman, 1967, p. 240)

Thus, the character contest is Goffman's term for situations in which we, as a result of modern life's lack of palpable danger and excitement, embark on risk-laden behavior in relation to other people for the purpose of adding value to our own character. Some people engage in this type of transaction more than others; some will indefatigably burst into heated remonstrations in the face of all their potential character-related losses and winnings. Yet, if you manage to maintain a clear head and carry yourself with a certain dignity, chances are you may win something; needless to say, if you lose composure or display signs of weakness, the risk of losing is imminent.

As we have briefly touched upon, it should be emphasized that when Goffman speaks of strategic interaction and employs the game metaphor in relation to social life (Goffman, 1969, pp. 113–114), he is well aware that empirical reality rarely presents us with such "pure games." Everyday games play out within the framework of constraining as well as opportunity-laden social norms. Thus, in "Where the Action Is" (1967), Goffman points to how character contests will only surface periodically, because people in everyday life fundamentally desire to sustain peace and ritual order. A crucial point made by Goffman is that it is the definition of the situation that orchestrates how players are expected to comport themselves and that this definition thus has a moral component in the sense that those participating have a right to be appreciated according to the social indicators they presume to possess. In this way there is an implicit coercion, often with a moral slant, involved in the situation. It is the definition of the situation that regulates how we are to act, which roles we should play, and what demeanor we should assume. So while players constantly make strategic deliberations in focused interactions, and while they sometimes act in a calculating manner in order to gain "character winnings," and while there may well be ongoing mutual surveillance or spying, all these efforts are made within a framework involving situational moral norms. This leads us to another central theme in Goffman's writings, namely the social and moral ritualization of everyday life interaction.

Interaction Rituals

In Chapter 2, we explored how Goffman found inspiration in the works of Émile Durkheim. This inspiration is evident as early as in his PhD dissertation, in which he observes the neglectful treatment sociology has afforded to the ritual aspects of interaction:

> The ritual model for interaction has been poorly treated in the literature, perhaps because of the stress given by G. H. Mead and by Weber to the fact that a social relationship, and hence social interaction, was a product of two persons taking each other's actions into consideration in pursuing their own action. This stress seems to have given an instrumental flavour to our thinking about the kinds of consideration we show in regard to others: the implication is that we take into consideration the actions of others (the better to achieve our personal ends, whatever these may be) and not so much that we give consideration to others. By "consideration" we have come to mean calculation, not considerateness. (Goffman, 1953b, p. 103)

In Durkheim's sociology of religion, Goffman found important theoretical components with which to build a perspective on social interaction emphasizing the ritual solicitude and respect displayed toward other people as "sacred objects." This line of thinking is also quite clear in the dramaturgical analysis; however, it is expressed in its clearest and most explicit form in Goffman's analyses of the so-called **interaction rituals** of everyday life (Goffman, 1967). In his essay "On Face Work," Goffman rationalizes the use of the ritual concept:

> I use the term *ritual* because I am dealing with acts through whose symbolic component the actor shows how worthy he is of respect or how worthy he feels others are of it. . . . One's face, then, is a sacred thing, and the expressive order required to sustain it is therefore a ritual one. (Goffman, 1967, p. 19)

The interaction rituals identified by Goffman are to be construed as a form of rules or "situational proprieties" (Goffman, 1963, p. 24) applying to everyday life interaction, manifesting themselves in stereotypical behavioral sequences and patterns of speech. Among the ways through which they express themselves are the small and seemingly insignificant courtesies that we daily extend to each other. Goffman (1967, p. 47) expands further on Durkheim's conception of the sanctity of the soul and thus claims that the faces of modern individuals have a kind of sacred character. This sanctity must be protected, affirmed, and maintained, and we do this, Goffman points out, by observing certain apparently insignificant interaction rituals.

Thus, by employing the concept of ritual, Goffman indicates that many of the interactions of everyday life are indeed symbolic actions aiming at endorsing individuals' faces and, thus, the microsocial reality of the social encounter. By treating each other with respect and dignity, by turning away our attention whenever others are about to lose face, in short, by engaging in "face work," we are actually protecting each other and the social reality involving us. It is the observance of this ritual collaboration, these many and varied interaction rituals, that makes Goffman assert that the individual, in modern society, has taken the place of the gods. As Goffman points out, many gods have disappeared, "but the individual himself stubbornly remains as a deity of considerable importance" (Goffman, 1967, p. 95). However, it is not people's uniqueness or individuality that is celebrated in the interaction rituals of everyday life. Rather, what is venerated is their commonality, that which they share and have in common; and it is through his analysis of the microscopic celebrations of commonality in everyday life that Goffman demonstrates how society's social order and structures are continually being reproduced (Album, 1996, p. 133). Hence, among Goffman's notable achievements is to have focused our attention on the significant rituals of everyday interaction. He demonstrated how, on the micro-level, these rituals are part of what ensures decent (and rule-following) social intercourse and how, on a global level, they form part of the *glue* maintaining societal cohesion.

Goffman was not interested in the interaction rituals that express themselves as explicit and verbalized injunctions or prohibitions but in those that come in the form of more or less unpremeditated ways of treating one another in everyday life encounters. In *Behavior in Public Places* (1963), Goffman explored the situational proprieties in "unfocused" and "focused interactions." In unfocused interaction, which is the dominating form in most public places, people are copresent without being mutually engaged in a shared activity, while in focused interaction people are gathered in and collaborate to sustain a shared focus of attention. A primary interactional task in unfocused interaction is to display a proper level of involvement, and here the body plays an important part. In unfocused interaction, people interpret and assess each other's behavior by way of a "body idiom," as there is "an obligation to convey certain information when in the presence of others and an obligation not to convey other impressions just as there is an expectation that others will present themselves in a certain way" (Goffman, 1963, p. 35). Exploring the dimensions of the body idiom, Goffman uses the term "body gloss" to describe the ways that individuals use their bodies to make otherwise unavailable things visible to others, and he identifies various subtypes of this body idiom. One such subtype is "orientation gloss," designating the behaviors that signal to others that we are engaged in normal and harmless everyday actions.

For example, when a person is standing in front of an office building, he may check his mobile phone or watch from time to time, displaying that he is engaged in waiting for someone and thus not engaged in another, suspicious activity. By performing body gloss, then, individuals can free themselves from undesirable characterological implications of their ongoing behavior (Goffman, 1971, pp. 128–129). Thus by managing the body according to the situational standards and by judging others' behavior through the body idiom, unacquainted people in unfocused interactions contribute to the orderliness and predictability in everyday life social interactions. Signaling proper involvement in the situation constitutes an important element of the body idiom. However, since a person's involvement is a cognitive or a mental state and thus is not directly observable, the level of his involvement is observed by others by perceiving indicators of his situational involvement. People, then, may use "involvement shields" to cover behaviors that signal improper situational involvement such as when hands "are used to cover closed eyes that are obliged to be open, and newspapers to cover mouths that should not be open in a yawn" (Goffman, 1963, p. 40). Furthermore, people need to allocate proper levels of attention to "main" and "side involvements," as when people sing or smoke while performing their work. Social situations, Goffman claims, prescribe what is to be perceived as the "dominant involvement" and thus what participants are supposed to engage properly in. Subordinate involvement, then, is the attention that the individual can pay to other activities while still respecting the dominant involvement:

> Thus, while waiting to see an official, an individual may converse with a friend, read a magazine, or doodle with a pencil, sustaining these engrossing claims on attention only until his turn is called, when he is obliged to put aside his time-passing activity though it is unfinished. (Goffman, 1963, p. 44)

In focused interaction, there is a shared mutual focus of attention; however, this is not always visible. In fact, Goffman demonstrated that although many everyday-life situations seem uncoordinated and without a shared focus of attention, this is often not the case. When passing strangers on the street, people usually glance downward or elsewhere before getting too close so as not to invade the other's personal space. Seemingly, no coordination or mutual focus is involved. Taking a closer look, however, the opposite might be the case:

> What seems to be involved is that one gives to another enough visual notice to demonstrate that one appreciates that the other is present (and that one admits openly to having seen him), while at the next moment withdrawing one's attention from him so as to express that he does not constitute a target of special

curiosity or design. In performing this courtesy the eyes of the looker may pass over the eyes of the other, but no "recognition" is typically allowed. When the courtesy is performed between two persons passing on the street, civil inattention may take the special form of eyeing the other up to approximately eight feet, during which time sides of the street are apportioned by gesture, and then casting the eyes down as the other passes—a kind of dimming of lights. (Goffman, 1963, p. 84)

According to Goffman, this interaction ritual may be the most overlooked, yet it is nonetheless a ritual constantly regulating the social interaction of human beings (Goffman, 1963, p. 84). **Civil inattention**, then, is an example of interaction with a minimum of mutual focus. As the example indicates, interaction rituals are to a large extent directed at showing the other person respect. The goal is to avoid intrusion and thus an invasion of the other's right to a private life. Differently put, the rituals ensure protection for the individual, but they are also part of what regulates the way we enter into relations with one another. In this context, Goffman (1963, p. 92) speaks about "opening moves" and "clearance signs," thereby referring to the different ways (typically by glances) we ask for contact and signal that we are available to each other. There are also rituals hinging upon the respect with which we should introduce ourselves. Because it is not enough to display respect for others, in order to receive the necessary recognition and acceptance from others, you must also be able to comport yourself in a respectful manner. In Goffman's analysis, we are interconnected through the interaction rituals whereby we respect, sustain, and acknowledge the images or faces that we present to one another. As has been mentioned, the rituals primarily involve protecting and caring for each other's faces; on a more general level, the ritual obligations serve to maintain a moral order.

By exploring how interaction rituals serve such face-saving purposes, Goffman's work was pioneering in integrating feelings into sociological theory. Thus, in the essay "Embarrassment and Social Organization," Goffman (1967) analyzed how social interaction strives to avoid the embarrassment that arises whenever an individual's self is threatened or discredited. In social encounters, individuals are expected to project a self that is suitable for the occasion into the interaction through the "expressive implications of his stream of conduct." More or less consciously, individuals will thus project a self into social situations, and the other players' contribution to that social situation is, according to Goffman, attuned to and composed of the demands thus projected. In everyday-life interaction, individuals will attempt to avoid the threat of embarrassment and, consequently, most people seek to avoid situations that threaten their own projected self as well as the self that is projected by the other players. This may be achieved by projecting relatively modest self-claims into the interaction and not overplaying one's hand, so to speak. It may also be done by deliberately charting a course skirting potentially dangerous situations and, finally, by showing consideration or tactful tolerance toward others. However, situations may arise in which certain events raise serious doubts as to the claims an individual has put forward concerning his or her self. The situation is then disrupted because the presuppositions on which it rested are seemingly no longer valid. These individuals therefore feel shame or embarrassment. As Goffman sees it, such feelings not only perturb the person whose self has been threatened. Often the confidence in whoever pretends to be tactful but actually causes the other person to lose face is weakened far more than trust in the person who is at first discredited.

People may also become embarrassed and flustered when persons who do not usually interact informally suddenly find themselves in situations in which the option of informal discussion cannot be ignored. When the cleaning lady and the CEO meet in the elevator, they may experience an awkward moment because, in adapting to this moment's demands, they have to, in a manner of speaking, abandon their usual roles. They may attempt to meet each other in an informal chat, but both may also feel uneasy at the situation because they have to "sacrifice" their roles. In such moments, Goffman identifies the social function of embarrassment. He points out that embarrassment it is not an irrational impulse but forms part of a group of actions that may seem spontaneous but are no less mandatory than the other, conscious acts that contribute to maintaining the social structure. Had the CEO in the elevator encounter insisted on his superior right to recognition—adhering to the principle that the nature of the work done determines a person's status— and had the cleaning lady on her part demanded an equal status according to the principle that belonging to the firm entitles you to such equal treatment, then the conflict between two opposite social principles of organization would have been expressed openly in the situation. But because both parties become embarrassed and thus temporarily sacrifice themselves, Goffman notes that "only" they and the ongoing social encounter are compromised. Thus, the individuals' embarrassment serves a specific function: In the example, it contributes to the maintenance or protection of the social structure as it prevents that inevitable clash between the organizational principles of different systems that are expressed too manifestly in the social encounter. As Goffman comments at the end of the essay, "Social structure gains elasticity; the individual merely loses composure" (Goffman, 1967, p. 112).

Besides describing and analyzing the microscopic interaction rituals and emotionology of everyday life, Goffman also developed a wide range of conceptual classifications and taxonomies. From Durkheim, Goffman (1967, p. 73) adopted the fundamental differentiation between positive and negative rituals. According to Durkheim, positive rituals are a kind of mandatory rules prescribing preferred modes of behavior, while the negative rituals are overt prohibitions or taboos. Goffman rephrased these concepts into "presentational rituals" that "encompass acts through which the individual makes specific attestations to recipients concerning how he regards them and how he will treat them in the on-coming interaction" (Goffman, 1967, p. 71). According to Goffman (1971), one type of positive ritual is so-called "supportive interchanges," such as the minor actions and behavioral patterns with which individuals display respect and courtesy toward others and that primarily revolve around preventing interactional crises or "ritual imbalance." Goffman calls the negative rituals "avoidance rituals," and they primarily concern keeping others at a distance and avoiding violation of what Simmel might have called people's "ideal sphere" (Goffman, 1967, p. 62). The pedestrians performing civil inattention in the quote in which they "dim the lights" are thus participants involved in an avoidance ritual aimed at mutually respecting each other's ideal sphere.

Of course, interactions in everyday life do not unfold without breakdowns, awkwardness, embarrassment, violations, and crises. Everyday life involves situations in which individual faces are violated to a degree, making it awkward or unbearable for the violated individual as well as for the other participants. Such situations call for what Goffman calls "remedial interchanges." Remedial interchanges are sequences of behavior or procedures that help people to repossess lost faces and thus reestablish the situation as a whole. The individual responsible for the violation or crisis may be confronted with negative sanctions explicitly and directly. In case of minor violations, situations may be repaired through imperceptibly directing the common attention focus of all participants in other directions. If the violation cannot be ignored, the general rule is that the violator is given the chance to make good on the damage. Through remedial rituals, he or she will offer compensation to the violated party as well as to the overall situation. This may be through an explicit and public apology. In so doing, not only will the violated individual and the overall situation be provided with compensation and repair; if the compensation is recognized, the violator (who in fact may have violated himself) also restores his self.

Goffman was particularly concerned with the positive, motivational, and supportive rituals. To him, the social interactions of everyday life are not an ongoing, comforting, and unproblematic process that participants may enter into risk free. A number of potential threats and dangers lurk in social interactions of everyday life, and they demand constant attention (Burns, 1992, p. 26).

The main part of the interaction rituals that Goffman identified emphasized how this fragile order unremittingly has to be repaired and maintained. In various ways, then, the interaction rituals contribute toward facilitating social interaction. As has been mentioned, there are rituals that contribute to soliciting togetherness and semaphore availability (Goffman, 1963, 1971). Similarly, there are rituals for "closure;" there are rituals for repairing broken-down situations (Goffman, 1971); and there are conversation-regulating rituals (Goffman, 1981a). Thus, by focusing on the everyday ceremonials, Goffman demonstrated how, in everyday social encounters, we make a certain sacrifice or pay a particular price for ensuring the problem-free proceedings of that encounter and interaction (Album, 1996, p. 133). This sacrifice or price is our humble and decent behavior, our display of a respectable and comprehensible personality. In return for making this sacrifice, we may expect a certain amount of security, interpersonal trust, and social recognition.

Conclusion

Anthony Giddens (1987) once asked whether Goffman should be considered a systematic social theorist. As did Giddens, we would not hesitate to answer in the affirmative. Although his overall theoretical model may be hard to discern due to his innovative writing style (Collins, 2004, p. 22), Goffman developed, through his studies of everyday-life behavior, a theory of interaction among copresent individuals, and one of his major achievements was the exploration and identification of an "interaction order" with its specific elements and entities. So although Goffman once insisted—perhaps teasingly—that his writings did not provide any concepts for the study of everyday life (Goffman, 1983c), this chapter has shown that he in fact did develop a substantial and comprehensive arsenal of relevant and useful concepts for studying and understanding everyday situations.

Summing up this chapter, it has demonstrated that Goffman's analysis of the ritualized unfolding of our face-to-face interactions and the elements of performance and deception should be viewed in a context involving efforts to sketch the outline of a so-called interaction order. Drawing the contours of this order, Goffman performed metaphorical redescriptions of everyday-life face-to-face encounters. These redescriptions revealed both "the promissory, evidential character" and the "social ritualization" of social life as well as the game-like character of social life, enabling actors to block or even misdirect the revealment of an individual's purpose or intent (Goffman, 1983a, p. 3). The interaction order is the order that exists in socially situated interactions among copresent parties. The orderliness of this order is "predicated on a large base of shared cognitive presuppositions, if not normative ones, and self-sustained restraints" (Goffman, 1983a, p. 5). Each of Goffman's analytic metaphors has highlighted important aspects of this order. The analysis of interactional behavior in public places explored how embodied information flows and governs much of our public behavior. The dramaturgical and game metaphor illustrated the deception-like character of everyday-life self-presentations and thus how we purposely give or unwillingly give off information about ourselves, while the ritual metaphor emphasized the elements of trust and moral engagement underlying everyday social behavior. It is thus important to note that by employing a variety of analytic metaphors, Goffman did not portray everyday life interaction as merely performative, strategic, or morally ritualized. Each of Goffman's metaphors reveals simultaneously existing layers of the complexities of modern social life. The dramaturgic, game-like, and ritualized interchanges are thus to be perceived as three sides of the same thing: the maintenance and production of a social order by way of performances and strategic moves that serve to uphold social situations as well as the perception of the performers as reliable members of a morally grounded interaction order. In the interaction order, strategic and calculative behavior coexists with a system of constraining interaction rituals. As Goffman points out toward the end of *The Presentation of Self in Everyday Life*, people follow moral standards because of their social nature. However, as performers, they are "concerned not with the moral issue of realizing these standards, but with the amoral issue of engineering a convincing impression that these standards are being realized" (Goffman, 1959, p. 251). Before we move on to Goffman's sociology of deviance, we offer a few questions for further thought.

Questions

- How valid is Erving Goffman's claim that the "interaction order" should be treated as a domain in its own right?
- How accurate is Erving Goffman's analysis of the dramaturgic, game-like, and ritual aspects of social life?
- How relevant is Erving Goffman's description of the processes, elements, and structures of the interaction order to understanding today's digitized and virtual interaction?
- In what ways is contemporary everyday-life sociology indebted to the works of Erving Goffman?

5

Goffman's Sociology of Deviance

I n this chapter, we examine Goffman's works on deviance. The primary focus will be Goffman's ethnographic studies at the psychiatric hospital, St. Elizabeth's, conducted in the late 1950s, funded by the National Institute of Mental Health (NIMH) and published in *Asylums* (1961) as well as his more formal sociological work on the management of **stigma** and spoiled identities in *Stigma* (1964a). Both books bear witness to Goffman's interest in the consequences and management of violation of social norms and social categorization and illustrate his concern with the question of social order.

A Sociologist's View of the Cuckoo's Nest

Not only did Goffman catalyze the interactionist interpretation of dramaturgy in order to understand human self-presentation (Tseëlon, 1992b, p. 501), he was also, together with scholars such as Howard S. Becker (1963) and David Matza (1969), a pioneer with regard to the development of the so-called **labeling theory**. This strand of theorizing focuses on how deviance is socially constructed in societal processes in which certain behaviors are defined and sanctioned as violations of societal regulations (Becker, 1963, p. 9; Collins & Makowsky 1993, p. 328; Manning, 1992, p. 100). In some of his books—*Asylums* (1961), *Stigma* (1964a)—and several articles, Goffman developed what might be called a *sociology of deviance* by focusing on mental illness and how this condition is managed and controlled by institutional frameworks and in everyday-life interaction. And in so doing, Goffman contributed substantially to the so-called antipsychiatric critique of the 1960s that directed serious criticism toward the psychiatric profession and the institutional treatment facilities that were offered to psychiatric patients. Almost simultaneously with the release of Goffman's *Asylums*, French philosopher Michel Foucault published *The History of Madness* (1961), which was a historical analysis of the transformations of the psychiatric profession from the 18th-century authoritarianism to contemporary medical psychiatry. But whereas Foucault's critique was based on investigation of large-scale historical transformation, Goffman examined how microsocial processes as well as the overall institutional and professional arrangement of the hospital undermines the individuality of psychiatric patients (Hacking, 2004). For Goffman, this type of research was meant to question dominant conceptions of normality and pathology and to examine the societal dimensions in the definition and treatment of human suffering as well as the institutional setups offered to people suffering from mental illness. Thus, Goffman is often associated with studies of deviant or rule-breaking people that pertain to the fact that in much of his writing, he draws on experiences and observations from his ethnographic fieldwork at St. Elizabeth's. However, there has been some speculation on whether Goffman was genuinely interested in deviance and in the people he studied. Some scholars (e.g., Fine & Martin, 1995) have claimed that Goffman saw himself as a partisan sociologist taking side with the patients, while others (e.g., Collins & Makowsky, 1993) have suggested that Goffman never really sympathized with the underdogs of the **total institution**. Despite such controversies, it is a fact that Goffman examined social deviance in close detail and that he added significant elements to the sociological understanding of the intricate relations between normality, institutions, and self. In the following, we will go into more detail with the most important ones.

Asylums

In various ways, Goffman's sociology deals with the relations between individuals and social structures as they show themselves in the micronorms and rituals in everyday life. In *Asylums* (1961), this theme is quite evident. The essays in the book are based on Goffman's fieldwork in a large psychiatric hospital, St. Elizabeth's Hospital, in Washington, D.C. For 1 year (1955–1956), he conducted participant observation of the daily life and routines at a hospital ward, and the analysis presented throughout the book continuously inspires research focusing on the relationships among patients/clients, institutions, and professionals in health or welfare institutions. *Asylums* contain four essays. The first one aims to outline the characteristics of total institutions, the second examines the moral career of the mental patient, the third focuses on the features of the institutional underlife, while, finally, the fourth essay investigates the characteristics and challenges of the medical model as it is practiced within the framework of a psychiatric hospital.

Total Institutions and Moral Careers

In "On the Characteristics of Total Institutions," Goffman critically examined what happens to a person's self during the process of hospitalization and how hospitalized persons become part of the inmate world. According to Goffman, total institutions are "the forcing houses for changing persons," and therefore they constitute important cases for explorations of "what can be done to the self" (Goffman, 1961, p. 12). At first, the person undergoes an admission procedure that marks a series of degradations, humiliations, and profanations of the self. The person undergoes a "rite of passage" involving the creation of a new identity with a new social status. Entering the hospital marks the starting point in a number of radical changes in their "moral career"—a career that, according to Goffman, involves progressive changes concerning the person's beliefs of himself and significant others. Furthermore, the hospitalization itself marks the beginning of various assaults on the person's civilian self. It represents, in Goffman's words, the beginning of a process "by which a person's self is mortified" (Goffman, 1961, p. 14) and that involves a gradual erasure of the person's significant relations with the outside world and the building of a self that corresponds with the institutional and social arrangements of the institutional establishment.

The mortification process involves various elements, starting with the fact that the individual no longer is connected to the outside world and thus needs to give up his past roles in favor of the role(s) offered by the institutional arrangement ("role dispossession"). Furthermore, during admission procedures the person is subject to a kind of "trimming" or "programming," such as taking the inmate's life history, photographing, assigning numbers, issuing standardized institutional clothing, haircutting, and introduction to internal rules and regulations, all of which are designed to transform the person into an object that fits into the institutional and organizational machinery and thus may be systematically worked on through the routine measures of the institution (Goffman, 1961, p. 26). On admission, the person is also likely to be stripped of his usual "identity kit" (e.g., the personal belongings such as clothes, cosmetics, or other tools for the management of his personal front), just as access to such things as needle and thread, towels, and soap may be denied him or kept in places to which he will have limited access. Being deprived of his identity equipment, the individual is prevented from "presenting his usual image of himself to others" (Goffman, 1961 p. 19).

The process of **mortification of self** is also likely to involve forced adoption of certain postures or movements that convey certain lowly images of the person. In mental hospitals, as Goffman points out, "patients may be forced to eat all food with a spoon," and by adopting such postures or movements, the patient engages himself in activities that are incompatible with his former self-image as a normal, grown-up person. The process may also involve various forms of "contaminative exposure." In ordinary everyday life, a person can keep his body, his mind, and his possessions clear of contact with things that pose contaminating threats. In the total institution, however, the person cannot effectively maintain a boundary between himself and the environment, and "the embodiment of self is profaned" (Goffman 1961, p. 21). Goffman mentions various types of such profanations. First, the person may experience a violation of his informational preserve in relation to the self as various kinds of (dis)creditable facts about the person being collected and recorded on admission. Second, the person's self is altered by confessional practices in which the person, individually or in groups, is expected to confess or expose thoughts and feelings to audiences of professionals and/or other inmates, as in certain therapeutic practices. Another and more extreme, example is "a self-destructive mental patient who is stripped naked for what is felt to be his own protection and placed in a constantly lit seclusion room, into whose Judas window any person passing on the ward can peer" (Goffman, 1961, p. 23). In addition to this, there is the concrete contamination of the body by unclean food, clothing impregnated with other users' sweat, dirty toilets and bath facilities, forced medication, and contamination of intestines by forced feeding. In addition to the self-violations that take the form of contaminations of or assaults on the self, the self-mortification process may involve another, more subtle characteristic that consists of a disruption of the "usual relation between the individual actor and his acts" (Goffman, 1961, p. 35). When experiencing assaults or violations outside the total institution, a person usually can defend or protect his self and his autonomy by establishing a distance between his self and the self-threatening situation. He can refuse to show signs of respect, or he can express contempt or irony regarding the situation. If he does so within boundaries of the total institution, the effect is, however, not a protection of the self but rather subsequent violations in the form of punishment from the staff rationalized by the inmate's lack of cooperation or naughtiness. In the total institution, then, acts of self-protecting are likely to be perceived as signs of the inmate's self rather than his attempts to distance or save his self from a degrading situation. Goffman termed such disruptions caused by the desegregating processes

looping. Looping thus underscores the labeling component in the hospitalized patient's illness identities as he to some extent is imposed upon by the institutional arrangement and the professionals who have the power to define resistant behavior as signs of illness.

Taken together, the elements in the self-mortification process bereave the individual of the resources that, in ordinary life, testify to the environment that the person is in control of his life, that he is a person with adult self-determination, competence, freedom, and autonomy. In Goffman's analysis, it is the violation of the adult executive competency and the things that symbolize it that leads to the progressive degradation of the self. During the process of self-mortification, the individual is stripped of his possibilities of experiencing himself as an actor owning his own acts and his abilities to project a self using territories and identity equipment. At the same time, the analysis demonstrates how Goffman moves beyond approaches that focus exclusively on (1) the individual's relations to his own self or (2) the self in a context of interaction, to an original position that relates the self and the social interactions to larger structures and system identities (Bergesen, 1984, p. 53).

In addition to his analysis of the process of self-mortification, Goffman also provides a general profile of the so-called total institution. Figure 5.1, which is inspired by the works of Philip Manning (1992, p. 115) and Nicholas Perry (2000, pp. 174–176), illustrates the four constitutive features of the

Figure 5.1 The Main Characteristics of the Total Institution

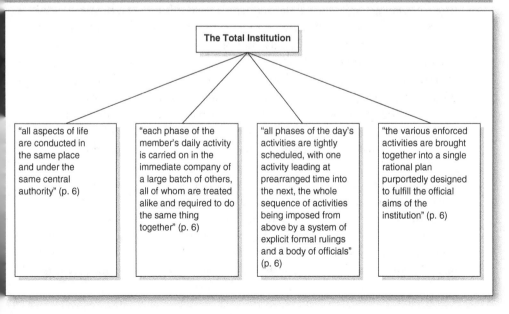

total institution and how their interrelations manifest themselves in an institutional establishment or form in which inmates, in varying degrees, are subject to the institutional structures and requirements of total subordination.

It is important to emphasize, however, that Goffman's concept of total institution is an ideal type in the Weberian sense, which means that Goffman proposes an abstract and formal concept that, on the one hand, describes and captures essential features of a phenomenon while empirical examples of its pure form do not necessarily exist. In the preface to *Asylums*, Goffman stresses that one cannot find institutions in the real world that display all the features laid out in the essay but that total institutions, in varying degrees, share some of the general characteristics.

As it appears, total institutions distinguish between two fundamentally morally and socially different types of people (the normal on the outside and the deviants on the inside), and this difference is manifested in the various social arrangements and rituals of the institution. According to Goffman, the inmate's specific way of adapting to these arrangements will, in turn, determine the specific development of his character, or in Goffman's words his **moral career**. This special career involves a series of progressive changes regarding the inmate's moral status and in his "framework of imagery for judging himself and others" (Goffman, 1961 p. 128). Once hospitalized, he is gradually changed from a free and normal person to an unfree and institutionalized patient. In the essay "The Moral Career of the Mental Patient," Goffman examines the prepatient and inpatient stages of the moral career. By admission and thus as prepatient, the person may pass through "a kind of betrayal funnel" consisting of "linked stages, each of which are managed by a different agent." One subtle characteristic of this betrayal that gradually decreases the person's free status is that each of the agents in this "circuit of significant figures" (family, friends, and professionals) not only attempts to reassure the prepatient that no further assaults on his freedom will occur but also tries to pass the prepatient on to the next while maintaining this illusion (Goffman, 1961, p. 140). An example of such "betrayal" may be the ways that close friends or relatives encourage a person to accept hospitalization, assuring him autonomy and that everything will be all right while passing on personal information and knowing that treatment of their friend or family member will involve discomfort and pain.

Once admitted, the inpatient finds himself in a situation of tension between his normal world and the life of the institution, and accordingly he needs to find a way of adapting to the tensions of identity produced by the total institution. Although the total institution violates and induces degradations of the self, it also provides for a new inmate identity who is offered a place in the institutional establishment by the issuing of certain privileges and positions in the internal hierarchy ("the ward system"). In adapting to these arrangements and thus finding a way through the mortifying experiences on the one hand and the ward system supporting inmate identity on the other, the inmate may employ various modes of adaptation such as situational withdrawal or conversion. These adaptations, then, mark the typical ways by which the inmate manages the moral experiences that accompany the loss of the usual settings of identity support (Goffman, 1961, p. 148). A key point in this analysis is that the moral career of the mental patient is closely related to an institutional system with its specific own norms, routines, and relationships. According to Goffman (and we shall return to this in more detail in Chapter 6), the self, then, should not be viewed as a property of a person; rather, it resides "in the pattern of social control that is exerted in connection with the person by himself and those around him" (Goffman, 1961, p. 154).

Hospital Underlife

According to Goffman, total institutions involve an unofficial life that occurs under the institutional surface, and this particular life is constituted, to a wide extent, by the so-called secondary adjustments. The first two essays in *Asylums* mainly analyze how total institutions gradually obtain control over the inmates' self-presentation resources and, thus, their selves. In the essay "The Underlife of a Public Institution: A Study of Ways of Making Out in a Mental Hospital," Goffman studies how patients can resist or free themselves from social control of the institutional arrangements. The patient, his analysis shows, may distance himself from the ascribed roles and identities, or he perceives them as nonsignificant. Secondary adjustment, then, is

> any habitual arrangement by which a member of an organization employs unauthorized means, or obtains unauthorized ends, or both, thus getting around the organization's assumptions as to what he should do and get and hence what he should be. Secondary adjustments represent ways in which the individual stands apart from the role and the self that were taken for granted for him by the institution. (Goffman, 1961, p. 189)

Examining the various resources that patients use in these adjustments, Goffman distinguishes between "making do" and "working the system." The first form involves the use and transformation of available artefacts in institutionally unintended ways such as making a knife from a spoon or making ink from extracts of *Life Magazine* (Goffman, 1961, p. 187). Working the system requires thorough knowledge of the institutional routines and involves how patients acquire things that they are not supposed to have. Goffman gives an illustrating example from the dining room: "On days when bananas were made available, a few of the patients would spirit away a cup of milk from the jug meant for those who required milk on their diet, and would cut their bananas up in slices, put on some sugar, and expansively eat a 'proper' dessert" (Goffman, 1961, p. 211). Secondary adjustments also involve private hideouts ("stashes"). These are places that allow the patient to keep some of his private or forbidden possessions that not only represent practical use value but also function as resources in self-presentation and in maintaining a minimal degree of privacy. Secondary adjustments, then, represent the inmate's resistance to the institutional threats to their selves and thus their attempts to maintain a self in the cracks and holes of the total institution. Following this line of thought, Goffman's analysis shows that through secondary adjustment, the individual defines and conceives his self in opposition to the self-definition forced upon him by the institution:

> Our sense of being a person can come from being drawn into a wider social unit; our sense of selfhood can arise through the little ways in which we resist the pull. Our status is backed by the solid buildings of the world, while our sense of personal identity often resides in the cracks. (Goffman, 1961, p. 280)

Thus, according to Goffman, the self develops in a dialectical process characterized by identification as well as resistance (Zeitlin, 1973, p. 203). At one level, then, *Asylums* is concerned with the meeting between mental patients and a psychiatric hospital. On another level, it involves an analysis of the maintenance and transformation of the social self. A similar interest in the micropolitics of power as well as resistance practices within institutional frameworks is found in the works of Michel Foucault (1961, 1977), who shared Goffman's interest in the ways society classifies and controls mental disorders and how institutions are "normalizing" in the sense that they are forcing inmates to conform to certain identities.

Secondary adjustments are closely related to another important theme in this essay: the spatial dimensions of the total institution. Goffman lists various types of spaces, each involving a special set of norms and characteristics. First, there are "out-of-bounds spaces" to which patients usually have no access but may be allowed access occasionally as a specially earned privilege. Furthermore, there is "surveillance space" (which constitutes the main part of the hospital), where the patient may freely stay, but under surveillance. In both restricted and surveillance spaces there is special attention to proper behavior and a formalized distance between patients and professionals. Additionally, Goffman identifies the so-called free places where behavior may be completely different and informal, where activities often are in conflict with institutional policies, and where rules and regulations may be creatively interpreted, bent, and perhaps even violated. There are also "group territories" where inmates are gathered, as in the dining hall, and the "personal territories" where inmates have their own private domain, such as the cell, the bed, or the toilet.

Toward the end of the essay, Goffman notes that whenever we study social establishments with their official expectations of what their participants owe to the establishment, one will realize the many often unrecognized and often unauthorized things that people do in order to decline the institution's view of them and thus to maintain an experience of being a normal person. It will be clear how such phenomena as private stashes and free places that are taken for granted in ordinary everyday life change character and may serve as frameworks for secondary adjustments. Similarly, it will be clear how inmates learn to use the various vulnerable places in the institution (e.g., the storerooms, the kitchen, or the workshops), and one of Goffman's conclusions is that these places are breeding sites for various forms of secondary adjustments. And as he remarks, "whenever worlds are laid on, underlives develop" (Goffman, 1961, p. 305). This notion has informed and inspired numbers of other sociological studies of human life in different social arrangements. Two such examples are found in the works of Norwegian sociologists Thomas Mathiesen and Sverre Lysgaard. In his book *The Defences of the Weak* (1965), Thomas Mathiesen analyzed how inmates in a Norwegian prison developed collective communities of solidarity as a response to the exertion of power by prison authorities. In a somewhat similar vein, Sverre Lysgaard (1976) conducted a study among workers at a timber processing plant and identified a form of *worker collectivity* that committed the workers to a set of social norms, some of which were challenging management goals of efficiency and productivity.

The Medical Model and Psychiatric Hospitalization

The last essay in *Asylums* differs from the three previous ones in terms of its focus and scope. Here Goffman is not primarily concerned with patients and their interactions with institutional arrangements but rather with the rationality and practices of the psychiatric institution. He thus picks up the thread from the first essay in which he briefly touches upon what he calls "the rational perspective espoused by the institution" (Goffman, 1961, p. 83). In "The Medical Model and Psychiatric Hospitalization," Goffman continues the analysis of the rationality of the total institution by an examination of the psychiatric profession as a service-providing expert system. Goffman is concerned with the service relationship that exists between service-seeking patients who more or less voluntarily enter into the custody of medical experts. As in other parts of his work, Goffman opens the essay by introducing a metaphor. He describes the service triad among the practitioner, the object in need of repair, and its owner as an example of a "tinkering service" (Goffman, 1961, p. 326), referring, however implicitly, to the service provided by groups of traveling people (such a Gypsies or Irish Travellers) earning their living from various minor services such as mending, repairing, or adjusting household utensils. Such craft-like professions tamper with broken or malfunctioning objects in order to make them function again. With this analogy, Goffman portrays psychiatrists as a special type of craftsmen who provide an emotionally unengaged service of mending objects. The medical profession, Goffman thus indicates, meddles with people just like the auto mechanic fixes his customer's car. As mentioned, this essay explores the social relation that exists between patients seeking treatment and professionals providing professional service within the institutional framework of a mental hospital. According to Goffman, this relation involves service-seeking people placing themselves in the hands of others:

> Ideally, the client brings to this relationship respect for the server's technical competence and trust that he will use it ethically—he also brings gratitude and a fee. On the other side, the server brings: an esoteric and empirically effective competence, and a willingness to place it at the client's disposal; professional discretion; a voluntary circumspection, leading him to exhibit a disciplined unconcern with the client's other affairs or even (in the last analysis) with why the client should want the service in the first place; and, finally, an unservile civility. (Goffman, 1961, p. 326)

Goffman uses this service pattern as a framework for understanding the organization of the relationship between psychiatrists and patients in the mental hospital. The patients are objects of service, and thus they constitute the organic systems in need of repair. Some of them seek the service voluntarily, while others are brought to admission against their will, and in both instances this marks the beginning of the characteristic cycle of repair or, as Goffman terms it, the rational-empirical treatment with its elements of assessment, diagnosis, prescription, and treatment. Psychiatric hospitals, Goffman contends, institutionalize a grotesque form of the service relationship that "brings together a doctor who cannot easily afford to construe his activity in other than medical terms and a patient who may feel he must fight and hate his keepers if any sense is to be made of the hardship he is undergoing" (Goffman, 1961, p. 369). Compared with patients, however, doctors do have far better opportunities to evolve mechanisms assisting them in coping with their problem:

> There are some features of the hospital situation that help the psychiatrist in the difficulties of his role. The physician's legal mandate over the fate of the patient and his institutional power over some elements of staff automatically provide authority that other servers must in part win through actual interaction with the client. Further, while psychiatric knowledge often cannot place the psychiatrist in a position to predict the patient's conduct correctly, the same science provides the psychiatrist with interpretive leeway: by adding *post hoc* qualifications and adumbrations of his analysis, the psychiatrist can provide a picture of what has been happening with the patient that can no more be disproved than proved. (Goffman, 1961, pp. 369–370)

The psychiatrist may of course attempt to manage his role problem by leaving the hospital in favor of a career in an institutional arrangement that better matches the service pattern. He may also—and this is the main focus of Goffman's analysis—in collaboration with other staff members try to build a protective skin of words, meanings, and sentiments that serves to "stabilize the medical-service definition of the situation" (Goffman, 1961, p. 373). Goffman finds examples of this stabilizing work in the hospital's public-relations work, where the medical service is displayed in exhibitions, brochures, magazines, and displayed medical equipment. In addition, Goffman argues, hospitals often have a collection of narratives illustrating the validity of the approach applied by the medical professions. One example might be the story of a patient who was released against the recommendation of the doctors and subsequently committed suicide or murder (Goffman, 1961, p. 373). This is one aspect of the stabilizing work and an aspect that concerns the nature of the hospital. Another important type of stability work concerns the nature of the patient. In the hospital, the general view of the patient is that

> were he "himself" he would voluntarily seek psychiatric treatment and voluntarily submit to it, and, when ready for discharge, he will avow that his real self was all along being treated as it really wanted to be treated. A variation of the guardian principle is involved. The interesting notion that the psychotic patient has a sick self and, subordinated to this, a relatively "adult," "intact," or "unimpaired" self carries guardianship one step further, finding in the very structure of the ego the split between object and client required to complete the service triad. (Goffman, 1961, p. 374)

In establishing this view of the patient, Goffman points out that the record plays an important role since it helps in building up a personal history of the patient that documents the gradual development of a mental pathology. The record, with its categories of pathology labels, then is a key element in the "magical ways of making a single unity out of the nature of the patient" (Goffman, 1961, p. 375). Further, in this process of redefining the patient's nature, the notion of a "danger mandate" is of critical importance. This mandate involves the idea that the service object has certain danger points and therefore may be damaged in the hands of unskilled persons. In the psychiatric hospital, Goffman observes, the danger mandate takes form in the view that wrong action can cause damage to the patient and that among the hospital staff, only the trained and skilled psychiatrist is capable of performing potentially dangerous service. Obviously, this reduces the psychiatrist's role problems since "the possession of the mandate confirms one's view of self as an expert server" (Goffman, 1961, p. 378).

During the course of the redefining process, the patient is transformed to an object that is suited for psychiatric service. The irony (or tragedy) is, however, as Goffman notes, that once this redefinition has taken place, very little service is available. The transformation of a person to an object suitable for medical service thus seems to serve interests other than those of the patients. Although officially and explicitly aiming at providing professional treatment, Goffman's analysis suggests that the redefinition processes also serve to stabilize and confirm the medical service model. At the other end of the process, at discharge, Goffman observes a similar pattern. Discharge is taken as evidence of institutionally catalyzed improvement and, as Goffman notes, phrases such as "'discharged as improved' imply that the hospital had a hand in the curing or improving" (Goffman, 1961, pp. 381–382).

The analysis of the rationalities of total institutions and the medical model thus seems to be concerned with "system maintenance." At the manifest or surface level, the medical service that is performed in total institutions is performed for and upon the patients. Going a step deeper, Goffman's study highlights at least three important mechanisms: (1) that the medical service, the various treatment programs, therapeutic approaches, and disciplinary measures are presented as individual service to the patient while it appears to be measures performed in service of the institution: "under the guise of medical-service model the practice of maintenance medicine is sometimes to be found" (Goffman, 1961, p. 383); (2) that the application of the medical service model within hospital psychiatry seems to worsen a patient's situation instead of bettering it; and finally (3) that one of the total institution's important achievements is the production of institutional identity and the maintenance of its staff's professional self-perception: "Inmates and lower staff level are involved in a vast supportive action—an elaborate dramatized tribute—that has the effect, if not the purpose, of affirming that a medical-like service is in progress here and that the psychiatric staff is providing it" (Goffman, 1961, p. 385). Thus, what Goffman's analysis implies is that apparently therapeutic institutions such as mental hospitals and apparently humanistic psy-sciences such as psychiatry and psychology function as systems of control and degradation of human selves. This observation is echoed in Michel Foucault's historical and sociological works on the treatment of mental disorder and the development of prisons in Western societies (see preceding).

Stigma and the Sociology of Spoiled Identities

As we have seen, the analysis in *Asylums* highlights how mental patients in total institutions go through moral careers, are gradually stigmatized and relate themselves—and their selves—to the role of a psychiatric patient. In *Stigma*, Goffman changes the focus from institutions—or perhaps more correctly, from institutional behavior—to the encounters and behaviors of everyday life. As the subtitle "The Management of Spoiled Identities" indicates, this work examines how people with spoiled identities manage themselves and their identity work in the complexities of the myriad of everyday-life encounters. The analysis unfolding in *Stigma* lies in natural continuation of *The Presentation of Self in Everyday Life* in which Goffman investigates how people collaborate in maintaining a workable definition of the situation and thus help each other in sustaining adequate selves. This theme is also evident in *Stigma*, but where *The Presentation of Self in Everyday Life* (1959) examined it by looking at the interactional cooperations of so-called normal people in everyday-life situations, *Stigma* focuses on the interactional management of inappropriate, discrediting, or stigmatized characteristics. For this reason, *Stigma* might appropriately have been launched under the title "The Presentation of Discredited Selves in Everyday Life" (Friedson, 1983, p. 361).

In *Stigma*, then, Goffman investigates the social interaction that takes place between the stigmatized and so-called normal people (Goffman termed people who do not bear a particular stigma "the normals"). More specifically, this work contains three interrelated themes: (1) the development of a sociological understanding of how stigmatization occurs and the examination of the processes that produce a stigmatized person; (2) an analysis of how stigmatized persons manage themselves and their stigma in social interactions; and finally (3) how this management affects the stigmatized person's self-conception.

Let us begin with the sociological understanding of stigmatization. According to Goffman, stigma is a deeply discrediting attribute or behavior, and he defined it as a discrepancy between a person's virtual and actual social identity:

> While the stranger is present before us, evidence can arise of his possessing an attribute that makes him different from others in the category of persons available for him to be, and of a less desirable kind—in the extreme, a person who is quite thoroughly bad, or dangerous, or weak. He is thus reduced in our minds from a whole and usual person to a tainted, discounted one. Such an attribute is a stigma, especially when its discrediting effect is very extensive; sometimes it is also called a failing, a shortcoming, a handicap. It constitutes a special discrepancy between virtual and actual social identity. (Goffman 1964a, pp. 12–13)

Stigma, then, is a societal reaction that spoils normal identities and perspective that is generated in social situations by way of norms that encroach on social encounters (Williams, 2000, p. 217). The distinction between "virtual" and "actual" identity points to another important notion in *Stigma*: the permanent threat to our identity in social encounters. No matter how self-confident we might feel, meetings with other people may bring our self-presentation into jeopardy. The fundamental issue here, as we shall return to later in this chapter, is that in fact we are all potentially stigmatized and that the course of the social encounter determines whether a potential stigma will have negative consequences for its possessor.

As it appears, Goffman describes a social process through which social identity is spoiled as a result of the reactions, categorizations, and evaluations of a social audience. Through such processes of definition and/or categorization, persons who display culturally nonaccepted attributes or behaviors are placed in discredited social stereotypes. Goffman, then, distinguishes among three different types of stigma: First, there is *physical stigma* or what Goffman calls "abominations of the body," which cover the various deformities of the body. Second, there is *character stigma* or "blemishes of individual character often perceived as weak will, domineering or unnatural passions, treacherous and rigid beliefs, and dishonesty;" and finally there is *tribal stigma* that results from belonging to a particular race, religion, or nationality. These three types of stigma are all characterized by the same fundamental sociological mechanism, namely that they attract attention from a social audience and subsequently lead to social rejection and lack of recognition of other, potentially creditable attributes.

Goffman begins his analysis by concluding that since the invention of the term by the ancient Greeks, the application and meaning of the concept have undergone certain and important changes. For the ancient Greeks, stigma referred to the physical signs that were applied to a person as a mark of his or her particular status. Such signs would be burned or cut into the body in order to signal that this particular person was a slave, a criminal, or in some other way a blemished person with whom public contact should be avoided (Goffman, 1964a, p. 11). According to Goffman, contemporary use of the term "stigma" comes close to the original Greek version as it refers to a person's deviant status. There is, however, a significant difference as the contemporary stigma concept emphasizes the personal shame and disgrace more than a person's physical signs or marks:

> By definition, of course, we believe the person with a stigma is not quite human. On this assumption we exercise varieties of discrimination, through which we effectively, if often unthinkingly, reduce his life chances. We construct a stigma theory, and ideology to explain his inferiority and account for the danger he represents, sometimes rationalizing an animosity based on other differences, such as those of social class. . . . We tend to impute a wide range of imperfections on the basis of the original one, and at the same time to impute some desirable but undesired attributes, often of a supernatural cast, such as "sixth sense," or "understanding" . . . . Further, we may perceive his defensive response to his situation as a direct expression of his defect, and then see both defect and response as just retribution for something he or his parents or his tribe did, and hence a justification of the way we treat him. (Goffman 1964a, pp. 15–16)

The quote contains some of the fundamental components in Goffman's concept of stigma and illustrates his interconnection of a number of classical sociological and social psychology concepts regarding the relations among the individual, groups, and society. First, there is the relation between observed differences and stereotypes. For Goffman, stigmatization involves a differentiation and categorization of persons sharing certain attributes or behaviors, and the members of such categories (their attributes and personal characteristics) are viewed through certain stereotypic understandings. Through this process, a perceptional erasure of the stigmatized unique personal qualities and characteristics takes place. Second, there is discrimination and the accompanying loss of social status. Stigmatized persons are excluded from a number of social arenas and the general respect that is enjoyed by normal people in society. Third, prejudices play an important role in stigmatization processes. As it appears from the quote, the aversion and segregation do not necessarily rest on thorough and nuanced information but rather on a kind of intuitive or automatic aggregation of negative views based on observed differences or deviances.

The second theme in *Stigma* has to do with how the management of stigma in social situations is affected by a number of different factors, and one reason behind the book's status as a classic in the sociological canon is Goffman's fine sense of the complicated interactions between the stigmatized and their social environment. In developing this understanding, he introduces an analytical distinction between "the discredited" and "the discreditable." It is important to recognize that these are analytical types. The discredited are bearers of a visible deviancy, while the deviancy of the discreditable is unknown and undetected by the social environment. In meetings between "the normals" or in so-called mixed contacts, these two different types will engage in fundamentally different forms of social interaction. For the discreditable, the stigma have not yet been revealed, and Goffman examines the various ways that such types (which in principle potentially involve all of us) try to manage and communicate identity. Specifically, this work has to do with controlling information about the self. The discreditable person may attempt to withhold and give off certain information about himself in order to keep his potential stigma hidden from the participants in a social encounter. The key phrase here is thus "information control." An example of this information control directed at hiding stigma is the practice of people with nonvisible stigmas (such as epilepsy or mental illness) to carefully select the audience to whom they talk about their condition.

Goffman often uses the verb "to pass" to describe such successful secret keeping of potentially stigmatizing attributes. Even though a person may successfully pass in a social encounter and thereby maintain his identity as "normal," these efforts have their costs and dangers. First, one lives with a permanent risk and fear of being revealed or exposed. Second, during passing attempts, persons may, by accident and involuntarily, expose other incapacities than those they initially try to conceal:

> slovenliness, as when a near blind person, affecting to see, trips over a stool, or spills drink down his shirt; inattentiveness, stubbornness, woodenness, or distance, as when a hard of hearing person fails to respond to a remark proffered him by someone ignorant of his shortcomings; sleepiness, as when a teacher perceives a student's *petit mal* epilepsy seizure as momentary daydreaming; drunkenness, as when a man with cerebral palsy finds that his gait is always being misinterpreted. (Goffman, 1964a, p. 105)

For the discredited, the interaction with the social environment has a different basis since his stigma is publicly known and thus affects its bearer and the social audience. Goffman demonstrates how a social audience may try to avoid noticing a person's discrediting attributes and how such efforts of "not noticing" add tension to the situation. On the other side, the stigmatized often feels unsure of what the other participants really think of him. The crucial problem to be solved here is to what extent the normals openly should notice the deviance of the stigmatized and how the stigmatized (with his knowledge of the normal's situational considerations) should act in such situations. The key phrase here is "tension management." Examples of tension management may be observable in the ways that highly overweight individuals or people with visible physical handicaps make jokes about their situation while in the presence of "normals" in order to facilitate unrestrained and smooth social interaction.

The third central theme in *Stigma* deals with how interactional management of discrediting characteristics affects the self-perception of the discredited. Goffman examines, among other things, how the so-called good adjustment (that is, when a stigmatized person presents a normal self without pressing his claim of acceptance too far) never results in a full social acceptance:

> The stigmatized individual is asked to act as to imply neither that his burden is heavy nor that bearing it has made him different from us; at the same time he must keep himself at that remove from us which ensures our painlessly being able to confirm this belief about him. Put differently, he is advised to reciprocate naturally with an acceptance of himself and us, an acceptance of him that we have not quite extended him in the first place. A *phantom acceptance* is thus allowed to provide the basis for a *phantom normalcy*. (Goffman, 1964a, pp. 147–148)

Here Goffman points to a subtle kind of oppression that takes place within the frames of the social order in Western societies. Although he is not perceived as fully normal, the stigmatized must pretend to be a normal person with a normal identity, and he must tactfully receive acceptance and help from the normals and even act to protect them by avoiding those situations that complicate the hypocrisy of their phantom acceptance. In other words, Goffman uncovers a somewhat unrecognized form of mundane oppression, or perhaps even symbolic violence, in the sense that discredited people are forced to act and understand themselves from the perspective of others, and in so doing they confirm and maintain the normative structure that excludes them in the first place. The management of stigmatized attributes in the course of social interaction thus supports the internalization of a degraded and deviant self-conception. Examples of the experiences of phantom normalcy can be observed among some ex-criminal offenders who have found that in the process of moving from deviant to normal, there may be a period involving a feeling that one is learning or gradually in the process of becoming a normal and socially acceptable person (see Farrall & Calverley, 2006).

One of the key points in *Stigma*, then, is that the normative structure of society in some situations is confirmed and secured by persons who receive little or no social recognition. Thus, *Stigma* contains a profound critique of modern, Western societies. Another key point is the rejection of stigma as an immanent, personal, and context-independent characteristic. Stigmatization occurs through certain social processes and situations. Therefore, we are all potentially stigmatized in the sense that we all possess characteristics that, in certain situations and contexts, would be perceived as deviant or inappropriate.

Stigma After Goffman

Since the release of *Stigma* in 1963, a considerable amount of sociological and psychological research has employed the concept and perspective developed by Goffman (see, e.g., Ainlay, Becker, & Coleman, 1968; Franzese, 2009; Katz, 1982; Link & Phelan, 2001). A wide and diverse range of empirical studies has been conducted, and many of these have focused on those types of stigma that relate to various mental and physical illnesses. Stigmatization processes and effects of stigma in relation to mental illness have been investigated in various qualitative and quantitative research projects. Among the many studies, we might mention Fred E. Markowitz's (1998) study of how stigmatization processes affect the quality of life among people with mental illness; Sarah Rosenfeld's (1997) study of negative and positive effects of the official medical labeling; and Jennifer B. Ritscher and Jo Phelan's (2004) study of stigma internalization among ex-mental patients.

The space here does not allow for a summary of this large and still-growing corpus of research (see Hinshaw, 2007, for an overview), but generally speaking, there is a polarization in the interpretation of stigmatization effects. On the one hand, some studies indicate that stigma that relate to certain mental illnesses involve experiences of social exclusion, loneliness, and shame. A somewhat consistent finding seems to be that the process of diagnosis mobilizes cultural stereotypes and negative prejudices and that these stereotypes are attached to the persons in question, resulting in social devaluation, negative self-perceptions, and limited life chances. On the other hand, some studies seem to suggest that the social exclusion experienced by mental patients is caused by the illness and its symptoms and not by labeling and cultural stereotypes. In this vein, diagnostic processes are not exclusively seen as negative elements in stigmatization processes but also as an access line to help, understanding, and treatment. Similarly, the investigation of stigmatization processes in relation to physical illness has taken place in a number of studies. Again we just mention a few: Neville Millen and Christine Walker (2002) have examined how chronic illness affects the patient's self-conception, ability to manage the illness, and their social networks, while Scott E. Rutledge and his research team (2008) have investigated the stigmatization process among HIV positives. Besides documenting the potential excluding effects of stigma, this type of research has shown how the differentiation and stereotyping described by Goffman have a significant impact on the stigmatized experience of themselves and their chances of managing their situation.

Although stigma focuses on microsocial interactions in everyday life and many subsequent studies have adopted Goffman's perspective in the study of stigmatization processes on the micro or intermediary level, Goffman's work has, as we have already indicated, several macrotheoretical implications. British sociologist Graham Scambler (2006) has proposed a macrotheoretical framework facilitating an extended understanding of stigma in contemporary societies. He suggests that the stigma concept involves a double perspective: the stigmatized experience of stigma ("felt stigma") and the various acts conducted by the stigmatizing ("enacted stigma"). Obviously, the interesting questions concern the relation between these perspectives: Does enacted stigma automatically lead to a felt stigma, and can a felt stigma occur without enacted ones? Answering such questions involves analysis of situational processes as well as structural features of society. Therefore, as Scambler suggests, it is relevant to engage in theoretical elaborations and extensions of Goffman's original concept in relation to other social and cultural contexts than those observed by Goffman.

Conclusion

This chapter has illustrated how mental illness, total institutions, processes of institutionalization, and stigmatization constitute important themes in Erving Goffman's sociology. His ethnographic case study at St. Elizabeth's in *Asylums* (1961) explored how total institutions, through various procedures, privilege systems, and institutional practices mortify the patient's selves, and today it stands as a landmark of microsociological institutional analysis. On a broader scope, his work explored how human selves and identities survive under critical circumstances, and thus it has added important insights to the sociological understanding of relationships and interconnection among self, roles, and social institutions. In *Stigma* (1964a), Goffman continued his work on deviance, focusing explicitly on how people, in everyday life, control potentially damaging information about themselves in order to protect their selves and identities. Stressing the situational character of stigma and thus challenging conventional understandings of deviance, Goffman observed that in fact we are all potentially stigmatized. Whether potentially discrediting information will result in spoiled identities depends on how actors, in everyday-life interaction, succeed in controlling information and how interacting actors manage the tensions that arise in mixed contacts.

Questions

- Discuss the validity of Erving Goffman's claim that deviance should be understood as situationally and socially constructed.
- What are the main differences between Erving Goffman's work on stigma and Howard S. Becker's labeling theory?
- Discuss whether a society without stigmatization is possible and whether negative effects of stigmatization of groups or individuals may be avoided or reduced by way of other mechanisms that produced stigmatization in the first place.

6

Goffman and the Self

I n this chapter we will explore and discuss Goffman's view of the self. We will explore how, in Goffman's sociological thinking, the self appears as a highly social product, which is the result of individually staged projections and responses taking place in social meetings as well as of situational and societal constraints. In so doing, we discuss how Goffman's self is intertwined with the interaction order.

A Dualistic View of the Self

So far we have seen how Goffman attempts to develop a theory of interaction between individuals in face-to-face encounters. But even though Goffman was probably primarily interested in understanding the aforementioned interaction order as "a substantive domain in its own right" or as an order *sui generis*, another of his ambitions was to further develop the sociological understanding of the human self, its formation, and maintenance. This interest in the self runs like a thread through most of Goffman's books, articles, and essays, and in the following we will attempt to summarize the most important elements in Goffman's view of the self. What we need to establish first, however, is that in Goffman's works the self, as well as a number of other matters, is not presented in one cohesive theory from the same perspective and definition (Miller, 1986, p. 177). Considerations on the self appear in many parts of Goffman's work and are analyzed from different perspectives, defined in various ways. By means of analytical perspectivism, Goffman developed his original conception of the self. With regard to this, Ann Branaman (1997) pointed out that it is possible to identify at least two apparently opposite perceptions of self in Goffman's works: on the one hand, the perception of the self as an exclusively social product without any actual personal core, and on the other hand, an image of the self that is, to a certain degree, able to release itself from social limitations and manipulate strategically the social situation so as to appear in the most favorable light.

This seemingly contradictory view of the self is evident in *The Presentation of Self in Everyday Life* (1959). In this work, Goffman applies a dramaturgical perspective to investigate the ways in which individuals present themselves and their activities to others and how they seek to manage the impression others form of them in everyday-life situations. One of the main arguments in this work is that all individuals attempt to communicate a certain picture of who they are and how they wish others to perceive them. In other words, in social encounters, individuals project an image of themselves, and from this projection the self emerges. This is done collectively through a performance involving actors and audience. Participants in everyday-life encounters or performances need to confirm the self-conception that is projected into the situation before the owner may experience congruence between his inner self-understanding and the external, socially confirmed identity. The confirmation of a person's projected self relies on both trust in the social environment and the credibility of the possessor's performance (Weigert, 1981). Echoing Mead (see Chapter 2), Goffman's self, then, is both social and mutable and the subject of negotiations between the possessor of the self and the social audience. The social audience may accept or reject the performer's presented self, emphasizing that the self is in fact a product of these social interchanges:

> While this image is entertained *concerning* the individual, so that a self is imputed to him, this self itself does not derive from its possessor, but from the whole scene of his action, being generated by that attribute of local events which renders them interpretable by witnesses. A correctly staged and performed scene leads the audience to impute a self to a performed character, but this imputation—this self—is a *product* of a scene that comes off, and is not a *cause* of it. The self, then, as a performed character, is not an organic thing that has a specific location, whose fundamental fate is to be born, to mature, and to die: it is a dramatic effect arising diffusely from a scene that is presented, and the characteristic issue, the crucial concern, is whether it will be credited or discredited. (Goffman, 1959, pp. 244–245)

Goffman thus presents the notion that analyses of the self ought not focus on its possessor, since he is merely a "peg" on which collectively and interactionally produced stuff may be hung for a period of time. Stressing this point, Goffman indicates that the self emerges from the scene that is performed by a team of actors, a team that makes use of available stage equipment and whose performance is interpreted and accepted by an audience. The Goffmanian self is, however, also dramaturgical in another sense. Besides being a product of an *active self-presentation* and creative impression management, it is at the same time a *staged* activity aiming at securing the smooth and successful flow of social situations (Holstein & Gubrium, 2000, p. 36). The self, then, is both something that individuals actively *do* while it is also something that *finds its place* and adapts to the various and differently framed social encounters of everyday life. Thus, for example, when in the classroom, students may present various self-images (e.g., critical, engaged, or rebellious learners), all of which, however, need to correspond with the specific social situation framed as education in order to secure a smooth flow of social interaction. This emphasizes the notion (which is not always apparent in interpretations of Goffman's view of the self) that it is social situations that constrain individuals to present a self, to take certain roles, and to appear credible, honest, and tactful, and therefore it is in fact society that makes individuals into actors (Collins, 1986, p 107). Once individuals have chosen a specific and situationally appropriate line, they will be constrained to stick to it, while on the other hand, the audience and coperformers are obliged to go along and maintain the jointly enacting definition of the situation and the presented selves (Collins, 2004, p. 16). Thus, according to Goffman, a person's self should not be understood solely as a driving force controlling and managing his role play. We do not act in certain ways because we possess a certain self. The self is a "dramatic effect" that is something that emerges from interactional collaborations in which performances are accepted, rejected, and corrected within a broader game that follows some more or less well-defined cultural and moral scripts. In other words, the self is produced through our everyday-life performances in which we take socially produced roles in ways that produce unique self-identities. Thereby, Goffman's analysis of the self challenges the notion of identity between self and consciousness, since the self is not perceived as a generator of actions but rather as a result of our abilities to, through creative role play, flavor our identity with private intentions and subjective characteristics (Elliot 2001, p. 33).

In exploring the concept of **role distance**, Goffman (1961) pursues a similar line of thought. Here he analyzes how individuals may deal differently with the socially situated roles they are placed in and how they, through the way we choose to deal with these roles, may convey a certain self to the social surroundings. We may engage in the role, be completely devoured by or immersed in the role, or distance ourselves from it. By relating to the roles, individuals actively try to relate to the self they imply. In certain contexts, the person will accept the role and be completely immersed in it, like the perfect waiter or 3- to 4-year-old children on a merry-go-round. In other situations, individuals try to distance themselves from the role and from the socially situated self as well in an effort to signal to the surroundings that they are in fact something else and more than what the social role would seem to imply. Examples include when a child of age 7 or more rides a merry-go-round with a bored and nonchalant attitude, signaling distance from the self-image of a small child who can barely stay on the horse, or when a surgeon, while performing his work, is humming obscene songs to assure his fellow staff that alongside his professional role as surgeon is an emotionally balanced individual. With the concept of role distance, Goffman thus refers to the actors' ability to drive a wedge between themselves and the socially situated role or, rather, between themselves and the actual self that the role implies and that should be valid for everybody accepting it and acting it out. Thus, role distance is the prerequisite for both filling out and entering into social roles while at the same time expressing a unique personality (Goffman, 1961). In later works, it is emphasized more explicitly how the competences of the individual regarding self-presentation are subject to significant limitations (Branaman, 1997). Thus, in the essay "The Insanity of Place," Goffman states:

> [T]he self is the code that makes sense out of almost all the individual's activities and provides a basis for organizing them. This self is what can be read about the individual by interpreting the place he takes in an organization of social activity, as confirmed by his expressive behaviour. The individual's failure to encode, through deeds and expressive cues, a *workable* definition of himself, one which closely enmeshed others can accord him through the regard they show his person, is to block and trip up and threaten them in almost every movement that they make. (Goffman, 1971, p. 366)

The social individual, then, is obliged to present a self-definition that corresponds with, or at least does not contradict, the definition others can accord him through social intercourse. In the essay "On Face Work," Goffman also presents a dual definition of the self:

> [T]he self as an *image* pieced together from the expressive implications of the full flow of events in an undertaking; and the self as a kind of *player* in a ritual game who copes honourably or dishonourably, diplomatically or undiplomatically, with the judgmental contingencies of the situation. (Goffman, 1967, p. 31; emphasis added)

Through this dual view of the self, Goffman suggests that the human self emerges in processes of autonomy and dependency (Laursen, 1997). Thus, theoretically speaking, the Goffmanian self is located somewhere between the socially determined "*homo sociologicus*" (Dahrendorf, 1973) and the living, intention-controlled, and symbol-creating human being of symbolic interactionism.

Territories of Self

As already touched upon, it is a central presumption in Goffman's thinking that the property and **territories** of the self are parts of or perhaps rather a type of an extension of the self and that violation of this property or these territories constitutes, at the same time, violation of the self. In the externalization of our selves, we as persons lay claim to shares of the physical and social spaces within which the interaction takes place, and at the same time we make use of certain personal objects or props. In other words, we need territories and props in order to launch and maintain our selves. The territory is both the symbolic and the material space of action required by the self. Thus, maintenance of the self presupposes maintenance of the territories of the self. Conversely, the absence of respect for these territories signals a lack of respect for the person's self.

In *Relations in Public* (Goffman, 1971, pp. 29–40), Goffman describes the different types of territory that correspond in terms of content with the elements of the mortification process described in *Asylums* and explored in more detail in Chapter 5. The territories may be divided into categories depending on their organization. Thus, Goffman operates with "fixed territories," which have a certain geographical extension and to which the person can claim formal legitimate title. One example might be real property. Another category is constituted by "situational territories," which are linked to a certain location and which the person may make his or her property for a limited period (a bench in the park). Finally, there are the "egocentric territories," which are carried about by the person. Goffman further divides the categories of territories into various subtypes.

First, we have (1) the "personal space," which surrounds the person and which may be violated when others step into it; (2) the "stall," which is the well-defined space a person may occupy temporarily and that he or she either owns or does not own. Examples may be a comfortable chair, a table with a view, or a telephone booth, and as charter tourists, most people recognize the battle for deck chairs at the swimming pool. (3) Third is the "use space," which is the territory immediately around or in front of the person, which is expected to be respected because it holds an instrumental use value. This may be the room a visitor to an art museum establishes around him- or herself and the work of art that is being watched. (4) Fourth is the "turn," which must be observed and respected, such as ladies and children first or one's turn in a conversation. (5) Fifth is the "sheath," in the shape of the skin of the body and the clothes we wear, which constitutes the smallest of all personal spaces and, at the same time, egocentric territoriality in its purest form. (6) Sixth is "possessional territory," which is any collection of objects that may be identified with the self and that are transported on the body. Typical examples are a jacket, gloves, cigarettes, and a wallet. (7) Seventh is the "informational preserve," which is the information about oneself that a person in encounters with others is expected to control: pocket contents, wording of letters, biographical information. And finally comes (8) the "conversational preserve," which covers a person's right to control, to a certain extent, who may draw him into a conversation and when. This is, in other words, a question of the person's conversational availability.

In connection with the territories of the self and the violation of these, Goffman dwells on what he calls "modalities of violation," or the ways in which violations may occur. He lists the following examples: (1) too short a physical distance, where the body is placed too close to the territory of others; (2) the body that can touch and thus defile the sheath or possessions of another; (3) the penetrating, intrusive, and immodest look; (4) sounds, made by others, that invade and allocate too much sound space to the maker; (5) inappropriate addressing, such as verbal approaches from a person who is not authorized or next in turn to make the address; and finally (6) bodily excreta, which are divided into four categories: (a) urine, semen, fecal matter, perspiration, vomit, (b) body smells, flatus, tainted breath, (c) body heat, which may be found on a chair, in overcoats, on a toilet seat, and (d) markings left by the body, such as in the shape of tooth marks in a bar of chocolate or food leftovers on a plate (Goffman, 1971, pp. 44–47).

Violation of the self, which is a central theme in both *Asylums* and *Relations in Public*, may also be committed as theft or destruction of props and other identity equipment, mutilation of the body, and, not least, as symbolic and concrete contamination of a person's body, whether this is a question of moving too close or actual defilement. Goffman's point here is that in principle, there is no difference between these violations, as they are all, albeit to different extents, expressions of territorial offense. According to Goffman, such offenses can be seen as prototypical violations that occur "when one individual encroaches on the preserve claimed by and for another individual, the first thereby functioning as an impediment to the second's claim" (Goffman, 1971, p. 50). Another type is the so-called self-violations, which may assume different forms. The individual may befoul himself. The most extreme examples in the West are when individuals smear themselves with their own feces. The individual may debase himself by using waste products of others. The third type has to do with exposure. This has to do with exposing sides of oneself that are normally considered too private or embarrassing to display (Goffman, 1971, pp. 52–56).

The Mask Behind the Mask

Although Goffman (in his works on stigma) maintains his distinction between "virtual identities" of persons on the one hand and "actual identities" on the other, he never reaches a clear determination of what the actual identity really is, let alone a clear conclusion as to whether this self does indeed exist (Chriss, 1999). We may add here that nor do the distinctions among social, personal, and ego identity assist our clarification of this question. In his essay on role distance, he writes, among other things, that human actors have both a profane and a sacred part. The sacred part has to do with more personal matters, with how the person really is once all profane layers have been peeled off. The sacred part is seen when the person is relaxing and displays to others how he really is (Goffman, 1972, p. 152). As James J. Chriss mentions, this might result in the impression that role distance is then not an option in the sacred part, where, as we know, a person appears in his authentic figure. But as Chriss points out, Goffman spends most of this essay documenting how role distance manifests itself not only in the profane areas of social life, but also in the sacred areas. In other words, there are elements in Goffman's sociology (this is perhaps most evident in his essay "Role Distance") of the self that point in the direction that no authentic self exists, understood as a human self, devoid of any social mask. The self in Goffman's view, then, is "the mask the individual wears in social situations, but it is also the human being behind the mask who decides which mask to wear" (Branaman, 1997, p. xlviii). Philip Manning (1992, p. 44) has developed the so-called "two selves thesis." In his opinion, Goffman points out that we have an outer masked self, which we use to manipulate people's idea of who we are, and we have an inner, perhaps more authentic self, which we protect against the audience. In Goffman, the self of the human being is to be seen as a function of society; it is, so to speak, oversocialized, and it is furthermore a characteristic that the identity concept, which plays the least prominent role in *Stigma*, is the phenomenologically inspired concept of *ego identity* (Rasmussen, 1975, p. 100). To Goffman, the self is the result of the surroundings in which it appears or *acts*. In other words, the self is not an ethereal and shapeless substance that can be designed according to need. It exists in and is constituted by social situations and connections. Danish philosopher

Dag Heede (1997) named his introduction to the works of Michel Foucault *The Empty Man*, because according to Foucault, it makes no sense to seek to uncover the original identity or essence of the human being. The same title might have been used as a (simplifying and provocative but still quite precise) headline for an analysis of Goffman's understanding of the self. To a certain extent, Goffman's studies of the self resemble, as do Foucault's, a peeled onion in the sense that we never find its center (Heede, 1997, p. 53) but merely the mask behind the mask.

Evidently, Heede's onion metaphor evokes associations with postmodernism, and Goffman's name has indeed (in, for instance, Battershill, 1990; Gergen, 1991; Schwalbe, 1993; Tseëlon, 1992a) been linked with the postmodern conception of the self. The postmodern idea of the self, if it is possible at all to speak of such a concept in the singular, suggests that the self does not exist as a definite and continuous entity. In *The Saturated Self* (1991), Kenneth Gergen actually claims that the postmodern self is a relational, nonessentialist, and discursive entity consisting of manifold and irreconcilable potential options of being (Gergen, 1991, p. 69). In *The Postmodern Condition: A Report on Knowledge* (1984), Jean-François Lyotard, one of the most significant advocates of postmodernism, also argued that the self has become decentralized and dissolved into a relational and episodic image, which is being created through communicative exchanges in various connections, contexts, or situations. Efrat Tseëlon (1992a, p. 121) bluntly claims that the Goffman self is "postmodern in the sense that it consists of surface or appearances, that it is situational and interactionally defined and a social product which does not exist outside the interaction." Therefore, it may in some way be justifiable to claim that with his role theory (the self is not a definite entity but a collection of personally colored, socially situated roles), his dramaturgy and his deduced idea of the self as a projected and interactionally confirmed image in fact forestalled the ideas of the postmodernists of the dissolution and decentralization of the self.

To summarize, we may conclude that in Goffman, the self is not a definite entity but, on the contrary, it is created in interaction and communication with others. As mentioned previously, in his reading of Goffman, Daniel Foss (1972) even goes as far as to claim that Goffman's accentuation of the tension between reality and appearance contains a critical view of the positivist idea of the self (e.g., the self as an entity we possess) and consequently the entire positivist knowledge concept (that true knowledge of objects in real life can be generated by an observing subject). Foss points out that when the audience in Goffman to a large extent influences and affects the nature of the actor, the thought of the self as a definite unit that can be possessed disintegrates. In Goffman, the audience, or the social surroundings, if you like, actually becomes the subject by means of which some people shape their assessment and definition of what true knowledge is (Foss, 1972, p. 298). Thus, false, nonauthentic actors in Goffman's dramaturgy may be viewed as indirect criticism of the knowledge concept of deductive science (Foss, 1972, p. 299). The implication of Goffman's dramaturgical presentation of the self is, in other words, that it makes no sense to speak about the self as a fixed entity inhabiting an individual, which, according to Foss, he attempts to illustrate by means of the connection between the concepts of actor and audience. Thus, the self is a type of articulation or projection that presupposes certain expressive equipment. In Goffman, this equipment is termed "props" and "territories." An aspect of this projection or self-presentation that has often been ignored is, according to Michael Schwalbe (1993, p. 336), that in actual fact this depends on circumstances outside the consciousness and control of the individual. Thus, as suggested previously, Goffman's view of the self does not involve the idea of a totally autonomous and context-independent self; rather, it encapsulates the ways in which the self is presented, projected, created, and changed by means of cues given in advance and in collaboration with the audience present. The self, then, is nothing but a dramatic effect:

> The self, then, as a performed character, is an organic thing that has a specific location, whose fundamental fate is to be born, to mature, and to die; it is a dramatic effect arising diffusely from a scene that is presented, and the characteristic issue, the crucial concern, is whether it will be credited or discredited. (Goffman, 1959, p. 245)

Hence, the self is the effect of the drama, it is the object of the rituals and the scene of strategic struggle (Branaman, 1997, p. lxiii), and consequently the drama, the ritual, and the performance are actually three aspects of the same issue: communicative and symbolic interchanges regarding the self. Goffman sees the self as something that is produced (and hence determined) through social performances and at same time as something the individual, taking into account his status and resources, is able to shape through his behavior. This duality in the presentation of the self is shown in Figure 6.1. The self is produced through encounters and relations between people; according to Goffman, it does not exist independently of the social encounter, and therefore the self is, in other words, tied to concrete situations.

The figure illustrates the way in which the self is, on the one hand, an acting and performing agent that fabricates impressions in a social drama and, on the other hand, the self is something that is produced through social encounters, in the sense that the "character" of the self is seen as the end

Figure 6.1   The Self in Goffman's Perspective

The self as performer → The social encounter

The social encounter → The self as a role

Source: Smith, Greg. (1988). The sociology of Erving Goffman. *Social Studies Review*, 3, 119.

product of the individual's interactional activity in the social encounter (Smith, 1988, p. 120). As to the understanding of the self as a product of social arrangements, Goffman writes as follows:

> There will be a back region with its tools for shaping the body, and a front region with its fixed props. There will be a team of persons whose activity on stage and in conjunction with available props will constitute the scene from which the performed character's self will emerge, and another team, the audience, whose interpretative activity will be necessary for this emergence. The self is a product of all of these arrangements, and in all of its parts bears the marks of this genesis. (Goffman, 1959, p. 245)

In the social encounter, the individual is concerned with maintaining a self that is respected by others, and, in addition, with defending this self against the discrediting threats and offenses to which he is exposed from time to time. Goffman's sociology about the self is, therefore, in many ways the story of how individuals (by means of impression management, dramatic realization, secondary adjustments, etc.) attempt to preserve and maintain what we might call "social creditworthiness." Or in other words, Goffman's sociology of self is about the way in which we as social beings, by means of different, more or less obscure techniques, attempt to maintain, for the world around us and for ourselves, an image of a respectable and worthy person. This does not mean, however, as Goffman stresses toward the end of *The Presentation of Self in Everyday Life* (1959), that a complete identity exists between the person and the projected and constructed self. According to Goffman, humans accommodate feelings and attributes that are "psychobiological" in nature (Goffman, 1959, p. 246) and that have a crucial effect on the choices made by a person and hence on the self presented by that person.

The self, therefore, is not only a question of communication; it is psychobiologically rooted, in a way Goffman does not, however, describe in any great detail. Thus, the fact that Goffman's self is primarily a *presented* self does not however imply a rejection of the individual's inner complexity (Mortensen, 2000, p. 95). Goffman is not concerned with, nor does he polemicize directly against, the possible inner authentic self. The object of his concern is the presented self, precisely in the same way as the interaction order and not the structure of society is his domain. Moreover, in his essay about role distance, he describes how we possess a plurality of different and *multiple selves* and how we may use these selves to supplement and vary the socially situated self placed at our disposal in the interaction and thus provide our own self with its unique and special character (Goffman, 1972, p. 133).

Following Durkheim, Goffman characterizes the human self as a sacred thing that must be guarded through proper ritual care and thus by individuals designing the symbolic implications of their acts (Goffman, 1967, p. 57). Employing the ritual perspective, Goffman revealed how in many social encounters, individuals are in fact concerned with a ritual celebration of the individual and simultaneously with protection of this vulnerable self by way of interaction rituals. Thus, in situations of copresence, "we become vulnerable through their words and gesticulation to the penetration of our psychic preserves, and to the breaching of the expressive order we expect will be maintained in our presence" (Goffman, 1983a, p. 4). In direct contact with others, then, the human self is exposed to various types of peril. By nature, we are fragile constructions that must make constant efforts to (1) avoid damaging the selves of others through "situational improprieties" and (2) protect our own selves. Through his many detailed analyses, Goffman has demonstrated how this fragility has to do with the way "our sense of ourselves, of what is real, and how we feel is bound up in—is inextricably knotted to—the ever-moving micro-dynamics of the immediate interaction order in endlessly complicated ways of which we are not aware" (Lofland, 1984, p. 9). This notion of the self as a fragile construction can also be deduced from his preoccupation with people in exposed positions, people whose presentation of self is particularly exposed to collapse and breakdown (Davies, 1997, p. 382). As we saw in Chapter 5, mental patients and other stigmatized and/or marginalized groups play an important part in Goffman's sociology.

A Strategic, Morally Engaged Self

Some commentators have suggested that by stressing the dramaturgical and game-like character of everyday performances, Goffman proposes a Machiavellian, manipulative version of self. The Goffmanian self is portrayed as being preoccupied with anything but carrying whatever mask and managing whatever impression will pay off in a given situation (Schwalbe, 1993, p. 336). Michael Stein (1991, p. 426) suggests something similar when he writes that this approach paints a picture of an unpleasant and problematic social world in which

> sincerity becomes secondary to manipulation and appearances. Whatever true feelings one has are constantly mitigated, guarded and masked by a presentation of self consistent with the official and appropriate definition of the situation. Accordingly, actors live externally with no interior specifications, letting situations specify who and what they are.

As may already be evident, we do not agree with such interpretations of Goffman's view of the self. Following Collins (1986, p. 107), we contend that Goffman's basic theoretical point was that ultimately society, the social system, is what constrains the individual to adopt different roles, to appear reliable, honest, and tactful, and that ultimately it is society that turns us into actors. As we saw in Chapter 4, Goffman was preoccupied with the tension between authenticity and covertness, between appearance and reality. This does not mean, however, that Goffman imagined that people are only manipulating and always playacting. He simply directs our attention to a central aspect of human interaction—an aspect we may not readily accept but that is indisputably an element of our social interaction—namely that we make use of the signs and props accessible in the situation and adapt our self-presentation to the current framework of action in which we find ourselves. The aim is not only to maintain the most profitable self-presentation and to protect our selves but also to live up to moral standards and to protect the remaining audience and hence the situation as such against breakdown. Strategic moves, then, may be performed in order to meet ritual requirements while the moral order of the situation constrains the strategic moves and information controlling behavior (Branaman, 1997, p. lxxiii). We might supplement this with the observation that different frameworks exist that demand different degrees of openness or honesty in the expression. Within certain frames, it is, for instance, embarrassing to display feelings, whereas in others it is embarrassing not to do so. Goffman's image of the self is, in other words, more complex (and seemingly contradictory) than a quick reading seems to display. Goffman recognized that on the one hand, the self is a pilot who is directing performers like *vehicular units* from the back region, and on the other hand, an image compiled by the expressive implications of social encounters (Branco, 1983, p. 180; Goffman, 1967, p. 31). Ultimately, however, Goffman's self is a social or situational self, produced during and dependent on the communicative exchanges taking place in social situations. And not even our superficially successful attempts at liberating ourselves from the socially structured self or the situated role are, in Goffman, expressions of real autonomy. To Goffman, role distance is a type of delusion in the sense that these resistance attempts, like the remaining social interaction, are structured by social and ritual orders. The fact that we consider a given behavior to be a relevant expression of the circumstance that a person is resisting and is not feeling at home in his socially situated role is also socially determined and serves the purpose of appeasing the actor who is under the illusion of being autonomous in his own role play (Branco, 1983, p. 199).

Goffman's view of self is not only interesting in relation to his understanding of the relationship between the individual and society. It also constitutes a shortcut to the understanding of his epistemology as this epistemology emerges from his view of the self (Waksler, 1989). As we have seen, the self is not a fixed, unique entity but a construct that is presented and presents itself when receiving and dispatching information, something that is created in interaction between people. According to Frances C. Waksler (1989, p. 5), Goffman accepted the premise that sociologists do not have access to the inner specifications of people but may learn about that which other people know and think by participating in the same social world. What sociologists may learn and the information they may receive from the inner being of other people have been filtered through the social interaction, which in this way acts as both the source of this information and its limitations (Waksler, 1989, p. 6). With Luhmann, we might say that social and psychological systems are the surroundings of each other but autopoetically closed around themselves. Goffman, Waksler maintains, did not pretend to be an omniscient sociologist who claimed to know the inner being of other people as they know it themselves. Instead, he suggested an epistemology based on the premise that the self is created and presented in communicative interaction with others and that information about the selves of other people is therefore, in principle, publicly accessible to the participants in this interaction. Proposing a dramaturgical approach in order to understand the self, Goffman then urged scholars to redirect attention from people's minds to public places (Lyman & Scott, 1975, p. 107).

Conclusion

As this chapter has shown, in Goffman's view, the human self consists of the multiple roles that individuals perform in various social situations. Thus, the Goffmanian self is *presented*, and the realization of this presented self depends on both the strategic impression management and self-monitoring of the actor as well as the support and ritualized care of the social environment. Therefore, the self "does not derive from its possessor, but from the whole scene of his actions," and accordingly, this self is not a *cause* of the scene that comes off but a *product* of it (Goffman, 1959, p. 245). Individuals' self-presentations are socially situated, and in every social encounter, individuals must take into account the prevailing set of situational proprieties, the other parties present, and the interactional frame in order to present an acceptable self-image. Moreover, Goffman did not support the idea of an essential, enduring, deep, or humanly inherent self, as he testified in *Frame Analysis*:

> It is hardly possible to talk about the anchoring of doings in the world without seeming to support the notion that a person's acts are in part an expression and outcome of his perduring self, and that this self will be present behind the particular roles he plays at any particular moment. . . . Something will glitter or smolder or otherwise make itself apparent beyond the covering that is officially worn. . . . So three cheers for the self. . . . [But] whatever a participant "really is," is not really the issue. His fellow participants are not likely to discover this if indeed it is discoverable. What is important is the sense he provides them through his dealings with them of what sort of person he is behind the role he is in. (Goffman, 1974, pp. 293–298)

Goffman's self, then was processual, performative, dramatic, and deeply intertwined with the ways that individuals embrace, adopt, and distance themselves from socially situated roles and social circumstances.

Questions

- Most commentators agree that Erving Goffman did not explicitly criticize modern capitalist societies. However, his sociology urges examinations of the effects of power relations and inequalities on the development of human selves. What aspects of Goffman's work do reveal a sensitivity toward the impact of societal forces on the development of self?
- What was particularly characteristic of Erving Goffman's understanding of the self?
- To what extent does Erving Goffman's view of the self correspond with that of symbolic interactionism?

7

Goffman on Frames, Genderisms, and Talk

E rving Goffman is perhaps best known among scholars as well as nonacademics for some of his early work on the intricate nature of face-to-face interaction and not least his dramaturgical metaphor deployed in *The Presentation of Self in Everyday Life*. In Chapter 1, we showed how Goffman's work—according to Randall Collins (1981a)—could be divided into three overall stages or phases. The final stage was called the "social-phenomenological" or "social-epistemological" phase, in which Goffman began to take an interest in more philosophically oriented themes such as, for example, how consciousness organizes human experience of events and how, in Goffman's words, we always "frame" the situations we enter into. This is also one of the reasons Goffman has been labeled by some a "phenomenologist" (Lanigan, 1988). Moreover, like the emerging perspective of ethnomethodology, during the 1970s Goffman also began to develop an interest in verbal communication, and therefore he has been described as one of the main forerunners to ethnomethodology and particularly to the conversation analysis strand within ethnomethodology (Attewell, 1974). Furthermore, at a time when so-called second-wave feminism began to flourish on the American continent and criticized the oppression of women by patriarchy and phallocentric capitalism, Goffman—from a more down-to-earth interactionist perspective—started to take an interest in how gender is performed and presented in social situations such as in the advertising industry. Thus, not only thematically but also more substantially, Goffman's work began to change quite considerably during the 1970s. Although still interested in the conceptualization and charting of interaction patterns and social situations, his writing style, exposition, and prose changed to the more conventional and less experimental scientific format. According to Allen Grimshaw, throughout his later years, "Goffman was moving toward systematic formalization of his work" (Grimshaw, 1983, p. 147). As this chapter shows, Goffman throughout his last decade turned his attention toward new areas of social life that simultaneously extended his previous interests but also paved the way for new ideas to flourish.

Frame Analysis

Goffman's latest works stretched from the early 1970s to the early 1980s. With his so-called **frame analysis**, he shifted attention from the microsociological study and description of relatively concrete instances of face-to-face interaction—and with it the study of the relationship between self and society—toward the study of the more abstract principles that govern our perception of reality and the organization of our experiences (Branaman, 1997, p. lxxiv). In a way, Goffman's book *Frame Analysis* (1974) can perhaps best be characterized as a sort of "meta-micro-sociology" (Park, 1990, p. 238), because it—despite its level of abstraction—is still concerned with what happens when people try to make sense of and navigate in their immediately surrounding world. Whereas some would regard this as a radical departure from Goffman's earlier areas of attention, others see it as a natural continuation of his ideas toward a more systematic, abstract, and theoretical treatise. Earlier, we have dealt in detail with how Goffman's writing style was very different from that of many of his contemporaries and how his sociology had a certain poetic edge. However, *Frame Analysis* (1974) is an exception. It is a voluminous and at times a dry piece of work stretching across almost 600 pages—not always a joyful or easy read but nevertheless full of insightful observations of something that we quite often take for granted or remain oblivious to. By many commentators (e.g., Smith, 1999a, p. 13), *Frame Analysis* has been described as Goffman's equivalent to Harold Garfinkel's *Studies in Ethnomethodology* (1967). The book differs from the other parts of Goffman's writings in its conventional dry, scientific exposition and its explicit and critical dialogue with the existing literature within the field, particularly the phenomenological tradition, which at this time had gradually established a stronghold in sociology. This may be one of the reasons for the more technical and tedious terminology deployed in the book. The foreword of the book, however, is written in typical Goffmanesque and teasing style, for example informing the reader about Goffman's considerations about the difficulties involved in writing a foreword and how words in their capacity as frame setters, explanations, and excuses may provoke the reader's distrust already from the start (O'Neill, 1981). One might say that with *Frame Analysis*, Goffman attempted to break away from his reputation as an anthropological essayist or impressionistic sociologist and establish himself as a serious and systematic sociological scholar. The subtitle of the book, *An Essay on the Organization of Experience*, at one and the same time betrays the reader and is quite informative: it gives the impression that the reader will merely encounter an "essay"—typically a term reserved for a shorter piece and certainly not a magisterial manuscript of more half a thousand pages—at the same time as it fulfills its ambition to explain how people organize their experiences of the social world's complex and chaotic stream of impressions into meaningful wholes. How is this possible? The answer, according to Goffman, is found in the concept of "frame," which he borrowed and appropriated from British anthropologist, biologist, and ethnologist Gregory Bateson.

So despite Goffman's use and subsequent development of the concept of "**frame**," the notion was not his own invention. In a rather temperamental reply to Norman K. Denzin and Charles Keller, one of the few times Goffman ever responded to criticism, he stated on his indebtedness to Bateson, who in his *Steps to an Ecology of Mind* (1972) used the concept of "frame": "That is enough for warranting my gratefulness to Bateson, and for saying that I will be using the term 'frame' in roughly the sense in which he meant it" (Goffman, 1981b, p. 64). Bateson's use of the notion of "frame" was in fact anticipated by philosopher Gilbert Ryle (1949), who wrote about "frames of mind." Also in the work of anthropologist Mary Douglas and psychologist Marion Miller, the concept of "frame" was used prior to Bateson's—and Goffman's—more publicized application. In Goffman's writings, a frame is here to be understood as the mental equipment we draw upon when trying to understand the situations and occurrences taking place around us. In fact, with the publication of *Frame Analysis*, the notion of "frame" in many ways replaced Goffman's earlier, frequently invoked idea of "definition of the situation," and the two concepts are used in an almost identical manner. In *Frame Analysis*, Goffman specifically defined a "frame" and "frame analysis" in the following way:

> I assume that definitions of a situation are built up in accordance with principles of organization which govern events—at least social ones—and our subjective involvement in them; frame is a word I use to refer to such of these basic elements as I am able to identify. That is my definition of frame. My phrase "frame analysis" is a slogan to refer to the examination in these terms of the organization of experience. (Goffman, 1974, pp. 10–11)

By "framing" our social perceptions and definitions of the situation—by putting them into general frameworks or what might be called "matrices of perception"—we systematize and organize the social world so that we can deal with it and move around in it. In other words, we create meaning with the chaos of events in the social world by placing them in particular frames. Frames help us in defining and deciphering the situation and provide a "header," as it were, so that we may act appropriately and in accordance with the requirements and expectations of the situation in question. An important insight from *Frame Analysis* is therefore, as Karl E. Scheibe expressed it, that "human beings seem incapable of regarding any social situation as not having some sort of frame, and that every frame is a manifestation of tacit piety" (Scheibe, 2002, p. 200). Goffman's concept of frames can thus be seen as a parallel to Alfred Schutz's notions of "recipes" or "types"—by way of frames/recipes/types, we are capable of organizing our impression of the situation and are thus more likely to understand and to control it. Just as definitions of the situation are not individual constructions invoked or maintained by the solitary individual (Thomas, 1923), neither are frames. Most often frames contain a collectively maintained and agreed-upon character, although this is, however, not always the case, which—as we shall see—can lead to the challenging, collapsing, or changing of frames. An important underlying assumption in *Frame Analysis* is therefore that there is not one singular understanding of social reality—situations and events can be understood from a wide range of sometimes mutually supportive, sometimes overlapping, sometimes conflicting points of view. This understanding of the existence and viability of "multiple realities" is an insight Goffman particularly derived from pragmatism and phenomenology (Berger & Luckmann, 1966; James, 1950; Schutz, 1945).

In his introduction to *Frame Analysis*, Goffman stated that one way to find out which frame is appropriate in a given situation is to ask the simple question: What is it that's going on here? He continued:

> Whether asked explicitly, as in times of confusion and doubt, or tacitly, during occasions of usual certitude, the question is put and the answer to it is presumed by the way the individuals then proceed to get on with the affairs at hand. Staring, then, with that question, this volume attempts to limn out a framework that could be appealed to for the answer. (Goffman, 1974, p. 8)

Whenever we are confronted with a new social situation or witness certain events, we read certain assumptions into the situation or event, and it is exactly these assumptions that Goffman by way of a particular conceptual apparatus sought to develop and chart in *Frame Analysis*. Let us look at parts of the comprehensive conceptual apparatus of the book.

The most important concept is obviously that of frames, which, as mentioned, is the underlying mechanism providing meaning to social situations and events. Under the heading "Primary Frameworks," Goffman discussed the most fundamental forms of frames, and here he differentiated between natural frames and social frames. Goffman insisted that "natural frameworks identify occurrences seen as undirected, unoriented, unanimated, unguided, 'purely physical.' Such unguided events are ones understood to be due totally, from start to finish, to 'natural' determinants" (Goffman, 1974, p. 22). One obvious example of a natural framework would be the weather. Social frames or frameworks, on the other hand, involve agency and, as Goffman states, "provide background understanding for events that incorporate the will, aim, and the controlling effort of an intelligence, a live agency, the chief one being the human being" (Goffman, 1974, p. 22). Social frameworks thus take as their point of departure how participants in a social situation interpret what is happening based on motives, interpretations, and intentions. Whereas natural frames are normally used within the physical and biological sciences, social frames are—obviously—primarily applied within the social and humanistic sciences. Goffman thus shows how a concrete social situation—such as an untimely death—might be framed in different ways, for example as an accident, as suicide, as manslaughter, or as premeditated murder by the coroner, by witnesses, by the police, and by the court. In the case of natural frames, no human agency might be to blame, whereas in the case of social frames, human intervention of some kind will provide the explanatory framework. Another central concept is that of "**key-ing**," which means something like "using a key." Goffman also borrowed this concept from Bateson, who developed it from his studies of animal behavior. Bateson claimed that when monkeys fight, a transfer of meaning takes place from one situation or frame (the real fight) to another equally structured frame (the playful fight). When playing, the monkeys bite each other as if it is meant seriously, but they do not bite hard. Goffman commented how "this play activity is closely patterned after something that already has a meaning in its own terms" (Goffman, 1974, p. 40), his point being that this transfer of meaning or "keying" is also taking place and is at work in our everyday interpretations of situations. Here situations that apparently look identical regarding their behavioral components might be defined differently depending on which key is used to understand or "unlock" them: "a "couple" kissing can also be a "man" greeting his "wife" or "John" being careful with "Mary's" makeup" (Goffman, 1974, p. 10). Goffman's point is that we subject all situations we witness or in which we participate to keying when we transfer meaning to them from other primary frameworks. We are probably all familiar with this from our own everyday lives when somebody interprets certain events or situations in ways that differ (sometimes quite radically) from how we would have interpreted the exact same situation. Everybody thus carries different mental frameworks around, which are then placed on reality in order to understand and organize it in meaningful ways.

Frames and Interaction

Frame Analysis is thus a comprehensive, thought-provoking, and metatheoretical attempt to understand how people systematize and use social experiences in order to make interaction with others adequate and meaningful to those involved. People's stocks of knowledge, prior experiences, and expectations are thus used to decode social situations and make sense of what is going on. An important point in Goffman's frame analysis is that frames simultaneously form the foundation for the interpretation of what is currently going on—how we define the situation at hand (McHugh, 1968)—in the same way as they enable us to anticipate and create certain expectations of what will happen next (Tannen, 1979). Frames invoked in interaction thus reach backward to the actor's prior experiences as well as point forward to expectations about future situations. Frames are, however, not merely mental constructs or frameworks of the world we confront—they may also serve as instructions for individual and collaborative action:

> These frameworks are not merely a matter of mind but correspond in some sense to the way in which an aspect of the activity itself is organized. . . . Given their understanding of what it is that is going on, individuals fit their actions to this understanding and ordinarily find that the ongoing world supports this fitting. (Goffman, 1974, p. 274)

According to Swedish sociologist Gerd Lindgren, "the frame is the key that actors seek out and most often identify; it helps them to create relations to others and gives coherence and meaning to reality" (Lindgren, 1994, p. 102). Lindgren here states something important about Goffman's concept of frame: namely, that Goffman with his frame-concept attempted to discover what Randall Collins (1988b) called a "middle road" between hyper-relativism on the one side and the objective determinism of sociology on the other, or, put differently, between constructivism and structuralism. As Collins proposed, in his introduction to *Frame Analysis*, Goffman argued that the phenomenological idea that the individual is constructing reality is too radical if it suggests that reality is constituted by what goes on in the minds of individuals in various social contexts. On the other side, however, Goffman did not surrender to structuralism, because structuralists routinely neglect the active and creative aspects of the individual's doings. Goffman instead insisted that the world exists as an external entity prior to the individual and that situations thus contain a structure that individuals enter into. Hence social reality and social situations are not exclusively the result of human construction work (something "made up," as it were), but they are also something that one steps into or arrives in (Collins, 1988b, p. 58). Consequently, Goffman's frame analysis is neither tied to a structural nor an agency-oriented perspective in sociology because although it clearly emphasizes that frames may be given in advance, it also stresses how actors have the ability and competence to find out which frame is at work, then to adjust their behavior according to the frame and ultimately also to propose a new or even to change the prevailing frame. Goffman thus showed how frames were vulnerable—frames are not fixed once and for all; they can be changed by the ongoing interaction. Frames can thus be broken, frozen, shifted, changed, challenged, bent, stretched, substituted, maintained, confronted, defrosted, transferred, destroyed, contracted, expanded, and so on. In fact, almost anything can happen to a frame when it is used.

Here Goffman clearly elaborated on the earlier parts of his writings, but he did so in a more traditional academic and less essayistic form. In *Frame Analysis*, he showed how we, through social experiences and knowledge about social symbols, can "decode" or define the situation and thus adjust our behavior according to it. We all—as phenomenologists would claim— have a natural attitude or "autopilot," as Lindgren (1994) calls it, which helps us intuitively to interpret and navigate in the welter of signs, symbols, and signals involved in a given social situation as the expression or crystallization of a meaningful and unified frame. Goffman also showed how we, as civilized individuals, are obligated to behave in accordance with the behavioral limitations and possibilities built into the frame in question, which we are simultaneously subjected to as well as participate in maintaining. Frames are thus normative devices explicating how we "ought" to behave. We must show appropriate respect for the frame—and by doing so, we also indirectly recognize the other participants as respectable people. Due to this normative dimension of frames, Goffman's understanding of frames has been compared to Émile Durkheim's idea of "collective consciousness" (Damari, 2012), although there is more room for change and less constraint in the notion of frame. However, Goffman is also careful to point out that we should not get equally involved in all frames: "All frames involve expectations of a normative kind as to how deeply and fully the individual is to be carried into the activity organized by the frame" (Goffman, 1974, p. 345).

Thus, excessive emotional outbursts during a service transaction with a shopkeeper would amount to overinvolvement in the transaction frame, whereas the same amount of emotional involvement might be expected in a funeral frame. Moreover, a lot of social interaction is concerned with—as a joint venture between participants—how to contribute in maintaining a shared frame. However, this does not mean that we passively accept the existing frame or that we are unable to propose another frame. According to Goffman, a lot of the communication taking place between people is in fact "communication about frames," meaning that it is communication about how situations must be defined or framed. When the course or intensity of the interaction begins to slow down, develops in an unpleasant direction, or becomes downright boring to one or more of the participants, they can— often successfully—suggest another frame. For example, we may try to pep up the uninspired and boring academic conversational frame with a more informal and humoristic frame of sociality. Making such active shifts in frames demands a certain amount of social skill, knowledge, and dexterity. A precondition is that we are able to read and understand the often apparently insignificant but important signals testifying to the need for or possibility of a shift in frame informing us—however vaguely—about our strength and authority to launch and force through a shift in frame. Only respected or powerful people may be successful in changing the frame.

Communication About Frames

As mentioned, *Frame Analysis* marked a continuation of Goffman's earlier interests as well as inaugurated a significant shift in his style of writing. "Communicating about frames," or "metacommunicating" as Goffman calls it, thus also concerns a central theme in his argument in *The Presentation of Self in Everyday Life* (1959): the question of how we, in face-to-face interaction, cooperate about defining situations in a way that makes sense to the participants and makes it possible for them to project the most favorable expressions of self to others. According to Adam Kendon (1988, pp. 23–24), in *Frame Analysis* Goffman returned to his separation between information one "gives"—that is, consciously, knowingly, deliberately, and quite often verbally—and information one "gives off," often in an unconscious, unknowing, and bodily manner, as we also have shown in Chapter 4, just as how he reinvented his interest from *Behavior in Public Places* (1963) in the separation between "focused" and "unfocused" interaction. He showed how in interaction among people, certain so-called attentional tracks can be identified. Goffman's point is that in every encounter or interactional sequence, there is a particularly prominent and conspicuous aspect that constitutes the main focus of participants' attention. Just as a picture frame or a window frame separates the picture or the window from the rest of the wall, so frames in interaction also set those activities or pieces of information deemed important by participants apart from those that, at least at the moment, seem less important. This is what the interaction according to the participants' current involvement is all about and what Goffman calls the "main line" of the interaction (Goffman, 1974, p. 201). According to Adam Kendon, one can talk about two different forms of behavior. First is behavior that relates to this "main line" and that is managed in a particular way. This behavior is seen as voluntary, and the information conveyed is given as opposed to the information that is given off. The other type of behavior is that which does not relate to the main line of the interaction, which contains pieces of information given off, and which is treated in a quite different yet by no means less important way by participants.

In his analysis of this apparently irrelevant "out-of-frame" activity, Goffman introduced a separation between, on the one hand, "directional tracks," which regulate, delimit, qualify, and articulate the different components and stages of the interaction (Goffman, 1974, p. 210) and, on the other hand, "disattended tracks" that cover a range of potentially distracting incidences regarded as threats to participants' appropriate or expected involvement in the situation (Goffman, 1974, p. 202). Behavior in the "disattended track" has nothing to do with the main content or line of the interaction. For example, it is when participants scratch their hair, pick their nose, or change their seating positions. "Disattended track" behavior is a sort of acceptable or admissible deviation from the behavioral discipline that is otherwise displayed by all participants. Behavior belonging to the "disattended track" is, according to Kendon (1988, p. 24), not just something that is sorted out or passes in an unnoticed and inconsequential manner. In fact, it often plays a significant role in regard to the organization of social interaction. For example, it is behavior that belongs to this track that makes it possible for participants in a conversation to signal to each other—for example, by pointing to their wristwatch, changing their visual focus, or gesticulating hand signals—when the conversation should stop or change tracks. When we in conversation with a colleague notice that he or she begins to move around impatiently on the chair, looks out the window, or lights a cigarette, such signals tell us something important, for example about how our conversational partner wishes to terminate the conversation, change the subject, or in other ways change the course or content of the situation (shifting frame). Goffman pointed to the interactional value of such small yet nevertheless very important signals and hints. They allow a person to adjust his or her behavior toward an increasingly impatient conversational partner, which might prevent a disruption or an abrupt termination of the social situation. A person who at the right moment becomes aware of these minute and subtle signals may avoid ending up in an awkward or embarrassing situation by changing the subject or allowing the other person to utter his or her perspectives on the situation. On this background, *Frame Analysis* can be read as a more academic continuation of an earlier topic in Goffman's writings, namely the idea of the information-processing actor who, through various impression-management strategies, attempts to manipulate the situation in order to stage a favorable self-presentation but also in order to make sure that the situation does not collapse.

With his frame analysis, Goffman in many ways modified or rectified some of the understandings from his dramaturgical metaphor and his previous conception of rules primarily functioning as limitations. In *Frame Analysis*, he thus analyzed how rules may also function as resources in interaction. We can use the implicit rules of the frame as resources because we know that other participants interpret our actions in relation to certain rules and vice versa. This knowledge is a resource in the sense that we may exploit it in order to manipulate or strategically influence the interpretations others make of our actions (Manning, 1991, p. 83). *Frame Analysis* is also concerned with how we communicate (or "metacommunicate") about the definition of the situation or the frame in order to obtain personal advantages or to save the faces of the other participants. But contrary to the earlier parts of his writings, Goffman here emphasized how the actors' strategic self-presentations and performances are not necessarily aimed at personal gain but just as often involve a search for understanding (Chriss, 1995b, p. 556).

Applying and Extending Frame Analysis

Goffman's development of frame analysis has been subject to criticism from various quarters of academia due to its—according to some critics—highly speculative, abstract, structurally detached, and empirically unsubstantiated character (see, e.g., Craib, 1978; Gonos, 1977; Jameson, 1976, Sharron, 2000). Others, however, have insisted that frame analysis was indeed a much welcome and major contribution to the understanding of how ideas about mental and cognitive processes may be put to theoretical and empirical use within various subdisciplines (see, e.g., Entman, 1993; Hazelrigg, 1992; Littlejohn, 1977). The potential—theoretical and empirical—of frame analysis is evident in the numerous studies that *Frame Analysis* has spawned throughout the years—studies that uncover, show, and dissect the various underlying frames used in ordinary and extraordinary social settings to make sense of social situations.

Even prior to Goffman's own explicit use of the frame concept, ideas not far from his had already been used in sociology. One of the most prominent and promising forerunners to Goffman's frame analysis—also mentioned by Goffman himself as an important source of inspiration for *Frame Analysis* (1974, p. 7)—was the notion of "awareness contexts" originally developed by grounded-theory protagonists Barney G. Glaser and Anselm L. Strauss (1964) in their studies of death and dying in American hospital settings (see also Glaser & Strauss, 1965). Glaser and Strauss introduced "awareness contexts" as an analytical tool particularly used to capture the institutionalized experience of dying, and they defined such "awareness contexts" as "a total combination of what each interactant in a situation knows about the identity of the other and his own identity in the eyes of the other" (Glaser & Strauss, 1964, p. 670). As such, "awareness contexts" have to do with knowledge about self and others and the interplay between different perspectives on what is at stake in actual social situations. Applied specifically to the social context of institutionalized dying, Glaser and Strauss proposed four prevalent awareness contexts in the hospitals studied: "closed awareness contexts," in which the terminally ill patient is kept in the dark about his or her actual situation by staff and relatives and thus is unaware of his or her identity as "dying"; "suspicion awareness contexts," in which the dying patient suspects that something is wrong but is unable to obtain verified knowledge about the actual situation; "mutual pretense awareness contexts" that are a charade in which staff and relatives suspect that the dying patient might know something about the actual situation, and the patient might be looking for signs or confirming clues, but both parties seem to conceal knowledge from each other about what they really know; and finally "open awareness contexts," in which all interactants have knowledge about impending death and talk openly about it (Glaser & Strauss, 1964, 1965). Obviously, in their studies Glaser and Strauss implicitly supported the normative necessity of opening up awareness contexts in order to make dying more openly accepted and to allow the dying person to have a say in his or her terminal phase. In many ways, the notion of "awareness contexts" thus anticipated Goffman's later development of frame analysis by showing how a set of—in this case institutionally maintained—awareness contexts shapes expectations and actual actions in social situations.

However, Goffman's frame analysis was not only anticipated by previous ideas but itself also inspired many later studies within a variety of empirical domains. Let us here briefly review some later applications of Goffman's frame analysis to illustrate its diversified appeal. American sociologists Peter K. Manning and Keith Hawkins (1990) used Goffman's concept of frame to understand the function of the juridical system. Among other things, they show how the participants in the system—prosecutors and defense lawyers—use different frames to present cases and through these cases thus make decisions about what types of evidence support their framings in a convincing way and may be used in the courtroom. Their conclusion is that the juridical decision process can be characterized as a process of dramatization in which juridical truth is constructed in an intricate struggle between often conflicting frames presented in an equally favorable light by prosecutor and defense lawyer (Manning & Hawkins, 1990, p. 204)—something that numerous American television series about courtroom drama throughout the years have also illustrated. In order to understand the full implications of this juridical framing process, one needs to carefully study and analyze the authoritative framing taking place in actual courtroom deliberations and presentations (Manning & Hawkins, 1990, p. 229).

American sociologist Phillip B. Gonzales (1993) used the notion of frames when analyzing what happens when people are convicted of driving while intoxicated and thus enter a so-called DWI frame (which is a legal frame) and the more specific frames used in actual social interaction when convicts meet families, friends, colleagues, and others in an American society known for its ambivalent attitude toward drunk driving. Based on interviews with first-time offenders, Gonzales came up with two particularly prevalent situational frames: the "shame frame" dictating how convicts, when confronted with their DWI sentence (e.g., when showing one's driver's license), for a long time feared being disclosed or discredited or losing social status, which meant that they either openly admitted their offense or instead decided to lie about or keep their sentence a secret, and the "peer frame," according to which the offender would perhaps be embarrassed but also supported or protected by his or her social network so that the feeling of shame and stigma was minimized. Gonzales's main point is that there may be a rather substantial difference and even a moral discrepancy between the overall frame (in this case the legal DWI frame) and the various situational and interactive frames at work in the actual interaction between convicts and their surroundings.

Finally, sociologist Mark Paxton (2004) used frame analysis in his study of how different local factions in a small town in Missouri, through the media and in courtrooms, fought about whether the symbol of a fish (commonly known as the ichthus) should embellish their town seal or not. This battle was an offshoot of a communitywide design contest aimed at finding the new logo for the town. According to some locals, this particular fish symbolized something religious, which infuriated those who insisted on maintaining a sharply drawn boundary between public (religious) symbolism and private faith. Based on an extensive analysis of news coverage, Paxton suggested that the media used four different frames (or journalistic angles) to report the story about the local fish fight. The first frame was a trivializing frame that partly ridiculed the local community and described the whole situation as out of proportion, grossly exaggerated, and much ado about nothing. A second frame, a stigmatizing frame, was used to describe and denigrate the plaintiff who was identified in the case—a local woman whom the media described as someone practicing witchcraft. According to a third media frame, the entire local community was described as an activist and idealist group of people fighting against "meddling outsiders" in order to defend their fish symbol. Finally, the media used a military-metaphorical frame to capture the nature of conflict, talking about "shots being fired," "skirmishes," "war," and "combat," in which the local community was "called to arms." All in all, Paxton showed how the news media in their coverage used a variety of different and colorful frames to create attention about even the apparently most insignificant and least sensationalistic of events.

Also researchers in a Nordic context—from where we come—have gradually embraced Goffman's frame analysis and used it in connection with various empirical studies. In a Finnish context, sociologist Anssi Peräkylä (1988) identified four so-called frames of death in modern hospitals—the "practical frame," the "semi-psychiatric frame," "the bio-medical frame," and the "lay frame"—each frame providing a particular professional or nonprofessional perspective on and meaning as to how death was in fact perceived and handled by staff and relatives in a hospital context. Norwegian sociologist Dag Album (1996) used the idea of frames in his study of interaction patterns among hospitalized patients. For example, Album specifically used the notion of frame when analyzing so-called illness talk among patients, and he discovered four different frames of illness talk: "the soliloquy of illness," "learning conversations," "conversations about momentary sensations," and "safe talk." Each of these frames dictated how, why, what, when, and with whom patients talked about their diagnosis and illness. Finnish childhood researcher Anna-Maija Puriola (2002) studied the frames used by childcare educators in a kindergarten to interpret their work situation. Based on interviews and observation studies, she was able to identify five frames used by the childcare workers: "educational," "caring," "managing," "practical," and "personal." Building on ethnographic material from observations of collegial talk, Hannele Fosberg and Åsa Vagli (2006) have used a frame-analytical approach to the study of how emotions are socially constructed realities among Finnish and Norwegian child-protection social workers. They developed two prevalent frames differing in the Finnish and Norwegian context—"frames of despair" characterized by nightmares, escapism, and the feeling of wishing to throw in the towel and "frames of concern" characterized by feelings of anger, sorrow, and commitment. As these few examples have indicated, Goffman's frame-analytical approach has been found particularly—although not exclusively—useful in studying behavioral patterns in specific professional, organizational, or institutional contexts.

Obviously, Goffman's development of frame analysis preceded the arrival of many contemporary advances within information technologies, electronic communication, and the media. However, also within media, communications, and technology studies, Goffman's frame-analytical ideas have later been found useful in the study of Internet communities, mobile telephones, and interactive behavior in online situations that Goffman's more physically bounded ideas of stages, frames, and regionalized behavior might not have anticipated. At the threshold of the emergence of Internet and virtual realities—which are nowadays an integral part of most people's everyday lives—Mary Chayko thus proposed a revision or extension of Goffman's bounded perspective on frames:

> In modern everyday life, it is difficult (and becoming impossible) to definitively classify experience as "real" or "not real"; it is more helpful to determine the degree or "accent" of reality in an event. The frames we once used, conceptually, to set the real apart from the unreal are not as useful as they once were; they are not as sturdy; they betray us. As they become ever more fragile, we require new concepts and understandings. . . . We must take the important teachings of James, Schutz, Goffman and Bateson, and others—specifically, that we must not take reality or literal experience for granted as a universally understood given—and must now interpret these works in light of technologies that create new social worlds which must be examined, yet cannot be located among the coordinates of our physical universe. (Chayko, 1993, pp. 179–180)

Chayko's proposal was indeed appropriate as well as useful, because so many aspects of people's lives today—shopping, dating, communicating, entertaining, working, killing time, and so on—now increasingly take place in virtual environments. Moreover, in media studies, David L. Altheide (1997) has shown how many news programs consciously deploy a so-called problem frame to sensationalize stories, to script and stage certain responses, and to frame events in ways that make them particularly interesting or pertinent to viewers. In relation to Internet behavior, Sarah Wanenchak (2010) has documented how different kinds of frames are used in virtual role-playing games. As is evident from these few selected examples, Goffman's frame analysis—in its original as well as revised shape—is still very much alive and kicking among students and scholars even in contexts unimagined and unimaginable by Goffman himself.

Advertisements, Genderisms, and the Arrangement Between the Sexes

One of the most fundamental ways we humans frame and organize our social experience with others such as our identity, social roles, and social function is based on binary gender categories. Gender, or sexual difference, is a primordial and generic category separating men from women, husbands from wives, brothers from sisters, waiters from waitresses, widowers from widows, and so on. Moreover, these different gender categories—far from mere biological or natural marks of distinction—also have social and cultural foundations and repercussions on a macro and micro level of society. In the case of microfoundations and microrepercussions, Goffman's preferred domain of analysis, gender differences are perhaps particularly evident in the way we present ourselves, in the way we perform gender roles, and in the way gender is publicly displayed, such as in commercials and advertisements.

In many ways, *Gender Advertisements* (1979a) is a rather uncharacteristic Goffman publication, particularly because his concern here was not with the analysis of interaction as such but instead with the visual or symbolic representation of gender—and, in fact, exclusively female—stereotypes. In this book, which contains hundreds of pictures from magazine advertisements, Goffman used his aforementioned frame analysis as a starting point for investigating the relationship between the sexes—something similar to what he also investigated in his article "The Arrangement Between the Sexes" (Goffman, 1977a). His main idea in *Gender Advertisements* is that the way men and women—and particularly their interrelationship—are portrayed in advertisements can tell us a lot about how we think about and live out this relationship in our actual interaction with each other. According to Goffman, advertisements in visually simplified or exaggerated form crystallize and explicate the often vague, unconscious, and unclear conceptions of the relationship between men and women. Advertisements make our vague conceptions clear cut, and they thus become pattern setting for our often stereotypical constructions of gender in society. Advertisements reduce the complexity of everyday experience, and these simplified displays are then used as models in our own lives. In Goffman's words, we try to identify ourselves with the simplified "gender displays" of the advertisements. Of the notion of "gender displays," Goffman stated that "if gender be defined as the culturally established correlates of sex (whether in consequence of biology or learning), then gender display refers to conventionalized portrayals of these correlates" (Goffman, 1979a, p. 1). Here we near the central thesis of Goffman's book—that our ways of expressing and understanding gender (and the relations between the different genders) in everyday life are highly ritualized in the sense that they rest on exaggerations and simplifications. Our gender displays convey ingrained ritualizations through action and expression, something that—in itself—hardly qualifies as a revolutionizing insight. However, the important thing, according to Goffman, is also that our displays

> can be lifted out of [their] original context, parenthesized, and used in a quotative way, a postural resource for mimicry, mockery, irony, teasing, and other sportive intents, including, very commonly, the depiction of make-believe in advertisements. . . . What was a ritual becomes itself ritualized, a transformation of what is already a transformation, a "hyper-ritualization." Thus, the human use of displays is complicated by the human capacity for reframing behavior. (Goffman, 1979a, p. 3)

Goffman's point, then, is that we can learn a great deal about presently existing gender relations by looking at advertisements as so-called hyperrituals exactly because they—in the last instance—refer to everyday life. We can gain insights about the micropolitics of gender by studying advertisements, and here the subordination of women to men is evident in advertisements because they are hyperritualizations of everyday-life interaction situations. Toward the end of his introduction to the extended series of pictures included in *Gender Advertisements*, Goffman formulated the following important proposition:

> I want to argue that the job the advertiser has of dramatizing the value of his product is not unlike the job a society has of infusing its social situations with ceremonial and with ritual signs facilitating the orientation of participants to one another. Both must use the limited "visual" resources available in social situations to tell a story; both must transform otherwise opaque goings-on into easily readable form. And both rely on the same basic devices: intention displays, microecological mapping of social structure, approved typifications, and the gestural externalization of what can be taken to be inner response. (Goffman, 1979a, p. 27)

This proposition is important because Goffman here showed how the advertising industry—in the same way as society at large—performs the task of securing a certain order and stability in society by providing unequivocal ritual signs allowing members of society or participants in interaction to enter into balanced and mutually calibrated and aligned relations with each other. He also showed how the advertiser performs a role similar to that of ordinary people in their everyday interactions—to present idealized and dramatized impressions of self (in the case of the advertisers, the self of others) to others, as Goffman showed in *The Presentation of Self in Everyday Life* (1959). In this way, the advertiser as well as society as such participates in sustaining social order by presenting and providing schemes of orientation indicating—or indirectly dictating—how (gender) relations between people should be constructed. In this respect, Goffman was in line with many feminist writers at the time who claimed that there is no innate masculine or feminine "nature" but only culturally constructed and socially defined images of what is respectively "masculine" and "feminine." Gender is thus partly socially constructed, and the study of the prevalent images of gender stereotypes according to Goffman does not tell us anything about gender as such but rather about how such images function in society. *Gender Advertisements* was by some champions within the feminist movement thus regarded as a powerful weapon in the struggle against the oppression of women. As Gaile McGregor (1995, p. 7) expressed it:

> Goffman's analysis of the gestural stigmata of infantilization not only confirms that women *are* being stereotyped in advertising—which is itself a politically useful accomplishment—but even better, it elucidates the equivocal implications of the particular gender relations signalled if not actually constructed by means of this process of stereotyping.

Despite its "feminist" analysis, *Gender Advertisements* also provoked less positive responses from female commentators in various magazines (see, e.g., Wedel, 1978), and on several occasions Goffman had to accept seeing himself presented as a male chauvinist. As we see it, Goffman neither wanted to provide ammunition for the feminist movement nor aspired to degrade the female gender. Rather, with *Gender Advertisements* he wanted to conduct a sober and objective study of the visual forms of portrayal of women in various social situations. But, as Randall Collins (1986, p. 108) reminds us, one of the major assets of Goffman's writings was that he wrote in layers, so that what was apparently signaled on the surface was one thing, whereas a closer reading would reveal that things were in fact much more complicated and less straightforward than indicated initially. So although *Gender Advertisements* by many was regarded as a feminist critique, it can—at the same time—also be seen as a defense of traditional and functionally derived gender roles. Whether intended as a feminist critique or as a functionalist defense, because of its object of analysis as well as its unconventional methodology, *Gender Advertisements* stands as a somewhat strange parenthesis in Goffman's writings.

The pertinent question of culture versus biology, which was noticeable between the lines in *Gender Advertisements*, Goffman treated much more directly in his article "The Arrangement Between the Sexes" (1977a). Here the main argument is that the scenes of social interaction "do not so much allow for the expression of natural differences between the sexes as for the production of that difference itself" (Goffman, 1977a, p. 324). The central concept here is "institutional reflexivity," which describes the process through which the social environment is organized so as to make whatever natural gender differences there are accentuated, visible, and significant (Branaman, 1997, p. lxxx). Goffman points out how five different features of the organization of social life (gender-divided work, siblings bringing up siblings, gender-segregated toilet practices, looks, and career choices, as well as identification systems) all contribute in confirming the biologically based gender stereotypes. His point is that although biological differences between the sexes do indeed exist, these are far from self-explanatory or from providing sufficient grounds for explaining the relationship between men and women in modern society. The arrangement between the sexes, the different gender identities, gender practices ("**genderisms**"), and the routinized subordination of women to men need to be explained socially and culturally instead of looking for biological explanations. In short, we need to look beyond biology. Goffman insisted that social life is organized in such a way that we unavoidably end up in situations (or frames) in which we more or less consciously participate in the ritual confirmation and maintenance of the socially constructed relationship between the sexes. Deeply embedded and ingrained institutional practices, Goffman claimed, are thus instrumental in transforming social situations into

> scenes for the performance of genderisms by both sexes, many of these performances taking a ritual form which affirms beliefs about the differential human nature of the two sexes even while indications are provided as to how behavior between the two can be expected to be intermeshed. (Goffman, 1977a, p. 325)

By participating in ordinary and trivial social situations, we, according to Goffman, often unknowingly take part in the confirmation of the different natures of the sexes. Philip Manning has described Goffman's texts about the relationship between the sexes as a practical use of frame analysis because they focus on the frames detectable in advertisements as well as in everyday interactions, which in either case function as guides to understanding the relationship between the sexes. The standardized and exaggerated presentation of the male person as the stoic and loving protector of the female person in advertisements is thus a hyperritualization of the parent–child frame describing a status difference between a (superior) man and a (subordinate) woman (Manning, 1992, p. 134). Gender differences can thus not be said to rely only on natural—that is, biological—differences but rather rest on the fact that the gender-based relationship between man and woman should be interpreted through an entirely different social frame. In the same way, Goffman stated about gender-segregated public restrooms that although there are indeed gender-differentiated physical organs based on differences in function,

> there is nothing in this functioning that *biologically* recommends segregation; *that* arrangement is totally a cultural matter. And what one has is a case of institutional reflexivity: toilet segregation is presented as a natural consequence of the difference between the sex-classes, when in fact it is rather a means of honouring, if not producing, this difference. (Goffman, 1977a, p. 316)

Goffman thus wrote himself directly into the at-the-time quite heated gender debate, but it is still important to ask if he really contributed with decisive or new knowledge in the question of culture versus biology. Cut to the bone, his message was rather banal—that gender is socially constructed. As one reviewer thus teasingly observed:

> None of the actual discussion of the photographic material [in *Gender Advertisements*] is very original. There is almost a feeling of strain about it, as though [Goffman] is trying to both pacify and also keep one jump ahead of a lot of bright girl post-graduates. (Carter, 1979, p. 9)

However, despite its lack of originality, the novelty of Goffman's analysis was his illustrations of *how* gender differences are structured after entirely different frames (e.g., child–parent relationships) and *how* frames in and by themselves produce and reinforce the differences between the sexes. Moreover, Goffman's work with gender and genderisms inspired a host of other writers who more systematically and theoretically elaborated how gender is something performative and something one "does" instead of merely being something natural, unchanging, and essential (see, e.g., Brickell, 2005; Butler, 1993; West & Zimmerman, 1987), and how gender is stereotypically portrayed in advertisements, television programs, commercials, women's advice books, and so on. Although the notion of "doing gender" had already been coined prior to Goffman's book *Gender Advertisements* and was indeed mentioned in a footnote in that book (Goffman, 1979a, p. 3), his work nevertheless was instrumental in providing backing for this performative idea. For example, Arlie R. Hochschild (1990) has shown how many American advice books for women present two different "gender codes," "traditional" and "modern egalitarian," constructed around how gender is presented and related to colors used, facial positioning, bodily posture, handshake, feeling rules, emotion control, and the like. Inspired by Goffman's ideas, Hochschild insists that despite the prevalence of these codes, we may also detect a certain mixing of codes pointing out how conventional gender roles and stereotypes are increasingly challenged and changed. Moreover, Goffman's original and extensive use and analysis of visual images in *Gender Advertisements* later inspired many other researchers into developing visual methodology within a variety of substantive research areas.

Forms of Talk

Goffman's last published book was *Forms of Talk* (1981a). This book, published only a year and a half prior to his death, consisted of an introduction and five subsequent essays—some relatively related, others appearing more as individual pieces—in which Goffman mingled many of his previous ideas and applied them to a new research context—that of talk. First, we find a continuous interest in the use of the frame metaphor. Thus, all the essays in *Forms of Talk*, at least according to Goffman's foreword, build on a frame-analytical approach that frames, as it were, the way Goffman approached the phenomenon and study of talk (Goffman, 1981a, p. 1). Second, the book also contained an explicit continuation of the dramaturgical metaphor now primarily applied to situations of talk. In the introduction, Goffman thus stated on the use of dramaturgical ideas: "In what follows, then, I make no large literary claim that social life is but a stage, only a small technical one: that deeply incorporated into the nature of talk are the fundamental requirements of theatricality" (Goffman, 1981a, p. 4). Moreover, in typical Goffmanesque fashion, Goffman initiated *Forms of Talk* almost in a self-apologetic manner when stating on the nature of the invented and proposed concepts in the book: "None of the concepts elaborated may have a future. So I ask that these papers be taken for what they merely are: exercises, trials, tryouts, a means of displaying possibilities, not establishing facts" (Goffman, 1981a, p. 1). According to him, *Forms of Talk* primarily centered on and elaborated three main ideas: "ritualization," "participation frameworks," and "embedding" (Goffman, 1981a, p. 3). Each in its own way, these ideas, however not systematically, are pursued in and undercut the essays included in *Forms of Talk* showing how talk is a highly ritualized activity dependent upon participants' engagement and perspective and always embedded in specific situational and interpretative circumstances.

Because *Forms of Talk* was not as concerned with nonverbal behavior as many of Goffman's previous books were, it marked a kind of "linguistic shift" (Phillips, 1983) in his way of thinking about and analyzing the (nonverbal as well as verbal) signs and signals people give and give off in interaction situations. Throughout the book, two underlying assumptions seem to be at work: (1) that the study of talk should not be restricted to the strictly formalized methods of linguistics but ought also to be seen within an interactive framework and (2) that talk—as social interaction—constantly involves instances of self-presentation and self-maintenance (Collins, 1994, p. 283; Corsaro, 1983, p. 220). Consequently, conversation is thus not merely reducible to action—rather, it ought to be regarded as *inter*action—something taking place between people. In the first essay of the book, "Replies and Responses," conversation or talk is seen as a case of a social "arrangement by which individuals come together and sustain matters having a ratified, joint, current and running claim upon attention, a claim which lodges them together in some sort of intersubjective, mental world" (Goffman, 1981a, pp. 70–71). In this connection the spoken word plays a significant role because "words are the great device for fetching speaker and hearer into the same focus of attention and into the same interpretation schema that applies to what is thus attended" (Goffman, 1981a, p. 71). Please note how the concept of "interpretation schema" here is equivalent to the previously discussed concept of "frame," insofar as it refers to that which offers meaning to verbal interchanges and provides rules for how one should appropriately behave. Throughout his analysis of talk, Goffman concludes that talk is not only a dialogical connection between two parties but rather constitutes a frame-based form of interaction that, for example, makes it possible to distinguish talk from the "moves" made by participants involved in formal games (Goffman, 1981a, p. 52). By regarding talk as such sequences of response, in which the various responses can either maintain, change, or introduce a new frame, one, according to Goffman, obtains a much more nuanced understanding of talk (Phillips, 1983, p. 114).

The second essay in *Forms of Talk*, "Response Cries," deals with the social significance of those utterances and verbal expressions that are apparently directed at or intended for nobody or that we produce whenever we think we are all alone. They are expressions that "stand alone" in the sense that they are neither to be regarded as expressions waiting for an answer nor as answers to a given expression. For example, this might be when during a dinner arrangement we are about to drop our coffee cup and then out of utter surprise express a "Whoops" or an "Oops." Such responsive cries are according to Goffman to be seen as

> exclamatory interjections which are not full-fledged words. *Oops!* is an example. These nonlexicalized, discrete interjections, like certain unsegmented, tonal, prosodic features of speech, comport neatly with our doctrine of human nature. We see such "expression" as a natural overflowing, a flooding up of previously contained feeling, a bursting of normal restraints, a case of being caught off guard. This is what could be learned by asking the man in the street if he uses these forms, and, if so, what he means by them. (Goffman, 1981a, p. 99)

The purpose of the essay is to document how these apparently trivial, spontaneous, and involuntary utterances contain a substantial amount of social and interactional significance (Watson, 1983, p. 104). According to Goffman, these utterances are important because they function as a kind of signal to our surroundings that explain or excuse our behavior. The "response cries"—no matter how spontaneous or involuntary they might seem to be—serve the purpose of ensuring our surroundings that our loss of control with the situation (and perhaps even with ourselves) is only momentary and will shortly be put back on track again. At the same time, they signal that we are indeed aware that something extraordinary just happened and that we made a mistake. When we leave the museum and in distraction walk straight past the exit and express an oops before discovering the exit, then we release an excusing and explanatory utterance to others present about our behavior. With our whoopses or oopses, we define to our immediate surroundings that certain aspects of our behavior are to be seen as minor accidents, thereby making sure that they are not interpreted as expressions of a more general behavioral incompetence (Goffman, 1981a, p. 102). This is also a theme that is evident in the subsequent essay titled "Footing," in which the notion of "**footing**" refers to the way participants in verbal interaction align themselves to others or to the content of what is being said, the management of the production, or the reception of utterances in a given social situation.

The final two essays of *Forms of Talk*, "The Lecture" and "Radio Talk," both analyze situations in which a single individual has the opportunity—either directly or in a mediated format—to approach a larger audience for a longer period of time without the minor disruptions so characteristic of many everyday conversations (Burns, 1992, p. 337). In "The Lecture," Goffman looks at the lecture, such as at a college or university, as a sort of speech action, and the essay is in fact itself a transcription of a lecture Goffman himself once gave—on lectures. The purpose is to investigate to what degree a lecture can be seen as an instance of social interaction rather than as a typical example of one-way speech communication. Here it is important for Goffman initially to specify that the success of the lecture is particularly dependent upon the ability of the lecturer to unite himself/ herself with the audience in a "special realm of being." Lecturing is thus about creating a shared situational room that the audience is absorbed by. This is probably something most lecturers can recognize from their own teaching experiences. From here Goffman moves on to analyze the minor mistakes or mishaps produced by the lecturer during the performance and the creative and ingenious ways he or she tries to make up for them—which is probably also recognizable to most lecturers. According to Goffman, these mistakes can be interpreted in two different ways: (1) as a disturbance in the lecture seen as a textual and informational transfer or (2) as the accompanying music that makes the lecture a living interactional scene for lecturer and audience, which, as Goffman eloquently expressed it, marks "the very difference between reading a lecture at home and attending one" (Goffman, 1981a, p. 186). Indeed, those behavioral mishaps and minor mistakes produced by the lecturer when he or she stumbles over words, when his or her voice snaps, when he or she becomes flustered, when the overhead or PowerPoint presentation is turned upside down, or when the book intended for quotation is left at home, this is in fact what opens up the interaction. Moreover, it is through the lecturer's subsequent correctional process, during which he or she explicitly addresses mistakes and tries to save the situation, that a connection between lecturer and audience is established, which makes it meaningful to see the lecture as an example of social interaction rather than merely as the delivery of information.

It is more or less a similar theme that is played out in "Radio Talk," albeit now it is the slips, blunders, and boners of the host of the radio show and not the lecturer, together with the subsequent attempts at excusing, correcting, and restarting the presentation, that is at stake. These are, as in "The Lecture," analyzed as instances of social interaction between the radio host and the abstract, nonpresent, and unknown audience of listeners. Apparently, this is a case of one-way communication during which the radio host speaks incessantly to the listeners, who are unable to respond, replicate, or interrupt—although they may obviously turn off the radio. According to Goffman, however, this is rather to be seen as an archetypal example of verbal interaction, and it is therefore the host's various speech mistakes such as mispronunciations, stuttering, tactlessness, and indiscretions (Goffman, 1981a, pp. 209–211), but also his or her subsequent self-corrections, cover-ups, and excuses that are analyzed as the source of interaction between radio host and listeners. Take the following example into consideration:

> Try this wonderful new bra . . . you'll especially love the softly lined cups that are so comfortable to wear. You gals who need a little something extra should try our model 718. It's lightly padded and I'm sure you'll love it. I do! . . . I mean I like the looks of it. . . . Well . . . what I am trying to say is that I don't need one myself, naturally, as a man . . . but if you do, I recommend it. . . . How do I know? I really don't. . . . I'm just reading the commercial for Mary Patterson who is ill and at home with a cold. (Goffman, 1981a, p. 302)

Not only is the example quite entertaining, but Goffman (1981a, p. 301) also regards it as an illustrative example of how the radio host in this threatening and delicate situation is willing openly to "break the frame" and to provide the listeners with information that was otherwise not intended in a desperate attempt to save what is left of his own reputation. "Radio Talk" is supplied with the subtitle "A Study of the Ways of Our Errors," which clearly indicates Goffman's strategy: to study talk as social interaction by looking at what happens when errors occur in speech and when what is regarded as the norm is momentarily breached.

Forms of Talk is simultaneously a typical and an atypical Goffman book. It is typical because with its various essays, it seeks to change our understanding of talk as interaction (e.g., lectures and radio broadcasts), but also because it deploys the characteristic Goffmanesque style: the extended discussions, at certain places quite abstract, at other places remarkably nonanalytical, with example following example without any notable accompanying comments (Stubbs, 1983, p. 78). It is atypical not only because Goffman here takes an interest in verbal communication rather than nonverbal interaction but also because he began to explore the systematic aspects of interaction rather than—as earlier—its more ritual aspects. Or rather, he studied how the normative precepts of action, the "ritual constraints," cooperate with the "**system requirements,**" which facilitate and structure the interaction taking place between people talking to each other in face-to-face situations. In short, Goffman moved the system requirements of interaction up alongside the ritual constraints. The system requirements of interaction are those preconditions or communication-technical demands that interaction must abide by if it is to succeed as interaction. In the essay "Replies and Responses," Goffman mentioned eight such "system requirements':

1. A *two-way capability* for transceiving acoustically adequate and readily interpretable messages.

2. *Back-channel feedback capabilities* for informing on reception while it is occurring.

3. *Contact-signals* such as means of announcing the seeking of a channelled connection, means of ratifying that the sought-for channel is now open and means of closing off a previously open channel.

4. *Turnover signals* such as means to indicate the ending of a message and the taking over of the sending role by the next speaker.

5. *Pre-emption signals* such as means of inducing a rerun, holding off channel requests, interrupting a talker in progress, etc.

6. *Framing capabilities* such as cues for distinguishing special readings to apply across strips of bracketed communication, recasting otherwise conventional sense, as in making ironic asides, quoting another, joking, etc.

7. *Norms* obliging respondents to reply honestly with whatever they know that is relevant and no more.

8. *Non-participant constraints* regarding eavesdropping, competing noise and the blocking of pathways for eye-to-eye signals. (Goffman, 1981a, pp. 14–15; emphasis added)

These "system requirements" each in their way function as a kind of model, which explains or systematizes the interaction taking place between people involved in sequences or exchanges of explicit signals with others, or, in other words, talk. But as already indicated, Goffman did not leave it at that. In *Forms of Talk*, he also showed how these system requirements or demands were supplemented, reinforced, or downright controlled by more normative ritual responsibilities to the situation—responsibilities that equally facilitate and constrain communication. For example, requests for access to or requests for the termination of communicative interaction with others are, according to Goffman, not only a matter of participants' compliance with communication-rational obligations but also cases of how microrituals express a demand for the protection of each other's faces (Goffman, 1981a, pp. 18–19).

Goffman's interest in language and conversation analysis is also evident in the extensive essay "Felicity's Condition" (perhaps one of the longest essays ever to appear in the *American Journal of Sociology*), which, aided and abetted by his widow, the linguist Gillian Sankoff, was published the year after Goffman's death (Goffman, 1983b). In this essay, Goffman—inspired by pragmatics, conversation analysis, and sociolinguistics—was concerned with the so-called background assumptions, "background expectations" or "presuppositions" in situations of verbal communication, meaning how we in conversation (and social interaction more generally) use and draw upon different expectations and assumptions about each other in order to make the interaction succeed. By drawing on insights from sociolinguistics and conversation analysis—which at this time began to attract increasing attention among researchers, particularly on the American continent—Goffman's aspiration was to develop a sociological understanding of the mechanisms that contribute to successful social interaction. Throughout the essay, Goffman—by way of various examples of verbal exchanges between, respectively, two strangers and two acquaintances—demonstrated how we to a large degree base our interaction on assumptions about the intentions, motives, knowledge, and so on of others, just as we, as producers of utterances and behavior, consciously as well as unconsciously incorporate elements that make it possible for the recipient to interpret what we are saying and doing as meaningful and reasonable. For example, when a person at the box-office window outside the cinema is desperately searching his pockets and to the salesperson then utters "Two, please," the salesperson can safely regard this as a meaningful wish to buy two tickets for tonight's screening (Goffman, 1983b, p. 34).

Based on his many examples, Goffman developed the point that all the different background assumptions that we as producers and recipients utilize in social interaction (whether in actual conversation or just by being together) serve the basic function of demonstrating to others that we are capable, competent, understandable, and accountable participants in interaction, and it is exactly this demand that he described as "**Felicity's Condition.**" Cryptically formulated, "Felicity's Condition" is the background assumption behind all other background assumptions. In Goffman's own words, it is "any arrangement which leads us to judge an individual's verbal acts to be not a manifestation of strangeness. Behind Felicity's Condition is our sense of what it is to be sane" (Goffman, 1983b, p. 27). Clearly drawing on ethnomethodological ideas of "indexicality," "accountability," and the "etcetera principle," Felicity's Condition is that which binds social interaction—verbal and nonverbal—together and makes it safe, recognizable, understandable, and meaningful. Felicity's Condition is the all-dominant and underlying assumption that ensures and secures meaningful interaction. Or put another way: Felicity's Condition is the underlying arrangement, which confirms to us that we can communicate knowingly with each other, that even fragments or sparse or disconnected information is received and understood as meaningful and coherent utterances, and that our assumptions about the behavior and utterances of others are not cast into doubt. When we live up to the expectations of Felicity's Condition, we, in other words, live up to the social demands to demonstrate to others the predictability and saneness of our actions. Goffman ended the essay by expressing this clearly with the following statement:

> Whenever we come into contact with another through the mails, over the telephone, in face-to-face talk, or even merely through immediate co-presence, we find ourselves with one central obligation: to render our behavior understandably relevant to what the other can come to perceive is going on. Whatever else,

our activity must be addressed to the other's mind, that is, to the other's capacity to read our words and actions for evidence of our feelings, thoughts, and intent. This confines what we say and do, but it also allows us to bring to bear all of the world to which the other can catch allusions. (Goffman, 1983b, p. 51)

Felicity's Condition is thus the rule that underpins all other interactional rules (Manning, 1992, p. 25). To analyze Felicity's Condition thus to a large degree means analyzing everything that we subconsciously take for granted and draw upon in social interaction.

Conclusion

In this chapter, we have been concerned with delineating and discussing what might be termed the "late Goffman," meaning the work by Goffman published throughout the last decade of his life. Although many of Goffman's later writings might come across as being concerned with utterly different topics—mental frames, gender, and talk—than his early work, there is nevertheless some method to the madness. In his later books, Goffman increasingly began to search the "backstage," as it were, of the organization of social interaction—the underlying, invisible, and cognitive structures and organizing principles that allow people to participate—verbally and nonverbally—in and make sense of social situations. The final three books written by Goffman—*Frame Analysis* (1974), *Gender Advertisements* (1979a), and *Forms of Talk* (1981a)—thus each in their way extended and elaborated on some of the earlier arguments about definitions of the situation, impression management, ritualized practice, and performances.

The most significant of Goffman's last books was probably *Frame Analysis*. Seen in hindsight, Goffman's notion of frame analysis was both a catalyst of and itself an incarnation of the so-called cognitive turn during the 1970s and 1980s in social, literary and humanistic studies showing how all facets of human life—organizational, institutional, and everyday—rely upon different cognitive frames that allow participants, professional and nonprofessional, to make sense of their social contexts (see, e.g., Rogoff & Lave, 1984). Moreover, perhaps Goffman's frame analysis also provided a caustic sociological diagnosis of the times. At least Kwang-ki Kim suggested that a certain civilizational critique—or perhaps rather relief—might be read into *Frame Analysis:*

Individuals are encompassed with unprecedented pandemonium in modern society. Yet, even under these conditions, they are not abandoned in a sea of chaos, having no help. Just like a beacon, frames provide individuals with perspectives or interpretations about the particular situation. . . . In other words, throughout the analysis of frameworks, Goffman wants to address the cognition of individuals facing increasing ambiguity and ambivalence. (Kim, 2002, pp. 65–66)

Frames thus ensure that individuals will "know how to go on," as Ludwig Wittgenstein proposed, in a society of increasing liberties and possibilities and with increasingly relaxed and informal codes of conduct. Perhaps a similar caustic or critical sensibility might also be discerned in *Gender Advertisements*, as a mischievous comment to contemporary gender stereotypes, and in *Forms of Talk*, as an exposure of a society obsessed with avoiding slipups, mistakes, and embarrassing performances. Although Goffman continued his commitment to studying the minutiae of social interaction, in his later works one senses a more distanced, more analytical, and perhaps also more ambitious endeavor to discovering, listing, and systematizing some of the overlooked organizing principles beneath or behind human participation in social life.

Questions

- How should we understand Erving Goffman's notion of "frames" and how does it relate to one of his previously favored notions such as the "definition of the situation"?
- Why did Erving Goffman begin to study talk, and how did his ideas developed in *Forms of Talk* and "Felicity's Condition" contribute to our understanding of the rules and rituals of everyday—verbal and nonverbal—interaction?
- How did Erving Goffman understand gender and gender differences?
- What were the main similarities and differences between Erving Goffman's early work and his last three books?

8

Reading Goffman "Forward"

I n Chapter 2, we conducted a so-called "backward" reading of Goffman
and attempted to outline the origins of his microsociological thinking in
variety of intellectual perspectives and theoretical traditions. In this chapter,
we shall try to read him "forward," as it were, and thus try to identify how
elements of his work have inspired other sociological thinkers and are
employed as building blocks in contemporary social and sociological theory.
Besides recording some of the most significant sociological analyses in the
field of everyday, modern life, Goffman's publications have, indisputably, left
distinct imprints in contemporary sociological theory. Not only has
Goffman's authorship acted as inspiration or a dialogue partner to some of
today's most distinguished sociological theory builders, his sociology has
also acted as a launch pad for what has grown to become a large number of
empirically oriented studies of individuals in different social situations and
contexts. In the following, we shall consider the links and inspiration from
Goffman to a number of central sociologists who have used or related to his
conceptual framework in their own, original theory construction. As
Goffman has been influential to many sociological thinkers, our listing here
of theorists with a Goffmanian flavor is not, of course, an exhaustive one.
We have selected a sample of well-known sociologists on whom Goffman's
ideas have had significant influence. These are Harold Garfinkel and his
ethnomethodological position, Jürgen Habermas and his theory on communicative action, Niklas Luhmann's systems theory, Pierre Bourdieu's reflexive
sociology, and Anthony Giddens and his theory of structuration. We conclude by touching briefly upon some of the recent theoretical innovations
building on Goffman's microsociology.

Harold Garfinkel

Goffman turned his back on American sociologist Harold Garfinkel's program of ethnomethodology, which, according to Goffman, was far too oriented toward theoretical problem matters, far too radical in its epistemological implications and conclusions (Collins, 1985, p. 225), and too individualistic in its conception that everything social is locally founded. Garfinkel (1967) did, however, develop his ethnomethodology during more or less the same period as Goffman launched his sociology, and in spite of their mutual disagreements, they allegedly also inspired one another. At any rate, it is a fact that Goffman refers to Garfinkel. For example, this is evident in *Asylums* (1961) and particularly in the analysis of the moral career of the mental patient, where Goffman draws on Garfinkel's (1956) concept of degradation ceremonies (Goffman, 1961, p. 130). Both represent a microoriented everyday-life sociology dealing with the ways in which people, in order to make everyday social meetings successful, employ special competencies and draw on a special tacit and congenial knowledge stock. Another common feature, which they both probably derive from pragmatism, is the conception of the social order as a practical result of human action. Goffman is indeed, from time to time, presented as an actual forerunner of many of the ideas later developed by ethnomethodology (Attewell, 1974). For the sake of completeness, it should be mentioned that Goffman did in fact encourage his students to read texts by Garfinkel, with the result that a number of these students left the University of Berkeley, where Goffman was working, for Los Angeles in order to attend Garfinkel's lectures and sociological experiments (Wallace & Wolf, 1999, p. 227).

With his so-called breaching experiments, Garfinkel was interested in illustrating what happens when the normative obligations of interaction are broken and the social order collapses momentarily. According to Garfinkel, individuals interact to define the situation, and Garfinkel is interested in these everyday methods and procedures used by the participants in these meaning-creating definition processes. This is where Garfinkel differs from Goffman, who was indeed interested in the meaning-creating procedures of the actors, but on the basis of a far more normative and less cognitive interest than Garfinkel (Album, 1995, p. 252). It might be claimed that whereas Garfinkel was interested in the *microtechnique* used by individuals in order to create meaning in social situations and constitute the basis of social order, Goffman was more involved in studying the way in which individuals in social interaction live in accordance with ritual obligations, and how, in this way, they are controlled by an external, superindividual social syntax (Knorr-Cetina, 1981, p. 3). Both were preoccupied with rules, but whereas in Goffman's view, rules expressed moral and normative demands on the actors, to Garfinkel they were merely practical tools that, when applied, will ensure the mutual understanding of participants. Or in other words: both Goffman and Garfinkel were interested in individuals in face-to-face situations, but whereas Garfinkel was mostly interested in the way the situation is determined and defined, Goffman was, in addition to this, also preoccupied with the ways individuals work out how to behave appropriately in the situation (Album, 1995, p. 253).

Hence, it is to a large extent in their view of the social actor and in their assessment of the normative element of interaction that Garfinkel and Goffman differ from one another. Whereas Garfinkel held the opinion that in Goffman the individual is reduced to a "cultural dope," a passive being who complies mechanically with rules and regulations, Goffman held the view that ethnomethodologists isolated themselves in a mystifying perspective detached from reality. It seems only fair to mention, however, that even though Goffman dissociated himself from ethnomethodology (particularly its exaggerated pragmatism, which refers everything to collective social pragmatics), his own authorship took a clear ethnomethodological turn with the publication of *Forms of Talk* (1981a). Here Goffman writes himself into the strand of ethnomethodology that is termed "conversation analysis."

Anthony Giddens

One of the examples of where Goffman's sociology has been employed in a more substantive theoretical manner is in British sociologist Anthony Giddens's development of his theory of structuration. Thus, in *The Constitution of Society* (1984), Giddens draws to a large extent on Goffman's analyses of interaction among copresent individuals. Giddens's ambition is to formulate a general social theory or an *approach*, as he calls it, that does not conceive the reproduction of society from either an actor-oriented action perspective or from a structuralist systems perspective but accepts that both these aspects are inextricably linked. Giddens highlights many of Goffman's concepts of the units of interaction order (gatherings, events, unfocused interaction, focused interaction, and encounters) as important building blocks in a general social theory, and he also claims that in Goffman's works we find important inspiration for the understanding of the role the *practical consciousness* of individuals plays in everyday life.

Giddens draws attention to Goffman, because he has demonstrated how individuals are equipped with a keen practical consciousness and that this very practical consciousness helps us make everyday interaction successful and unproblematic. As Giddens points out, with his analyses, Goffman shows how, in everyday life, we draw on a large amount of internalized tacit knowledge, which provides everyday encounters with the quality of regularity and ritual. Therefore, according to Giddens, understanding this practical consciousness is an absolute must for a sociology that wishes to explain the reproduction of society and, at the same time, to bridge the gap in the dichotomic relationship between structure and actor. Drawing clearly on the works of Goffman, Giddens states:

> I think it highly important to emphasize the fact that encounters typically occur as routines. That is, what from the angle of the fleeting moment might appear brief and trivial interchanges take on much more substance when seen as inherent in the iterative nature of social life. The routinization of encounters is of major significance in binding the fleeting encounter to social reproduction and thus to the seeming "fixity" of institutions. (Giddens, 1984, p. 72)

It appears that Giddens borrows from Goffman, among others, knowledge about the practical consciousness (and the social significance of the body) of individuals for a theory that is intended to explain the preservation of social life without ending up in either structuralist determinism or voluntarism. According to Giddens, Goffman and ethnomethodologists have demonstrated how individuals in everyday life make use of rules and knowledge to ensure what he calls "social integration." In his so-called *structuration theory*, Giddens uses the concepts of system integration and social integration to describe the fact that both social systems and individuals in face-to-face interactions may generate types of social order and integration, and here Giddens draws on Goffman to show how individuals with a certain practical consciousness produce and maintain a more or less stable social order through a seriality of interchanges. According to Giddens, Goffman has been criticized for taking the motivation of actors for granted and for presupposing a cynical and voluntaristic actor, who adapts and adjusts to the given situation on the basis of egocentric motives. Goffman may certainly be interpreted in a voluntaristic direction, but such interpretation disregards, as we have established and as is also pointed out by Giddens, that Goffman emphasized the tactfulness displayed in social encounters and the solicitude felt by individuals on behalf of the situation and the participating parties. So what Giddens points out is that not only did Goffman practice microsociology, in actual fact he displayed an interest in the innermost mechanics of social reproduction (Giddens, 1984, p. 70). In other words, Giddens argues that a nuanced understanding of human behavior in face-to-face situations is an essential element of a social theory that intends to explain how society is reproduced.

Drawing on Goffman, Giddens also explores the nature of the practical consciousness that makes life predictable in the sense that it becomes comprehensible and nonchaotic. At the same time, Goffman and the ethnomethodologists are employed to display that everyday routines are not fixed and absolute entities that are unconsciously repeated but rather the subjects of a constant, diligent, and reflexive adaptation effort (Giddens, 1984, p. 86). In other words, the (inter)action processes of individuals may very well be governed by routines, but these "constraining elements" are to a large extent the more or less conscious results of exchanging processes between practically conscious actors, processes that are constantly being changed and developed. In his formulation of the concept "ontological security," Giddens also draws on Goffman. His point of departure is Erik Erikson's developmental psychology, but Goffman's concept of frame is also included, since, according to Giddens, "framing may be regarded as providing the ordering of activities and meanings whereby ontological security is sustained in the enactment of daily routines" (Giddens, 1984, p. 87). Frames, thus, constitute the tools actors use to understand and create meaning in their social surroundings, and thus they help them to ensure the sense of predictability and security necessary to maintain the self.

Jürgen Habermas

Another central contemporary sociologist who makes use of concepts and theoretical insights from Goffman is German sociologist Jürgen Habermas. In his analysis of legitimacy problems in late capitalism (*Legitimations probleme im Spätkapitalismus*), which was published in 1973, he employed the concept of total institution (albeit without referring to Goffman) to describe the social organizational principles characterizing primitive societies. But it was not until the publication of his influential work *Theory of Communicative Action* that Habermas in an integrated way explicitly referred to elements of Goffman's thinking. He did so mainly in his discussion of four different action concepts (theological, normatively regulated, dramaturgical, and communicative). With regard to his formulation of dramaturgical action, Habermas refers explicitly to Goffman's work:

> From the perspective of dramaturgical actions we understand social action as an encounter in which participants form a visible public for each other and perform for one another. "Encounter" and "performance" are the key concepts. The performance of a troupe before the eye of third persons is only a special case. A performance enables the actor to present himself to his audience in a certain way; in bringing something of his subjectivity to appearance, he would like to be seen by his public in a particular way. (Habermas, 1984, p. 90)

In this way, Goffman's investigation of dramaturgical action is included in major theoretical construction work concerned with the development of a special communicative rationality that may serve as a tool for the establishment of norms. This integration is quite natural, considering the fact that Habermas and Goffman actually share a common interest in the communicative interactions of individuals. Habermas does, however, present a somewhat one-sided reading of Goffman's dramaturgical model, as he seems to overaccentuate the element of information manipulation and cynicism identified by Goffman in the role-playing actor. Thus, when Habermas (1984, p. 93) states that "Goffman's model of action does not provide for his behaving toward the social world in a norm-conformative attitude," he seems to neglect an important dimension of Goffman's work. Not only does Goffman demonstrate in *The Presentation of Self in Everyday Life* (which is the only one of Goffman's publications Habermas explicitly draws on) that the role-playing individual does indeed have a moral side and that interaction is indeed concerned with collaboration, but later on, in *Interaction Ritual*, he also points out that our everyday interactions are successful and do not break down in situations because we live by and comply with certain ceremonial and thus normative rules, as we illustrated in Chapter 4. Such reading of Goffman as seen in Habermas has, indeed, caused Goffman interpreters to react. Thus, James Chriss (1995b, p. 562) stated that "what Habermas and other astute social thinkers have failed to understand clearly is that, although all deceptive presentations are staged, not all staged presentations are deceptive or geared toward obfuscation or distortion."

Niklas Luhmann

Earlier, we mentioned Anthony Giddens as one of the sociologists who draws substantially on Goffman. German sociologist Niklas Luhmann is another. In *Trust and Power*, which is the forerunner of a number of subsequent substantial books on systems theory and constitutes Luhmann's attempt at illustrating how such phenomena as "trust" and "confidence" are manifest in differentiated and complex societies, there are numerous examples of his direct indebtedness to Goffman's sociology, while Parsons and Husserl also supply substance to the creation, application, and analysis of concepts (Luhmann, 1979). For the main part, Goffman's contribution here is the minute and detailed analyses and examples of the ways individuals assist one another to maintain face and help one another keep interaction going. Here trust is essential if interaction is not going to collapse. In Luhmann, this interactional trust is split up into *personal trust* and *trust in systems*, respectively. Personal trust can be taken as whether individuals seem confidence inspiring and trustworthy. In Luhmann, this trust is, to a large extent, based on whether individuals are successful in their self-presentation. It appears from the quotation below that Luhmann's conception of self-presentation draws on Goffman's thinking:

> People and social systems strive, in their self-presentation as we have already shown, to draw a consistent picture of themselves and make it socially accepted. Since other people and social systems also have an interest in building up reliable expectations with regard to the people around them, in seeing them as persisting identities, there develops in social interaction a type of expressive language which enables actions to be attributed to people or social systems, and not only causally, indeed, but also symbolically, as expressing their essence, their self. (Luhmann, 1979, p. 82)

Thus, according to Luhmann, it is trust, both the personal and that displayed in abstract systems, that contributes to reducing complexity in society. Furthermore, Luhmann utilizes Goffman's thinking on mistrust and deception displayed in *Strategic Interaction*. It may be stated, then, that Goffman legitimizes central elements in Luhmann's discussion of trust by providing sociological substance to the micro level in the analysis of the necessity of trust for all types of social systems, and Luhmann draws broadly on a large number of Goffman's works.

In Luhmann's extensive systems-theoretical work, *Social Systems* (1995), Goffman's thinking is also present. Here, Luhmann's mission is quite different, as this is where the more abstract thoughts on autopoiesis, observation, and communication strings dominate and must create the basis of a general sociology that can relate to and analyze all imaginable social contexts. Here, a strong parallelism exists between Goffman's idea of interaction order and Luhmann's concept of interaction systems as a particular type of social system. Goffman also plays a certain role in Luhmann's formulation of the concepts of "inclusion" and "exclusion," since here, Luhmann refers directly to Goffman's concept of total institutions. According to Luhmann, in stratified societies, total institutions play the role of including individuals who have been excluded by society (Mortensen, 2000, p. 98). Goffman is also incorporated, albeit briefly, in connection with Luhmann's idea that an action is always an action open to the perception of others, an action "for you," "against you," or "in front of you" (Luhmann, 1995, p. 130). Finally, it should be mentioned that in *The Reality of the Mass Media*, Luhmann draws on Goffman's concepts of objects and frames, and, initially, Luhmann makes use of the game metaphor with a view to understanding entertainment.

It may be added that the connection between Goffman and Luhmann is quite obvious. Both are deeply interested in communication: Goffman in communication processes that create and maintain the selves of individuals, Luhmann in communication processes in different types of systems. Finally, it may be said that to a certain extent, Luhmann carries on one of the analyses Goffman embarked upon: the coupling between the macro level of society and mundane everyday interactions (Luhmann, 1995, chapter 10). Moreover, examining the Goffman–Luhmann relationship, it is a noteworthy coincidence that Goffman's somewhat vague conceptualization of the relationship between the interaction order and societal structures did in fact have clear systems-theoretical features. As we saw in Chapter 4, Goffman used the term "loose coupling," which may indicate some level of systems-theoretical inspiration (most likely found in the works of Gregory Bateson, who also happened to inspire Luhmann).

Pierre Bourdieu

Although it has only been sporadically examined, there was a professional connection between the work of Goffman and that of French sociologist Pierre Bourdieu. In fact, it was Bourdieu who introduced Goffman in France through his editing of all five French translations of Goffman's books, and together, Bourdieu and Goffman had planned a joint presentation at the American Sociological Association's annual conference in 1982, which was, however, obstructed by Goffman's stomach cancer (Winkin, 1983, p. 109). Thus, Bourdieu had great respect for Goffman and his contributions to sociology, and Bourdieu's subtle sensation of the duality in the *social game*—that on the one hand individuals seek to advance and achieve advantages within different fields of social competition through adaptation to the rules of the game in that field (thus developing a particular habitus), thus, at the same time, reproducing and cementing the social order—contains clear parallels to Goffman. In an article published immediately after Goffman's death, Bourdieu paid tribute to him by writing,

> This vision of the social world, which may have appeared pessimistic, was that of a warm, friendly, modest, considerate man who was perhaps made the more sensitive to the theatricality of social life by his own profound impatience with all the ordinary forms of academic ceremonial and intellectual pomp. (Bourdieu, 1983, p. 113)

Bourdieu's positive assessment of Goffman's work and perspective was, however, not unambiguous. While acknowledging and appreciating the empirical sensitivity and the urge to conduct direct observations of the social world, Bourdieu expressed reservations regarding the interactionist tradition of which Goffman was seen as a leading exponent. Thus, in *An Invitation to Reflexive Sociology*, which was coauthored with Loïc Wacquant, Bourdieu expressed skepticism toward interactionist epistemology, as it, in Bourdieu's words, involves a certain blindness to objective and macro-level power structures (Bourdieu & Wacquant, 1992). According to Bourdieu, Goffman and interactionist sociology fail to grasp important societal power dimensions such as the "symbolic violence" that may be embedded in the language or in the actual structuring of interaction. According to Bourdieu, individuals move about between different "fields," bringing their own "habitus," which is shaped by the surrounding social space, their concrete position in the field in question, and their amount of "capital." Thus, habitus is the embodiment of historically produced and reproduced patterns of relations between these social trajectories, which provide individuals with certain dispositions for action that are expressed in social interactions. In other words, according to Bourdieu, the interaction and dispositions of individuals are predominantly expressions of the structure of society. To Goffman, on the other hand, it is in the *actual* interaction, in the concrete meeting between individuals, that the social aspect is unfolded—almost without past history or sequel. Whereas Bourdieu postulated a presituational shaping and definition of human encounters, Goffman was instead oriented toward the immediacy and unconditionality of the situation, and the former is therefore more structuralistic, whereas the latter represents a distinctly interactionist perspective. According to Goffman (1983a, p. 11), there is a "'loose coupling' between interactional practices and societal structures," whereas in Bourdieu, these structures are embedded in the minds of individuals and their actions through habitus. In one of his latest books, *Masculine Domination* (1998), Bourdieu did at times draw directly on some of the insights pioneered by Goffman and others. As its title indicates, the book describes how the structures that cause one gender to dominate the other are apparently reproduced in our society and come to shape our consciousness, acts, and discourses. Here Goffman's theory on gender relations—which we dealt with in Chapter 7—is brought into play, and on a couple of occasions Bourdieu mentions how the thinking behind "the ritualization of femininity" (Goffman, 1977c) may be used to elucidate some of the gender-based disparities in modern society. According to Bourdieu, these disparities are social constructions describing men as protectors and supervisors and women as delicate and submissive creatures (Bourdieu, 1998, p. 86). In other words, this is not a question of difference in habitus as such, but rather of differences in the "gender schemata" that have developed historically from different societal institutions such as family, church, state, school, and so forth.

The Sociology of Emotions

As we suggested in Chapter 4, much of Goffman's work was pioneering in integrating feelings into sociological theory, and it is evident that his work on the interactional dynamics and social function of emotions has opened a door to a sociological subfield: the sociology of emotion counting. Goffman's dramaturgy as well as his writings on social ritualization explore how the management of feelings of embarrassment and shame constitutes an integral part of individuals' everyday-life interaction. Building on these insights, sociological scholars such as Thomas J. Scheff, Randall Collins, and Arlie R. Hochschild have advanced and expanded Goffman's thoughts into a new sociological subdiscipline focusing, among other things, on emotion management. Reading Goffman as a symbolic interactionist in the Cooley line, Scheff (2005) has directed attention to two central aspects of his work: (1) the analysis of the process of living in the minds of others (shared awareness) and (2) how this process produces emotion. As pointed out by Scheff, the individual in much of Goffman's work is constantly attentive and responsive to his own standing in the eyes of others, implying more or less constant states of emotion such as embarrassment. Individuals in everyday life interaction are concerned not to lose face or to end up with a discredited self and thus with feelings of embarrassment. Early interactionists like Cooley acknowledged this, but according to Scheff, Goffman went beyond Cooley and explored how individuals manage the emotions related to this process:

> Although Goffman has nothing to say about the pride option, his examples suggest that actors usually do not accept shame/embarrassment passively. Instead they try to manage it, by avoidance, if possible. Most of the embarrassment/shame possibilities that Goffman's examples explore are not about the actual occurrence of emotions but anticipations and management based on these anticipations. (Scheff, 2005, p. 159)

In Scheff's view, individuals' management of emotion serves a crucial function in terms of sustaining social order. Scheff (1990, 2006) proposes that maintaining social bonds through *bond work* is an essential human activity. In everyday life, individuals make efforts to maintain normal social bonds through recognition and ratification of each other's faces. As lack of recognition may result in feelings of exclusion and embarrassment, such emotions should be considered important drivers toward conforming to social norms and situational standards.

In another vein, Arlie R. Hochschild's (1979, 1983) works on emotion management are heavily indebted to—but also critical of—Goffman. According to Hochschild, most of Goffman's analyses focus on what she calls *surface acting,* that is, the kind of acting that is performed before an audience, implying that the performer acts for the benefit of the audience. Surface acting thus involves the management and control of (emotional) expressions in social situations, but this management, Hochschild argues, does not go below the surface of the individual. In Hochschild's view, then, Goffman did not concern himself with the ways that individuals actually control their feelings and how social situations constrain this feeling control. Addressing this alleged shortcoming in Goffman's work, Hochschild proposes the term *deep acting* for describing the process by which individuals control or induce feelings in themselves and act according to these feelings. In this view, individuals may manipulate their own emotions in order to act "authentically" in social situations. This is, however, not entirely an internal project, as individuals' emotions must be aligned with the social norms and conventions applying to the social situation. Hochschild (1983) termed these situational emotional scripts *feeling rules,* as they induce a sense of obligation that guides the emotion work. Moreover, Hochschild has followed Goffman's ideas on interactional power asymmetries in exploring how considerations of feelings are unequally distributed in society, as people of lower social status are often expected to manage their emotions, especially in their contacts with people of higher status. And what is more, she has shown how such asymmetries are often integrated parts of jobs in the service industry:

> When rules about how to feel and to express feelings are set by management, when workers have weaker rights to courtesy than customers do, when deep and surface acting are forms of labor to be sold, and when private capacities for empathy and warmth are put to corporate uses, what happens to the way a person relates to her feelings or to her face? When worked-up warmth becomes an instrument of service work, what can a person learn about herself from her feelings? (Hochschild, 1983, p. 89)

Expanding on Goffman's ideas, Hochschild thus demonstrates how feelings and emotions may be commercialized and sold as commodities and how such use of feelings reflects societal hierarchies and places the heaviest burdens of emotion work on people in subordinate positions.

Conclusion

Concluding this chapter, it can be said that key themes and insights from Erving Goffman's work have inspired a number of social thinkers and sociological theory builders. Goffman's sociological legacy is thus revitalized and cultivated by prominent members of the social science community, of which a selection have been brushed over in this chapter. Goffman himself lived long enough to witness how several of his students, including Harvey Sacks and Emmanuel Schegloff from the time at Berkeley, earned international acclaim (Collins, 1985, p. 216), while a number of other Goffman-inspired theory constructions have been published since his death in 1982. A clear strand of Goffmanian thought is found in the works of another Goffman student, Randall Collins, who most evidently illustrated his indebtedness to Goffman in his works on emotions and social stratification (Collins, 1990) and in his theory of so-called interaction ritual chains (Collins, 2004). In the latter, which may indeed be regarded as a contribution to a ritual theory within the "sociology of emotions" (Summers-Effler, 2007), Collins draws extensively on Goffman's (and Durkheim's) conception of ritual in building his theory of "momentary encounters among human bodies charged up with emotions and consciousness because they have gone through chains of previous encounters" (Collins, 2004, p. 3). Adopting from Goffman a focus on moments (situations) rather than their men, Collins advances a theory of interaction rituals that makes visible the conditions that determine the things that happen in social situations (Collins, 2004, p. 9). Collins's theory of interaction ritual chains is a theory of social dynamics. Its central mechanism is that in social occasions with high levels of intersubjectivity, emotional entrainment produces emotional energy, and in some of these moments (those with a high degree of ritual intensity), old social structures are torn up while new ones come into shape (Collins, 2004, p. 42).

Finally, it is worth mentioning that although critically assessing some of Goffman's fundamental constructs (that we are emotional creatures seeking recognition in interpersonal encounters), another contemporary sociological theorist, Jonathan H. Turner (2002), adopts several constructs from Goffman's microsociology in exploring the embeddedness of social interaction in the development of his sociological theory of interpersonal behavior. Turner's main ambition in this work is to present a grand theory of the microdynamics of interpersonal behavior, and in pursuing this task, he builds a conceptual base founded on the works of George Herbert Mead, Sigmund Freud, Alfred Schutz, Émile Durkheim, and Goffman. Turner's first step in unfolding his theory is an exploration of the sociocultural embeddedness of human interaction. According to Turner, sociologists have yet not "adequately conceptualized the structures and cultural systems in which encounters are embedded" (Turner, 2002, p. 27), and in addressing this issue, Turner conceptualizes the dynamics of sociocultural embeddedness by elaborating on Goffman's model of social interaction. Thus, he adopts from Goffman the conception that human encounters are lodged in various institutional systems and domains, each of which contain structures and cultures that impose themselves on human interactions. By way of Goffman, then, Turner develops the idea of "normatizing of encounters," which denotes "the point at which cultural systems impose constraints on the symbolic dynamics of the encounter" (Turner, 2002, p. 47).

Closing up, it needs mentioning that Goffman's intellectual influence is also apparent in a multitude of empirical studies. Goffmanian concepts and perspectives are applied in analyses of the protests of the underprivileged against unreasonable working and living conditions in India (Oommen, 1990), the identity formation of American baseball players (Adler & Adler, 1989), the orchestration of funeral ceremonies (Turner & Edgley, 1976), interaction rituals and etiquette among cancer patients in a Norwegian hospital ward (Album, 1996), and desexualization of the female body in connection with pelvic examination (Henslin & Biggs, 1978), to mention but a few.

Questions

- In what way is contemporary sociology particularly indebted to the works of Erving Goffman?
- How is Erving Goffman's sociology similar to and different from the various types of sociology of emotions in contemporary sociology?
- What kinds of theoretical issues and empirical issues may benefit from Erving Goffman's perspective?

9

The Legacy of Erving Goffman

As shown throughout the preceding chapters, Goffman left behind a substantial as well as a stylistic legacy to sociology and related disciplines. His substantial contribution consisted in conceptually carving out—with great detail and originality—a realm of social life titled the "interaction order," according to him deserving of analysis in its own right. Moreover, his writings on performance, stigma, total institutions, self, and framing have also left an impact and proven to be of lasting importance. His stylistic legacy consisted of an unmistakable Goffmanesque and exquisite methodological style that, among other tricks of the trade, comprised such writing and rhetorical techniques as irony and sarcasm, essayism, metaphors, and abductive reasoning (see, e.g., Atkinson, 1989). Goffman's legacy was inspired by a variety of classical social thinkers and traditions such as Émile Durkheim, Georg Simmel, the early Chicago sociologists, American pragmatism, ethology, existentialism, and the work of Norbert Elias. Moreover, Goffman's own ideas also went on to inspire as well as provoke many contemporary social thinkers, among them, for example, Anthony Giddens, Jürgen Habermas, Niklas Luhmann, Pierre Bourdieu, Thomas J. Scheff, Arlie R. Hochschild, Randall Collins, Jonathan H. Turner, and Judith Butler. That Goffman would leave the discipline with such a treasure trove of insights is rather surprising taking his consistently pursued outsider position into consideration. Perhaps this is one of the main reasons his work remains so alive and kicking within the social sciences. As Thomas Scheff suggested: "Since there don't seem to be any new Goffman on the horizon, perhaps we all need to practice his art of deconstructing taken-for-granted assumptions in social science. . . . To be as effective as Goffman, we need to be marginal persons, like him" (Scheff, 2003, p. 66). As we have shown earlier in this book, Goffman was indeed a marginal person, a maverick.

Goffman's Legacies

The main strength of Erving Goffman's sociology was its ability to spot and to refine the analysis of that which heretofore no one else seemed to take any serious notice of. Throughout all of his career, he had a keen eye and an incisive sensitivity toward seeing the meaningful and important in the apparently trivial and unnoticed features of everyday situations. We want to suggest that from Goffman's writings, some rules or procedures about how to approach and conduct social research can be extracted that may inspire coming generations of sociologists. Overall, we see Goffman as an exponent of some sort of "creative sociology" (Kristiansen, 2000) that critically deconstructed many taken-for-granted assumptions about social research, as the following propositions will show.

Sociology beyond induction and deduction. Sociological research can draw upon either inductive or deductive approaches to knowledge construction. This means that general insights are either generated through intensive empirical studies of concrete and unique single cases from which knowledge (theories or typologies) is then abstracted and generalized (data shapes the model) or that research contains a deductive dimension through which theories are tested against empirical findings at the same time as social reality is simultaneously tested against existing theories and models that are imposed on this reality (the model shapes data). In Goffman's work, the inductive approach, which can already be glimpsed in his PhD thesis, is not a strictly formalized or systematic procedure as that of grounded theory (Glaser & Strauss, 1967). Goffman's induction is much more intuitive, open ended, and searching. The deductive approach is mostly prevalent in Goffman's general use of metaphors and particularly in *The Presentation of Self in Everyday Life*, in which he already in the book's preface informs the reader that a specific and catch-all metaphor will be imposed on the social reality he investigates (Goffman, 1959, p. 9). With his metaphorically inspired work, Goffman actually transcended the conventionally closely guarded boundary between induction and deduction. Borrowing an expression from Richard Harvey Brown (1976, p. 171), we may say that Goffman performs a "metaphorical redescription of the explanandum," meaning of the empirical phenomenon he wanted to explain. If we accept this proposition, then it follows that Goffman's metaphorical redescription and perspectivism should be sought exclusively in neither the inductive nor the deductive approaches but rather in the abductive approach. The idea of **abduction**, as defined by pragmatist philosopher Charles Sanders Peirce (1979), proposes that scientific discovery (which means the generation of new knowledge) follows its own logical steps, and these steps cannot be understood as either (statistically probable) induction or as (theoretically necessary) deduction, but rather as abduction, which entails qualified guesswork and analogous reasoning, which can be either verified or falsified through further investigation (Brent, 1993). Peirce's argument—which Goffman in parts of his work seemed to follow—is that the creation of new knowledge does not occur only through conventional inductive or deductive procedures (at times referred to as contexts of "discovery" and "justification") but that researchers making new discoveries start out abductively and then subsequently make use of inductive and deductive approaches (see Jacobsen, 2014).

Theory as conceptual discovery. Sociological research and theory construction does not as its goal (necessarily) aim at presenting a complete, comprehensive, and static theory but is rather a constantly concept-testing process. Concepts must continuously be proposed, corroborated, or rejected, revised, redefined, and reintegrated in an ongoing constant confrontation with new data. Goffman constantly confronted his own concepts with data material from a variety of sources and saturated his metaphors with data in order to reach the limitation for their descriptive and explanatory potential. Goffman thus supplemented his dramaturgical metaphor with the ritual metaphor, because it explored aspects of the human encounter left out by the dramaturgical metaphor (e.g., the moral character of social life building on care and trust). Data collection, the development of concepts and hypotheses, and the discovery of theory take place synchronically in one smooth process that seeks to capture the changing, ambiguous, and complex character of social reality. By this we do not mean to suggest that such a strategy cannot lead to the formulation of an integrated (or even grand) theory but only that it fundamentally is more concerned with viewing research as an ongoing and searching process, stretching out and seeking to understand, rather than as a set of rigid and stepwise procedures claiming a tight grip on reality. Greg Smith once observed in a footnote that "cumulative theory construction was never part of Goffman's expressed agenda (which is not to deny that his ideas might contribute to general theory)" (Smith, 1999b, p. 17). True, Goffman's ambition was—as a sociological incarnation of Aristotle or Linnaeus or, in the apt words of Peter K. Manning (1980, p. 253), as a "diabolical taxonomist"— rather to propose and develop an impressive arsenal of classificatory and analytical concepts that could help set a sluggish sociological imagination in motion. We want to repeat and stress that Goffman's project consisted in understanding the depths of social interaction and that his books and essays should therefore be seen as attempts at approaching and conceptualizing a new and independent area of sociological investigation: the "interaction order." Such a project called for an intuitive and searching approach, and although one, in Georg Simmel's well-chosen words, would never "be completely satisfied upon a basis of vague instinctive treatment of details, yet science would be condemned to sterility if, in presence of new tasks, a completely formulated methodology were the condition of taking the first step" (Simmel, 1909, p. 309). Throughout his work, Goffman argued that what we see on the surface is not all of reality, and we may only get a deeper understanding of the many layers of reality by describing them from different—sometimes tentative and sketchy—perspectives. Even though many of his concepts and metaphors evade conventional validation procedures, they nevertheless represent, as heuristic, exploratory, and hypothesis-generating devices, a significant scientific contribution.

Comparative sociology. Sociological research is comparative in the sense that it seeks to identify and infer general features across many and often quite different social situations. The comparative method is typically understood as the comparison of cases or units and is primarily known from comparative studies of nation-states or organizations. When Goffman's books abound with detailed descriptions of social encounters, it is not because he was interested in these encounters in themselves but rather because he, based on these often varied situations, wanted to discover the resources, competences, and procedures individuals in general draw on and use in order to make face-to-face situations succeed. In a similar vein, like the principles of Barney Glaser and Anselm Strauss's (1967, pp. 101–115) "constant comparative method" from their grounded theory methodology, Goffman was also searching for the similarities among many (at least on the surface) different social situations, groups, and phenomena. The comparative aspect of his approach consists in his detailed comparison of these many examples in order to articulate transversal and formal concepts. At the same time, this comparative procedure functions as a sort of concept modifier, because new findings constantly test the existing concepts. In Goffman's last text—his undelivered presidential address—he argued that the study of social interaction must break away from the misleading preconception that urban life is fundamentally different from rural life, that public behavior is fundamentally different from private behavior, and that the interaction between strangers fundamentally differs from the interaction between close friends:

After all, pedestrian traffic rules can be studied in crowded kitchens as well as in crowded streets, interruption rights at breakfast as well as in courtrooms, endearment vocatives in supermarkets as well as in the bedroom. If there are differences here along the traditional lines, what they are still remains an open question. (Goffman, 1983a, p. 2)

The quotation captures how Goffman worked in a comparative, case-by-case manner that sought to identify and define those interactional parameters that are common to human face-to-face situations across many different social contexts (Drew & Wootton, 1988b, p. 8).

An amphibological sociology of social synergies. Sociological research must seek to discover and preserve what Norwegian sociologist and philosopher Dag Østerberg (1993, p. 110) termed the "amphibological" about social situations. This implies that sociologists should focus on the forms of social interaction that are neither grounded in instrumental-rational action nor circumscribed by transindividual motives but seek to incorporate both at the same time. One must, in other words, on the one hand avoid the traps of a purified action-individualism, in which the shape of social situations can be reduced to the motives and intentions of individual participants, and, on the other hand, steer clear of the pitfalls of functionalism, claiming the preexistence of a "social body" with an independent, collective, and constraining conscience different from that of individual actors. It was this duality or "amphibological" character of many of the face-to-face interactions in everyday life that Goffman attempted to capture through, on the one side, dramaturgical-game theoretical metaphors and, on the other side, his ritual- and trust-based metaphor. By way of these often incommensurable metaphors, Goffman indicated that the human encounter contains both strategic and instrumental-rational aspects as well as ritual and normative dimensions and that social life consists of action-individual as well as transindividual motives. Goffman's proposition that a synergy effect is created in the social meeting between two or more people points in the same direction. This *unio mystico*, as Goffman called it, is a form of social trance in which the spontaneous and shared involvement of participants contributes to the integration of the situation (Goffman, 1967, p. 113). A central point here is that the situation is integrated, succeeds, or even becomes euphoric and ecstatic not because participants intentionally want to involve themselves spontaneously in such a way but rather because they impulsively and unthinkingly are carried along and in some kind of "social unself-consciousness" give in to the situation (Goffman, 1953b, p. 244). According to Goffman, social situations have a certain binding or hypnotic effect, and it is our prereflexive, impulsive, and spontaneous involvement and immersion in them that makes them—at least most of the time—succeed. In the meeting or encounter, there is thus a preconscious, nonindividual, and momentarily shared motivation between participants, and it is this peculiar aspect that sociologists need to take seriously. First, it is therefore important to understand that social situations are constituted and carried forward by motives and intentions that cannot be reduced to identifiable individuals but, as it were, exist in the air between them. Second, when people are united with each other in social situations, this is not necessarily because they aim at integrating themselves into a commonly shared and maintained world, in which the boundaries between their own motives and those of others are blurred (Østerberg, 1993, p. 100) but because people qua their social nature orient themselves toward others and allow themselves to be carried along in a shared coordination project.

Sociology beyond ideology. Sociological research must always seek to strike a delicate balance between distanced or disinterested observation on the one hand and social engagement or political sympathies on the other. Sociology parading as too distanced and disinterested risks rendering itself irrelevant, whereas sociology embracing political ideology or social activism ends up diluting or even betraying its own scientific potential. It is well known that traditionally, sociology has often been associated with liberal or left-wing political observations. As Howard S. Becker once famously testified, "It is no secret that most sociologists are politically liberal to one degree or another.... We usually take the side of the underdog; we are for Negroes and against Fascists" (Becker, 1967, p. 244). This was also—and perhaps particularly—the case during Goffman's lifetime. Anyone seeking to find support for specific political ideas in the work of Goffman, however, will search in vain. Like many positivists of his time, Goffman was politically "unmusical," at least in his sociological self-presentation, if by "politics" is meant normative prescriptions regarding the desired constitution of society. In his writings, Goffman remained clinically apolitical and even seemed to find pleasure in joking about his lack of convictions. For example, William A. Gamson quotes a story of how someone had once asked Goffman about his politics: "[Goffman] seemed momentarily taken aback by the question. 'My "politics"?' (pause), 'I don't think I have any "politics."'" (Another pause). 'If anything, anarchist'" (Gamson, 1985, p. 605). Goffman's "politics," if understood as his personal sympathies or worldview, were those—as so many other students of symbolic interaction, deviance, and other morally debatable topics in those days—of an open-minded and tolerant man. Goffman never saw himself as a spokesperson for any political movement or aired macropolitical visions, and Marshall Berman noted on Goffman's increasing political silence in the heydays of student revolt, racial riots, and antiwar demonstrations: "Although Goffman's works articulate the sensibility of the 1960s, his voice grew suddenly, strangely still just around the time the real action began" (Berman, 1972/2000, p. 267). But as books such as *Asylums* (1961) and *Stigma* (1964a) clearly indicate, Goffman was far from unsympathetic to the plight of mental patients, deviants, and underdogs. Gamson thus went on humorously to suggest how, "in the eternal hunt, Goffman ran with the hares" (Gamson, 1985, p. 605). Goffman's view on power and politics was therefore much more "bottom up," with an emphasis on how the less powerful—in institutional and noninstitutional settings—resist surveillance and stigmatization and create a meaningful and viable sense of self (Alaszewski & Manthorpe, 1995, p. 39). In a microsociological and micropolitical sense he was thus a very sensitive person—far from the politics concerned with state deficits, war campaigns, poverty, racial inequality, or nuclear disarmament. As Goffman teasingly declared in one of his books—especially aimed at those believing that social science should work as a vehicle for political purposes or serve as an alarm clock for the development of critical consciousness:

> He who would combat false consciousness and awaken people to their true interests has much to do, because the sleep is very deep. And I do not intend here to provide a lullaby but merely to sneak in and watch the way people snore. (Goffman, 1974, p. 14)

As Goffman elegantly showed in his own work, to write about sensitive topics such as stigma, institutionalization, deviance, and other latently or manifestly political matters without falling prey to sympathetic statements or political declarations is indeed possible, and perhaps his blatant, almost flaunting apolitical observance contributed to his continued relevance within contemporary studies of underdogs, minorities, and the downtrodden. Being apolitical, as Goffman's work demonstrated, does not amount to being without conscience or concern or without analytical depth and sophistication, but it requires that the sociologist be ready to acknowledge that the task of social science is to generate knowledge (and indeed also and perhaps preferably innovative, thought-provoking, counterintuitive, and even dangerous and disliked knowledge), not to provide ideological gunfire for political campaigns.

Goffman's Problems

There was little doubt about Goffman's genius and his gift for writing interesting, witty, and thought-provoking sociology. However, Goffman was not equally popular in all camps or circles of academic life. Everett C. Hughes, Goffman's teacher at the University of Chicago, in a book review testified to the potential for opposition against Goffman's observations and revelations of some of the most intimate aspects of human life:

> Observation of this measure of intensity is indeed a threat to the face of the observed subjects, if they are moral beings. Laden with guilty embarrassing knowledge, Goffman saves the face of all who are content to let themselves be considered normal, fallible human beings. Those who cannot take his analysis are no doubt tempted to do away with him. (Hughes, 1969, p. 426)

Goffman was not good at dealing with criticism—either he seemed to ignore it or, in a few instances, provided comprehensive and biting counter-replies. One of these latter instances occurred when Norman K. Denzin and Charles Keller (1981) in the early 1980s critically assessed his position and perspective. Goffman carefully commented on their understanding of his work in an extended, sophisticated, and irascible reply (Goffman, 1981b). Robin Williams aptly summarized the whole situation:

> Quite apart from [Goffman's] dissatisfaction with their understanding and description of the details of that particular book [*Frame Analysis*], two additional characteristics of the essay earned his special disapprobation. First, their tendency to treat his work as a substantive whole, a collection of studies structured so as to constitute a unity of effort, able to be characterized by some algorithm, reference to which would permit an understanding of work accomplished and prediction of work yet to come. Second, their desire to locate his work within some definable "tradition," "school" or "paradigm," the more easily to evaluate the nature of its contribution to modern sociology. Both of these tendencies he saw to be more regrettable, representing to him a colourless pedagogical interest in the discipline rather than a lively engagement with its practice and products. (Williams, 1983, p. 99)

Despite Goffman's own reluctance to give in or accede to some of the criticism raised against his ideas, several critical or inquisitive points can be, have been, and should indeed be raised against Goffman's work. Here we will merely mention three points of criticism.

Situational limitation. Goffman once provocatively stated about the nature of his own work: "I make no claim whatsoever to be talking about the core matters of sociology—social organization and social structure" (Goffman, 1974, p. 14). Indeed, Goffman's work—no matter how it is twisted and turned by either epigones or critics—*is* primarily microsociological. Although Norman K. Denzin has claimed that "those who are preoccupied with turning [Goffman's] theory into another micro-model perhaps do the discipline a disservice" (Denzin, 2002, p. 111), Goffman's ideas *were* indeed microsociological and have been subsequently used in microsociological contexts. This, however, does not mean that his ideas cannot be used for other analytical purposes, but their groundwork is microsociology. Anthony Giddens thus rightly observed how Goffman "deliberately avoided any sort of engagement with issues concerning the large scale or the long term" (Giddens, 1988, p. 251). In a more critical review, Alvin W. Gouldner once stated that Goffman's work is "a social theory that dwells on the episodic and sees life only as it is lived in a narrow interpersonal circumference, ahistorical and noninstitutional, an existence beyond history and society" (Gouldner, 1970, p. 379). Goffman himself also willingly admitted the limitations of his own microperspective when he—in one of his few interviews—stated:

> If you take a substantial institution like a mental hospital you could say that my treatment of the hospital was not seated in a historical perspective, nor, more damaging, did it deal much with the relationship between the mental hospital and the system of institutions of which it is an interdependent part. . . . That failure is a characteristic of what I do and a weakness of it, although that is not to say that anybody is doing it well. . . . I defend with no apology treating "small entities" as my subject matter. (Goffman in David, 1980, p. 7)

However, as mentioned, from this does not necessarily follow that Goffman's work might not have important implications for macroscale theorizing. As we saw in the preceding chapter, many contemporary social theorists—perhaps particularly those concerned with grand theory-building projects—have used parts of Goffman's ideas as important building blocks in their own abstract theorizing about modernity, society, class, communication, social change, gender, social order, and other predominantly macroscale phenomena.

We thus suggest that Goffman's work might fruitfully be played against or integrated with more macrosociological concerns. Let us provide an illustrative example. Few have addressed Goffman's implicit vision of social change—and the question remains if Goffman's largely situational microsociology is at all suitable for shedding light on the impact of some of the major social and cultural transformations. While some seem to point out that Goffman's stressing of the art of "impression management" in encounters and meetings supports the thesis of the rise of an "other-directed" personality type in modern society (Riesman, Glazer, & Denney, 1953/2001) obsessively concerned with the validation of self from others (Zussman, 2001), others have rather seen Goffman as a protagonist of the rise of recognition claims and reciprocal courtesies in contemporary polite society (Jacobsen, 2010b; Jacobsen & Kristiansen, 2009). Yet others, Marshall Berman for one, in his review of *Relations in Public* published in the *New York Times* in 1972, attempted to look beyond Goffman's somewhat stationary view and saw some disturbing signs for the future of society in his depictions of social relations:

> If this is so, it forces us to face some disturbing questions about the break-throughs of the sixties. For so many Americans these were years of unprece-dented personal expression and political confrontation. In every sphere, we "refused to keep our place," we broke boundaries, tore down walls, acted out what we felt, encouraged others to do the same. And where are we now? Goffman's final vision seems unrelievedly bleak. Life in the streets appears as a Hobbesian nightmare, life in the family an existential battleground. It seems terrifying both to go out and to stay in. And social life turns out to be far more fragile, more vulnerable than we thought. (Berman, 1972/2000, p. 276)

American sociologist Lauren Langman followed Berman's lead and suggested that:

> Goffman's analyses of self-presentations and interaction rituals of everyday life, strategies of winning interpersonal and material games in the context of a cul-ture of consumption, inform the nature of modern alienation. . . . Commodified self-presentations and interaction rituals often can be seen as expressions of alienated selfhood, characteristic of today. (Langman, 1992, pp. 108–109)

The question thus arises if these sinister views of a "commodified" and "alienated" life and the "Hobbesian nightmare," which Langman and Berman spotted in Goffman's microsociological writings, can be substanti-ated by real-life, macroscale events. Some signs point in a direction that may support Berman's and Langman's bleak readings of Goffman—for example, how we apparently and increasingly have come to live in a society of the spectacle obsessed with surface identities, staged impressions, and shallow images (e.g., on Facebook, Twitter, and reality-TV shows), how "life in the streets" may appear more dangerous than ever before (e.g., due to increas-ing crime rates, the threat of terrorism, and a concomitant tendency to become part of moral panics), and how many of the certainties and securi-ties that guided generations before have now been either demolished or diluted (e.g., due to globalization and financial crises)—while many other developments admittedly point in quite the opposite direction.

Despite several attempts to read into Goffman's writings hidden political statements, critical potentials, or diagnostical tendencies of a more general or macroscale nature, it is, however, important to recognize that Goffman never ventured into presenting a timeless or universal model of social life, nor did he want to present a diagnosis of the times or a critical social theory. His aspirations were—some would say more modestly, others more ambitiously— to provide the discipline of sociology with a conceptual apparatus and a focused gaze with which to capture and comprehend those microaspects of social life, which until then had seemed either unimportant or incomprehensible. So contrary to, for example, Michel Foucault, who, armed with his archaeology of knowledge and genealogy, studied institutions—the prison and the clinic and indeed society as such as a "generalized prison"—in a historical context focusing on changing power relations, discourses, games of truth, and regimes of knowledge, Goffman was content to provide a much more situational, inside view of the "interaction order" existing within the mental hospital without turning it into a grand narrative of modernity or civilization (Hacking, 2004)—although he insisted that the traits of the "total institution" might also be found in as diversified settings as schools, army barracks, and concentration camps.

What Goffman thus perhaps lacked in regard to analyzing macrosocial change and structural transformations he more than compensated for with his well-developed sense for descriptive detail and colorful and catching concepts when analyzing the intricacies and minutiae of microsocial settings. Thus, as Robin Williams boldly observed in an obituary tribute to Goffman, his work met "the most important requirements of modern social theory—to be self-conscious about the meaning of what it is to know" (Williams, 1983, p. 102). What Goffman wanted to investigate and obtain knowledge about was the "interaction order" and its contours, components, and content as an analytical microdomain in its own right.

Lack of systematic scientific methodology. As shown in Chapter 3, Goffman was critical of much of the conventional research methodology and techniques taught and practiced during his lifetime, perhaps particularly because these "abstracted empiricists"—C. Wright Mills's (1959) term for quantitative sociologists—believed that the truth about social life was apparently to be found in the methods used to capture, measure, or understand it. According to many critics, however, Goffman's own methodology lacked much of what would normally be expected of scientific work and what would be taught to most sociology students in their first year at university: replication, generalization, validation, or qualified discussions with existing work within one's research area and so on. Goffman's methods admittedly suffered from some of the same problems as did those of many other qualitative researchers—that their work is subjected to an evaluative terminology and stance derived from quantitative studies. True, Goffman was never good at telling his readers how his findings were necessarily obtained, how he arrived at certain analytical points, or how far his conclusions could be stretched. As to the question of the scientific quality of Goffman's own work, it has been proposed:

> Goffman is also much misunderstood, or perhaps misapprehended would be better, since to judge from many of the critical commentaries on him, he strikes some people as shallow, without significance, his work espousing a cynical attitude towards human nature, as well as being overly dependent on non-sociological sources and findings. It is thought to be "impressionistic," riven by problems of inference and validity, and by no means a contribution to the development of an "objective" social science. The primary test of this inadequacy is the sheer impossibility of replication. Goffman's contributions are unique, and illuminating and insightful, though they might be, in the end, unscientific. (Anderson, Hughes, & Sharrock, 1985, p. 144)

No doubt, Goffman's methodology *was* different—indeed impressionistic, alternative, alternate, and, last but not least, unarticulated. This made him vulnerable during a time when sociology struggled hard to obtain the much-desired status as an actual (meaning exact and "hard" science). During this period, Polish sociologist Stanislav Andreski observed how "the worshippers of methodology turn like a vicious hunting pack upon anybody branded as impressionistic, particularly if he writes well and can make his books interesting" (Andreski, 1972, p. 117). This is indeed an apt description of what perhaps happened to Goffman. Compared to the large-scale, collaborative, government-funded, quantitative studies collecting heaps of systematically sampled survey-based information from thousands of respondents and conducting sophisticated, computer-assisted statistical correlations on the material, his work—often consisting of hunches, small-scale observations, idiosyncratic cases, dubious data material, and catchy concepts—was destined to be labeled unscientific. However, his methodology was far from unscientific. True, his methodology—particularly the metaphors—straddled the artistic and the scientific genres, but Goffman's work should not be evaluated according to strict quantitative or statistical criteria. It was a completely different ballgame. We do, however, propose two warning indicators regarding Goffman's unconventional methodology.

First, the use of metaphors as sociological sources of explanation implies a risk of mistaking affinity for identity (Burke, 1984, p. 97). This metaphorical fallacy consists in taking metaphors too seriously. Goffman would no doubt insist that sociological knowledge can never be true, by which he would mean as an objective mirroring of social reality. In his view, sociological knowledge is always knowledge produced and conceived from a certain perspective—there is no view from nowhere—and sociological analysis is necessarily always limited or influenced by the perspective of the sociologist. This circumstance, however, does not detract from the fact that the metaphorical methodology proposed and employed by Goffman to a large degree leaves the reader in the dark regarding the question of the actual character of the concepts. Are they to be regarded as primitive and relatively loose suggestions, or are they rather more systematically developed analytical constructs (Manning, 1976, p. 21)? Goffman's metaphorical methodology makes it possible to discover aspects of reality that were previously hidden or incoherent, but at the same time there is a tendency to blur the transition from or the dividing line between loose hypotheses and well-founded ideal types. This was perhaps also what Goffman attempted to express when he wrote that "all the world is not, of course, a stage, but the crucial ways in which it isn't are not easy to specify" (Goffman, 1959, p. 78).

Second, the scientific abstraction of the complexity of the social world into simplified concepts necessitates considerations about the relationship between the concepts of sociology and those of everyday life. Alfred Schutz (1970) introduced a separation between "first-order concepts" (the concepts used by ordinary people to describe and make sense of their everyday life) and "second-order concepts" (the researcher's interpretations of those first-order concepts). A sociology aimed at generating theoretical knowledge about people's lives must necessarily invoke questions about how the second-order concepts of the sociologist relate to the first-order concepts of the people studied. In other words, the proposed relationship between the abstracted concepts of the sociologist and the phenomena of everyday life that they are supposed to replace or recapitulate must be clarified. Typically Goffman, regarding this point, remained enigmatically silent. In his work the reader will find no explicit answers, on the one hand, whether, if, and how the content of sociological theories transcends the consciousness of the people studied and thus must be formulated by the professionally trained sociologist, or, on the other hand, if and how generalized social facts are actually constructed by actors at the microlevel of social reality, which would obviate any notion of a "transcendental macroworld." Even though it is possible between the lines in Goffman's work to detect a certain predilection for Émile Durkheim's (1982) theory of "social facts" (which for all intents and purposes not only exert coercive constraint on social situations but are also external to the consciousness of the individual and may thus only be known or unearthed by the almighty sociologist), he never gave any instruction as to how sociological concepts relate to those phenomena of everyday life that they purport to encapsulate and conceptualize (Sharrock, 1999, pp. 121–122). When Goffman thus avoided explicit discussions of

what Derek Layder (1998) refers to as the "concept–indicator link," he, in
fact, skipped the important discussion of how the researcher at different
levels adequately documents and secures the relationship between his theory
and data.

Amorality of the actor. All sociological theories—implicitly or explicitly—
contain an image of man as a so-called "cognitive apriori" (Bauman, 1967)
that to a large degree determines many other facets of the theory such as the
understanding of structure, action, intention, power, responsibility, rationality, morality, and the like. In Chapter 6, we extendedly delineated and discussed Goffman's notion of the individual or "the self." As was obvious,
Goffman was not always clear about how he specifically understood people—
at times they were depicted as players, conmen, or performers preoccupied
with their own impression management, at other times as ritual and ceremonial beings celebrating and defending a "cult of the individual," at yet other
times as spies, private eyes, or manipulators concerned with disclosing or
revealing information about self and others. Goffman insisted that "universal human nature is not a very human thing" (Goffman, 1967, p. 45), which
may be one of the main reasons he resisted specifying the interior or mental
makeup of people. He did not want to psychologize the self. To him, the self
was ostensibly nothing but a dramatic effect in the eyes of the beholder
rather than something people could lay claim to. However, a common
(mis)conception—no doubt due to the widespread reception and reading of
The Presentation of Self in Everyday Life (1959)—among many Goffman
interpreters has been that Goffman primarily expounded a Machiavellian,
amoral, cynical, shallow, and strategic image of man (see, e.g., Brittan, 1973;
Gouldner, 1970; Habermas, 1984; Hollis, 1977; Lyman & Scott, 1970). As,
for example, Martin Hollis asserted,

> Goffman's actor is not in the altruistic business of investing effort and ingenu-
> ity for the benefit of later "selves" just like him. He is working for himself, to
> preserve and foster what is strictly himself from one time and one role to
> another. (Hollis, 1977, p. 103)

This image of man as a hypocrite hiding behind many masks, theatrical
performances, exquisite props, and elaborate self-presentations is, however,
neither accurate nor exhaustive. Goffman's many different metaphors—
and particularly the ritual metaphor with its focus on care and respect—
revealed that his view of man was much more nuanced and that there was
in fact also room for the moral, benevolent, and altruistic individual in his
writings (Smith, 1988, p. 118). Norman K. Denzin defended Goffman's
way of presenting his human subjects by indicating that he equally avoided

the (at the time of his writing) prevalent pitfalls of functionalists' oversocialized conceptions of the individual on the one hand, and, on the other, the undersocialized conception of human beings from behaviorist studies:

> Midcentury American sociology required a sociologist like Goffman. Perhaps we all got what we deserved when we started taking him seriously. He put a human face on the sociological subject. He gave life, meaning and purpose to the faceless human being that functionalists and exchange theorists wrote about. He brought nuance and moral meaning to the interaction order. (Denzin, 2002, p. 106)

Goffman's trick consisted in constantly shifting the perspective on the human subject, never becoming too firmly fixed in any one image. Thus his different snapshots of the individual were not portraits but rather lenses used to capture an elusive target.

Many of these points of criticism listed obviously depend on who reads Goffman and for what particular purposes. Moreover, they undoubtedly had to do with Goffman's own reluctance to deal with criticism and the self-assertiveness of his work, which was poignantly summarized by Mark Wexler:

> If one remains silent, or mostly so, when attacked, and most believe you capable of an ardent defense, it is not unlikely that you will be perceived as an enigma. Contradictory views of your work will emerge. . . . Lend to the silence and exacerbate the enigma, Goffman does not provide his colleagues or readers with a map to his intellectual turf. . . . What is essential in Goffman's silence is that in formulating a passive form of authorship, Goffman incites the kind of uncertainty which requires that others—readers, conflicting theorists, admirers—actively propagate their perception of his work. (Wexler, 1984, pp. 41–42)

No doubt Goffman's enigmatic silence contributed to frustration among those who in his work sought clear-cut answers or doctrinal guidance, but the elusiveness of his work also stimulated an interpretative openness that secured continued discussion and guaranteed Goffman a posthumous spot among the immortals of his discipline.

Embattled Goffman

Most sociologists—and social scientists more generally—as part of their formal education are carefully trained in the fine and important art of classifying, subsuming, categorizing, placing, pigeonholing, and lumping together. Everything apparently fits neatly into its little categorical box. However, today sociologists are divided about where Goffman's writings belong.

Howard Schwartz and Jerry Jacobs thus once mused: "Goffman is fine, but how many Goffmans are there?" (Schwartz & Jacobs, 1979, p. 184). The short answer is apparently: many. In fact, there are not just many Goffmans—meaning many layers in Goffman's own writings—but also many readings and interpretations of Goffman around. Although N. G. Hartland (1994, p. 251) claimed that "it is difficult for social theorists and researchers to appropriate Goffman," after Goffman's death, the quest from almost any quarter of sociological theory to appropriate his legacy quickly intensified.

When Goffman died in 1982, he was known to be one of the most widely read sociologists in the world. This status also made his intellectual legacy particularly eligible to appropriation and monopolization by those of his successors who regarded Goffman as an iconic representative of or an intellectual forerunner to their own particular theoretical perspective. Consequently, there have been several attempts at appropriating Goffman and subsuming his ideas under the headings of specific academic camps, schools of thought, paradigms, or research traditions. As Greg Smith proposed as one of the main reasons for these "framing" exercises of Goffman's work: "Attempts to frame Goffman's sociology in terms of the major traditions and perspectives of sociology and the human sciences in part arise from the disturbance many readers experience when confronted with its evident singularity" (Smith, 1999a, p. 4). Perhaps Goffman even deserved it, as Polish sociologist Marek Czyżewski insightfully seemed to suggest: "Goffman has fallen into a situation he described himself: in the eyes of a wide circle of readers his personal identity has been constructed around fragmentary, selectively chosen pieces of information and quotations which serve as an 'identity peg'" (Czyżewski, 1987, p. 40).

It was, however, quite surprising that someone like Goffman, a maverick and loner, would leave such a contested legacy. As Thomas Luckmann observed on Goffman's status at the time of his death,

> [Goffman] was working in an area definitely not considered to be "socially significant"; and working in a manner which did not endear him to those others whose shibboleth in social science was not "significance" but "hard science." He seemed diffident, even uncertain and at the same time dryly sarcastic in manner; he was not attached to any influential clique of professional patronage, and he neither joined nor founded a marginal sect devoted to the propagation of the master's fame and mutual protection from outside evil. (Luckmann, 1985, p. 175)

Goffman thus never intended to leave behind a following of disciples or to establish a school of thought in his name. He was, and regarded himself as, a maverick. We agree with Ian Hacking, who noted that Goffman was "an independent spirit, impossible to classify" (Hacking, 2004, p. 292). Despite this, several sociological traditions have laid claim to Goffman, insisting that his work belonged to or embodied their particular perspective. Symbolic interactionists, pragmatists, postmodernists, ethnomethodologists, phenomenologists, existentialists, conversation analysts, Durkheimians, Simmelians, critical theorists, symbolic realists, social semioticians, and so on—all have attempted to include Goffman as part of their particular paradigm (see Jacobsen & Kristiansen, 2010). Despite these numerous appropriation attempts, Goffman—especially during his final years—resisted association with any paradigm, although acknowledging this as an inevitable part of the sociology game and a price to be paid for intellectual stardom:

> I appreciate that graduate students in sociology might have need for this ideological format (a need also for schools of thought and of "paradigms"), in order to show their examiner that they have sociological convictions and some sense of sociology as a field, and I appreciate that their instructors might have recourse to the same slogans in order to establish standing in the classroom. (Goffman, 1981b, p. 61)

As it is often the case in introductory textbooks, it would be relatively easy to place Goffman's sociological contribution among the pragmatists and symbolic interactionists in direct extension of the work of such prominent names as Robert E. Park, William I. Thomas, John Dewey, George Herbert Mead, Charles H. Cooley, and Herbert Blumer (Abraham, 1982; Bottomore & Nisbet, 1978). Others have seen Goffman as a microfunctionalist who consciously positioned himself within the lineage of Émile Durkheim's theories on everyday life as a ritual and the socially constructed world as a moral order (Collins, 1988b; Collins & Makowsky, 1993; Jacobsen, 2010b). In fact, Goffman took a hybrid position betwixt and between symbolic interactionist microsociology and Durkheimian macrosociology (Collins, 1985), between an interactionist and a functionalist position, because the ceremonies he investigated—contrary to those of Durkheim—were not large scale, formalized, or extraordinary, that created barriers to human action, but rather the all-too-ordinary rituals that permeate every aspect of our everyday lives. As a sociological institution, Goffman could therefore be seen as a copious parenthesis in the historical development of the discipline squeezed in between the heights of structural-functionalist abstraction and universalism in the 1940s and 1950s and the depths of cultural relativism and particularism from the sociologies of everyday life during the 1960s and 1970s.

We thus claim that Goffman occupied an interesting intermediary position in sociology. He turned his back on both the sociologistic and the psychologistic/existentialistic—in Edward Tiryakian's (1962) terms—camps and instead turned his attention to "where the action is," as he said, by which he, eloquently expressed, meant "a field for fateful dramatic action, a plane of being, an engine of meaning, a world in itself, different from all other worlds" (Goffman, 1972, p. 26). The time–place constellation "where the action is," according to Goffman, was identical to the universe of human copresence and interaction. Where functionalists, for instance, believed that society as such—as a unified entity and an overall social order—should be analyzed *sui generis*, in itself, with the disclosure of all the connection points between structures and their functions, Marxists, based on the notion that the economy in the last instance determines political and societal conditions, rather looked at the conflicts, chasms, and cracks in society, and phenomenologists and existentialists looked at the connections—and sometimes also disconnections—among consciousness, action, and society, Goffman instead believed that the task of sociology consisted in studying interaction *sui generis* (Goffman, 1983a; Rawls, 1987). Obviously, this idea reached back to the work of Georg Simmel and the early Chicago School in the 1920s and 1930s and to the studies of small-group dynamics conducted by, among others, George C. Homans and Kurt Lewin. However, as is evident from his last text, "The Interaction Order" (Goffman, 1983a), Goffman—as we saw— never gave voice to the same ideological concern, political engagement, or personal sympathy for his subjects as did so many other sociologists coming from these traditions. In fact, Goffman was much more distanced. One of Goffman's former students, Gary T. Marx, thus reports how "Goffman presented himself as a detached, hard-boiled intellectual cynic, the sociologist as 1940s private eye. His was a hip, existential, cool, essentially apolitical (at least in terms of the prevailing ideologies) style" (Marx, 1984, p. 653). Also in this sense, he was an outsider who calmly and objectively recorded social life. This made the inventors of the so-called sociology of the absurd— Stanford M. Lyman and Marvin B. Scott—comment on Goffman's vision of man: "Machiavelli's prince and Goffman's social actor have no interior specifications. Rather, situations specify them. . . . Man's success arises not from the presence or absence of humanity, but rather from the strategic employment of appearances" (Lyman & Scott, 1970, p. 20). In such a view, there is little room—or need—for incorporating an interest in unjust social conditions or internalized human habits, preferences, or predilections. The world can basically be boiled down to social situations, performance rituals, and strategic interactions.

When it comes to pinpointing or analyzing social problems, Goffman is therefore often depicted as a distanced, disinterested, and apolitical sociologist, or as a spokesperson for white, conservative, American, middle-class values. But is this a justified picture? Despite the fact that Goffman never explicitly aired political sympathies, no doubt he was politically conscious. His work exhibited a moderate and balanced form of political awareness, and according to American sociologist T. R. Young, "Goffman neither celebrates the priest nor castigates the prostitute" (Young, 1971, p. 276). In fact, during his studies, Goffman did uncover and report some disturbing conditions in mental hospitals and some heartbreaking stories about stigmatized people, but he never used this material for political purposes. His ideas thus contained the potency for activism but were never—at least from Goffman's own hands—forged into political programs or ideological outbursts. Goffman was apparently the distanced, cynical, and objective researcher who moved freely among the Shetland Island population, psychiatric patients, and dealers in a Las Vegas casino while carefully collecting intimate details about what they did. Michael Stein once proposed that "[Goffman's] own presentation of self leaves the audience enlightened and amused even as they are kept guessing as to what was really going on behind the many masks" (Stein, 1991, p. 432). In the end, perhaps the best way to describe and capture Goffman's academic self and legacy is to say that it was nothing but a "dramatic effect," to employ one of his own favorite expressions.

Conclusion

Although the years have passed and the book covers have faded, although the novelty and allure of the new and different have subsided, although some of the expressions now seem dated, and although some of the examples used (of phone booths, dinner table etiquette, saluting gestures, and so on) have long since been deemed passé by new social norms or outpaced by technological developments, Erving Goffman's work has still retained its vitality. We have listed some of the most important legacies left by him to his own and related disciplines, we have discussed certain points of criticism voiced against his work, and we have shown how various schools of thought and theoretical traditions have continuously struggled to frame (or rather reframe) and appropriate his ideas to become part of their own paradigmatic setup. So despite his status as a maverick, a loner, and an eccentric, Goffman left an ineradicable and influential mark on his discipline, his age, and his posterity. As David Elkind elegantly summarized:

> Despite his influence, Goffman is something of a maverick as an investigator. His anthropological methods (his use of his own field notes, newspaper and magazine clippings, quotes from novels and books of etiquette as data) are regarded by many workers as unscientific. Likewise, Goffman's tendency to overgeneralize, his failure to consider alternative interpretations and the

absence of indexes in his books set many social scientists' teeth on edge. Finally, his reputation as a loner and his skill at intellectual putdowns have not endeared him to all of his colleagues. And yet, the sheer brilliance of some of his interpretations, his genius at giving unity and conceptual integrity to a polyglot collection of behavioral flotsam and jetsam, have won him a unique place in American social science. (Elkind, 1975, pp. 25–26)

We believe that Erving Goffman continues to attract attention, to be interpreted, criticized, applied, appropriated, and imitated because what he did was basically interesting. Murray S. Davis once insisted that the notion of "the interesting" is reserved for that which constitutes "an attack on the taken-for-granted world of [its] audience" and involves "a certain movement of the mind of the audience" (Davis, 1971, pp. 311, 342). Was Goffman's work interesting? Indeed—his work critically deconstructed many deep-rooted truths in social science (about methodology, interaction, self, deviance, gender roles, and so on) and was acknowledged even by nonacademics as a refreshing and recognizable view of how the world of everyday life looked. Was it scientific? We believe so—if our notion of science is not unnecessarily narrowed down to a one-size-fits-all definition. Was it useful? Apparently so—taking into consideration the number of theoretical traditions and schools of thought trying to appropriate and capitalize on his work as well as the magnitude of the literature devoted to and the research drawing on his ideas. This latter point is the topic of the final chapter to follow.

Questions

- What were the main legacies Erving Goffman left to the discipline of sociology?
- What do you consider to be the most problematic aspects of Erving Goffman's work?
- Was Erving Goffman's work scientific—and what do we mean by applying the notion of "science" to the social sciences?
- How should we classify and categorize Erving Goffman's sociology—as symbolic interactionism, ethnomethodology, existentialism, phenomenology, dramaturgy, microfunctionalism, or other?

10

Further Readings

Throughout the years, many things have been written and said about Erving Goffman, many stories and snippets of gossip wander, many myths prevail, numerous pieces of recollection and remembrance are published by former students, colleagues, and friends, and a lot of labels and epithets have been suggested to capture his life and work. For example, Albert Bergesen (1984) once called Goffman a "world calibre American contribution to sociological theory," Randall Collins (1981a) termed him a "hero-anthropologist," an "explorer of our social unconscious," and a "theoretically oriented empiricist," Allen Grimshaw (1983) named him a "genuine original," Pierre Bourdieu (1983) shortly after Goffman's death described him as the "discoverer of the infinitely small," Paul Bouissac (1990) labeled him a "comedian-experimenter," while Alvin W. Gouldner (1970) characterized him as a "young turk." Apparently, Goffman was a man whom many different epithets fitted. Contrary to this publicity around Goffman as a sociologist, there is also a great silence surrounding Goffman as a private person. His family has vehemently resisted leaking information about Goffman to inquisitive researchers, journalists, or students as a way to avoid him becoming a commodity.

As we saw in the preceding chapter, Goffman left a legacy—a substantial as well as a stylistic legacy. He introduced the idea of the "interaction order" to sociology, he argued for the relevance of microstudies, he investigated everyday events as well as studied deviance, stigma, and institutionalization, and he developed a comprehensive argument for frame analysis. But perhaps most important of all, Goffman had a special gift of coining many concepts that are now household items in sociology and related disciplines.

Randall Collins once listed some of the most important contributions from Goffman's conceptual cornucopia:

> Face-work, deference and demeanor, impression management, and the presentation of self; frontstage and backstage, teams and team-work, discrepant roles; a typology of secrets: dark, strategic, inside, entrusted, and free; moral careers, total institutions, and ways of making out in them; commitment, attachment, embracement, engagement, and role distance; focused and unfocused interaction, face engagements, accessible engagements, situational proprieties and improprieties, and the tightness and looseness of situation rules; vehicular units and participation units; territories of the self; personal space, use space, turns, information and conversational preserves; territorial violations; markers and tie-signs; supportive interchanges (access rituals) and remedial interchanges (accounts, apologies, body gloss); frames, keyings, fabrications, frame-breaking and out-of-frame activity. (Collins, 1981a, p. 222)

Obviously, this list is just the tip of the iceberg. As Robin Williams—following Susan Jane Birrell's thorough work sorting out and indexing Goffman's many concepts developed and utilized throughout the years—points out, Goffman invented close to 1,000 concepts and neologisms (Williams, 1988, p. 88fn). The fact that Goffman coined so many colorful, useful, and almost immediately recognizable concepts is also one of the main reasons so many successors wanted to appropriate his name and ideas, as the preceding chapter showed. In this final chapter, we want briefly to discuss how our own reading of Goffman has proceeded and point to its merits and limitations. We also show how Goffman's work has continued to inspire studies and research within various disciplines and subdisciplines, and finally we provide some suggestions for further reading. Although Goffman may have left the building, he most surely has not left the surface of sociology.

Reading Goffman

Goffman was indeed different—perhaps even deviant (Posner, 1978, p. 72). As we have shown earlier, he thoroughly detested intellectual pigeonholing and vehemently resisted and opposed any attempt at placing his sociology within any one school of thought or theoretical tradition. He mixed, borrowed, imported, and toyed with insights from a variety of sources and theoretical traditions and in the process consciously blurred the dividing lines between different genres and disciplines with his own unique perspective. Goffman happily accepted—perhaps even encouraged—the view of him as a hybrid, a loner, a maverick. Even though we have provided this book with an introduction, which—as Goffman would have claimed—frames the following presentation, we have wished to resist the temptation to propose an authoritative version of how Goffman must necessarily be understood or read. Obviously, we subscribe to a specific view or perspective on Goffman, but our purpose with this book has been to present as open, sensitive, and unbiased a reading of Goffman as possible—a reading that aspires to show the many nuances, peel off the layers, and excavate the depths in his writings. In one of the few interviews Goffman ever agreed to do, he revealed to Jef C. Verhoeven:

> It seems to me that you can't get a picture of anyone's work by asking them what they do or by reading explicit statements in their texts about what they do. Because that's by and large all doctrine and ideology. You have to get it by doing a literary kind of analysis of the corpus of their work. . . . If you just take a person's version of what they do, you will end up with a very superficial view of what goes on. (Goffman in Verhoeven, 1993, p. 322)

We have taken this challenge seriously and have dug our way deep into Goffman's work in order to discover an idea of his project. This book thus opposes different research traditions' attempts at monopolizing or conquering Goffman and especially turns against what might be called the "Americanization of Goffman." A central characteristic of much American sociology—at least as opposed to much European social theory—has been the celebration and analytical privileging of the individual and the subjective at the expense of the social and the structural. This is deeply embedded within the libertarian and pragmatic traditions so prominent in the United States. By many, Goffman was therefore also read as an exponent of middle-class ideas or conservative values. However, Goffman in his work rather showed how subjectivity and self were always shrouded in social and contextual circumstances, and in many ways he was capable of, in paraphrasing Ernest Gellner (1975, p. 450), "re-enchanting subjectivity" (which according to Gellner was a trademark of Californian-style interactionism and ethnomethodology in the 1960s and 1970s) without it being at the expense of the social. Although his work is often associated with the wave of "creative sociologies" (Morris, 1977)—such as ethnomethodology, symbolic interactionism, dramaturgy, phenomenology, and the sociology of the absurd—that particularly emerged throughout the late 1960s and early 1970s, he never presented an image of the social world in which the individual was free floating, self-contained, and unconnected. If someone were to suggest that we with this book want to fob the reader off with a specific reading of Goffman, it is that he is most definitely not to be seen as a prophet of the isolated and atomized individual. In Goffman's writings, the individual is never alone—he or she is always engaged in some sort of interaction with others, whether focused or unfocused, whether dramaturgical, ritual, or strategic. In fact, the individual would not exist were it not for the fact that it is intimately connected with and woven, as it were, into social life. Goffman's contribution is thus thoroughly *sociological*, whereby we stress the social dimension of his depictions of interaction, the individual, norms, self-presentations, encounters, stigma, frames, deviance, manners, situations, strategies, and so on. Remember, as he himself once wrote: "Not men and their moments, but moments and their men" (Goffman, 1967, p. 3).

Beyond Goffman

Already before his death, it was observed how "there are no heirs apparent to Goffman's sociology, but there are numerous sociologists who have followed in his footsteps. . . . Goffman has inspired a new generation of sociologists" (Fontana, 1980, p. 76–77). More than a quarter of a century has now passed since Goffman's departure, and many new social, cultural, intellectual, and technological developments have taken place since his death. Just think of globalization (and with it increased mobility, trade, and tourism), the rise of the surveillance society, the invention and spreading of new information technologies, new scientific developments, new theoretical terminology appearing on the academic market, the coming, going, and rehashing of political ideologies, new ideals, values, and new norms, new forms of human togetherness and cohabitation, and so on. Sociology has always been a science consisting of a multitude of mutually competing and incommensurable, self-proclaimed and time-honored, constantly upcoming and perishing -isms. In the discipline of sociology, for example, new theoretical terrain has been covered by adherents of social constructivism, poststructuralism, neopragmatism, actor network theory, postcolonialism, third- and fourth-wave feminism, postmodernism, and the like. The world Goffman wrote about is no longer quite the same.

Such a long time has now passed since Goffman's death that he should almost be counted among the classics of sociology—a classic because he contributed to the discipline with invaluable insights into the specific time and age in which he and his contemporaries lived. However, he is also a "contemporary classic" because his work not only captured his own lifetime—his view was not locked in time and place—but also pointed to more fundamental and lasting features of human togetherness in face-to-face situations. In recent years, the utility and use of Goffman's work, his basic ideas and specific concepts, have expanded to a variety of different research areas. Much has indeed happened since two editors of a volume dedicated to Goffman in the late 1980s claimed that "there is a paucity of empirical research which actually picks up Goffman's 'golden shovel'" (Drew & Wootton, 1988b, p. 2). Some of the most important and unmistakable features of Goffman's work—despite being conceived within a specific sociocultural time and context (American society in the 1950s to the early 1980s) and within a specific academic discipline (sociology)—are perhaps its relative *timelessness*: its ability or invitation to be used even in times and places far from its point of origin—its *versatility*: its ability to be applied in connection to studies of areas far away from its original or intended use—and its *elasticity*: its ability to be stretched and angled to fit a vast variety of different situational settings, research programs, and theoretical perspectives. Whereas Goffman's own list of publications is fixed once and for all (unless some obscure unpublished or undiscovered material should suddenly appear), all lists of publications of secondary literature (see, e.g., Waksler & Psathas, 1989) are already deemed outdated and obsolete or at least incomplete when published because Goffman's work continues to be used and applied so many places around the world. This is particularly true in the age of Internet publishing, when so many new texts are poured out in torrential pace.

To provide a few illustrative examples of this proposed timelessness, versatility, and elasticity, Goffman's overall perspective as well as more specific conceptual apparatus can be and have been used in and on a variety of contexts including analyzing the dramaturgical dimension of the presidential campaigns of Bush versus Kerry (Brown, 2005), the impression management of members of the American power elite through display of their "public wives" (Gillespie, 1980), the delicate impression management and orchestration of conduct of funeral directors (Turner & Edgley, 1976), impression management at the Ritz-Carlton Hotel (Dillard, Browning, Sitkin, & Sutcliffe, 2000), the "cynical performances" of waitress-dancers in topless clubs (Sijuwade, 1995), the face work of kindergarten children (Hatch, 1987), the postexam impression management of "aces" and "bombers" (Albas & Albas, 1988), analyzing the relationship between humans and their companion pet animals (Sarmicanic, 2004) as well as other companion animals such as pigeons (Jerolmack, 2004), the identity work involved in obituary writing (Bonsu, 2007), interaction patterns among patients in a hospital setting (Album, 2010), legalized gambling (Cosgrave, 2008), the ethics of naturalistic observation among postgraduate students (McDonald, Higgins, & Shuker, 2008), collaborative interaction processes in elementary school mathematics (Brandt & Tatsis, 2009), attendees' experiences and emotions at staged events (Nelson, 2009), gender display in public places (Gardner, 1989), sport as ritual (Birrell, 1981), experiences in homes for older people in Slovenia (Mali, 2008), dramaturgical teaching exercises (Brown, 2003), the presentation of the political self in public life (Eliasoph, 1990), face saving and maintenance of social order in religious ceremonies (Donnelly & Wright, 2013), recovery from drug use (Neale, Nettleton, & Pickering, 2011), developing public relations theory (Johansson, 2007), international relations theory (Schimmelfennig, 2002), shame induction, shame management, and shame avoidance (Gardner & Gronfein, 2005), family life (Collett & Childs, 2009), corporate reputations and reports (White & Hanson, 2002), bodily communication (Heilman, 1979), the social experiences of driving while intoxicated convicts (Gonzales, 1993), stigmatization of families of children with severe medical problems (Carnevale, 2007), the gestural dynamics of modern selfhood (Handler, 2009), modern theology and religious practice (Boulton, 2001), the behavior of elite youth football coaches during games (Partington & Cushion, 2012), struggles between relatives and administrators in nursing homes (Richard, 1986), the impact of the "new individualism" on self and interaction (Branaman, 2010), the rise of a new interaction order both on the Internet and in our bodily movements in everyday traffic situations (Jenkins, 2010), and tenant–landlord conflicts (Borey, 2004). And Goffman's classic analysis of "gender advertisements" has now been updated, revised, and criticized many times since then (Belknap & Leonard, 1991; Bell & Milic, 2002; Kang, 1997; McGregor, 1995; Smith, 2010), and his understanding of "stigma" has been continuously extended and refined empirically and theoretically in several later studies (see, e.g., Link & Phelan, 2001; Renfrow, 2004; Scambler, 2006). Goffman's work has thus been able to stand the test of time. And this list is by no means nearly exhaustive but merely illustrative of the frequent use of Goffman's original work in a variety of specific—empirical or theoretical—research contexts.

As is evident from this listing, everywhere there's interaction—which basically means almost everywhere—Goffman's concepts and perspectives have proved useful and inspirational. Some of the aforementioned topics may at first hand seem somewhat obscure or marginal (something that never troubled Goffman himself), but nonetheless they show how his terminology has struck roots even in the most diversified and surprising of fields. Moreover, in recent years, Goffman's conceptual arsenal has frequently been a reference in and applied more comprehensively to the study of the rise of new information and communication technologies, especially in studies of mobile phones and Internet behavior (see, e.g., Dell & Marinova, 2002; Hancock, Toma, & Ellison, 2007; Jenkins, 2010; Meyrowitz, 1990; Miller, 1995; Pinch, 2010; Rettie, 2009; Ross, 2007; Sannicolas, 1997; Williams & Weninger 2012), and we are certain there are many more journal articles, books, and student reports in the pipeline using Goffman's terminology in the context of the Internet, mobile phones, iPads, iPods, and other types of information and communication media (see particularly the recent book by Winkin & Leeds-Hurwitz, 2013). Goffman even—posthumously—gave name to a computer program titled ERVING, which by way of artificial intelligence techniques is intended to teach students to reason and think sociologically from his dramaturgical perspective (Brent et al., 1989).

Throughout the years also, a substantial number of international books in a variety of languages, especially edited volumes, have been published commenting on, describing, developing, extending, modifying, critiquing, and, last but not least, celebrating his work (see, e.g., Bovone & Rovati, 1992; Burns, 1992; Ditton, 1980; Drew & Wootton, 1988a; Fine & Smith, 2000; Gregersen, 1975; Hettlage & Lenz, 1991; Isaac, 1989, 2002; Jacobsen, 2010a; Jacobsen & Kristiansen, 2002; Lemert & Branaman, 1997; Manning, 1992; Nahavandi, 1979; Neri, 2002; Nizet & Rigaux, 2005; Persson, 2012; Raab, 2008; Riggins, 1990; Scheff, 2006; Smith, 1999a, 2006; Treviño, 2003a; Winkin, 1988). Besides this, Goffman has throughout the years been adopted or appointed as the intellectual forerunner to a variety of schools of thought within the social sciences such as ethnomethodology (Attewell, 1974), dramaturgy (Branco, 1983; Brissett & Edgley, 1990; Combs & Mansfield, 1976; Hare & Blumberg, 1988; Hopper, 1981; Messinger et al., 1962), labeling theory (Petrunik, 1980), the sociology of the absurd (Lyman & Scott, 1970), postmodern sociology (Battershill, 1990), the sociology of the body (Crossley, 1995), urban sociology (Hannerz, 1980; Jensen, 2006), the sociology of sport (Birrell & Donnelly, 2004), and the sociology of the familiar (Birenbaum & Sagarin, 1973). Moreover, he has been seen as one of the founding fathers or main sources of inspiration for a variety of conventional as well as emerging fields of study or subdisciplines such as political sociology (Gamson, 1985), medical sociology (Strong, 1983), organization theory (Manning, 2008), psychological anthropology (Bock, 1988), social psychology (Sarbin, 2003), disability studies (Drake, 2005; Ewing, 2002), recognition theory (Jacobsen & Kristiansen, 2009), the politics of dignity (Scheff, 2010), mass media studies and new information and communication technologies (Ling, 2010; Ytreberg, 2002, 2010), tourist studies (Larsen, 2010), mobility and urban studies (Jensen, 2006, 2010), surveillance studies (Marx, 2004), power studies (Jenkins, 2008), terrorist studies (Weigert, 2003), and environmentalism (Brewster, 2009; Hargreaves, 2011), just to mention a few but far from exhaustive examples. Add to all of this the thousands of student reports, working papers, book chapters, Internet publications, and all the citations of his work across a multitude of scientific disciplines and fields of study, then it becomes more than clear that many others picked up and renewed Goffman's legacy after his death. All of this also testifies to the contemporaneity and continued relevance of Goffman's work. So Goffman's work has proved inspirational for subsequent generations of sociologists and others who—each within their discipline—in his writings have found legitimation for an overlooked subject matter and stylistic inspiration as well as a way of approaching scholarship that is quite different from the mainstream. Therefore, Goffman's legacy continues to live on in the work carried out by established scholars and aspiring students who utilize his ideas in their own work. So just as there is an annual C. Wright Mills Award, a George Herbert Mead Award, a Walter Benjamin Award, a Robert MacIver Award, and so on, every year since 2004 there has also been an Erving Goffman Award bestowed to the winner for "Outstanding Scholarship in the Ecology of Social Interaction." The list of recipients of the award can be seen in Table 10.1.

Table 10.1   Recipients of the Erving Goffman Award 2004–2013

Year	Name of Award Winner	Title of Work
2004	Corey Anton	*Selfhood and Authenticity*
2005	Aaron Ben Ze'ev	*Love Online: Emotions on the Internet*
2006	David Berreby	*Us and Them: Understanding Your Tribal Mind*
2007	Richard A. Lanham	*The Economics of Attention: Style and Substance in the Age of Information*
2008	Paul Mason Fotsch	*Watching the Traffic Go By: Transportation and Isolation in Urban America*
2009	Rich Ling	*New Tech, New Times: How Mobile Communication is Reshaping Social Cohesion*
2010	Kenneth J. Gergen	*Relational Being: Beyond Self and Community*
2011	Richard S. Hallam	*Virtual Selves, Real Persons: A Dialogue Across Disciplines*
2012	Corey Anton	*Sources of Significance: Worldly Rejuvenation and Neo-Stoic Heroism*
2013	Valerie V. Peterson	*Sex, Ethics and Communication: A Humanist Approach to Conversations on Intimacy*

As is evident from this list of recipients, new generations of social scientists have successfully related Goffman's original ideas and perspective to emerging fields of study, new social conditions, and surprising areas of social research that he had perhaps not even anticipated.

There is little doubt that if Goffman had lived today, his penetrating look would have taken notice of the cornucopia of new cultural trends and macrosocial developments characteristic of contemporary society, although he would have insisted on studying its microsociological implications and crystallizations. Randall Collins (1986) once mused at what Goffman would have worked on if his life had not been cut prematurely short by cancer. According to him, Goffman had at least two more books in him waiting to be written. One book would probably have been an incisive and biting analysis of the intellectual world, a sort of sociology of science or sociology of sociology that perhaps—in typical Goffman manner—would have focused on the microdynamics of intellectual life inside the ivory towers of academia. Such a piece of work would doubtlessly also have had to touch upon the impact on intellectual work of the incessant rat race for research funding, the quantification of academic production, the deference and demeanor in research departments, and how intellectuals (such as sociologists) increasingly parade as media darlings, public witnesses of truth, and soothsayers (something Goffman would have despised). Another book to be expected—perhaps given Goffman's interest in the most delicate matters and his early interest in the work of Sigmund Freud—would have been on sexuality, because sex, and with it social norms in the shape of the superego, revolves around so many wonderful yet often almost invisible microrituals in everyday life. Moreover, had Goffman lived into the new millennium, he would surely have taken a keen interest in the rise and spreading of the Internet and the endless possibilities for self-presentation, focused and unfocused interaction, secrecy, identity play, behavioral rituals, and etiquettes made available to people online. Apart from these books, one can be sure that there would have been many more titles from Goffman dealing with much of that which is either neglected, overlooked, or intended securely to be kept under wraps in society.

Recommended Reading

As should be obvious from the cited works, for scholars or students interested in the work of Erving Goffman, a vast amount of secondary literature already exists—alongside Goffman's own 11 published book titles and his few but highly important journal articles—dealing with a variety of aspects of his life and work. Whereas some of the published books—edited volumes as well as monographs—are primarily attentive to biographical details, others are more analytical or introductory, and whereas some of the books available on the market have been published in English, others are only available in more localized languages such as German, Italian, French, Swedish, or Danish. For example, the French title by Yves Winkin, *Erving Goffman: Les moments et leurs hommes* (1988), is primarily concerned with presenting translated texts by Goffman himself but also contains Winkin's highly interesting and extended commentary on the life and background of Goffman. The most comprehensive introduction to date is still Tom Burns's *Erving Goffman* (1992), providing an insightful and thematically organized tour de force through most facets of Goffman's personal life and professional achievements. Another important book published around the same time is Philip Manning's *Erving Goffman and Modern Sociology* (1992), which also—and in more chronologically structured manner—digs into the theoretical themes and methodological engine room of Goffman's oeuvre. Greg Smith's (2006) more recent introduction is recommendable because of its relative brevity and its focused presentation of and preoccupation with the most central tenets of Goffman's life and work. For students who want the quick overview, this latter title is indeed the place to start.

There are also several edited volumes around that contain important interpretations and recommendable chapters by leading Goffman interpreters, such as, for example, Jason Ditton's *The View from Goffman* (1980), Paul Drew and Anthony Wootton's *Erving Goffman—Exploring the Interaction Order* (1988a), Stephen H. Riggins's *Beyond Goffman* (1990), Greg Smith's *Goffman and Social Organization: Studies of a Sociological Legacy* (1999a), and A. Javier Treviño's *Goffman's Legacy* (2003). Besides this, Charles Lemert and Ann Branaman have collected and published *The Goffman Reader* (1997), containing extracts of Goffman's own writings as well as intriguing interpretations and discussions by the two editors. Moreover, Gary Alan Fine and Greg Smith have collected a large proportion of the secondary literature (at that time) on Goffman in an impressive four-volume set (Fine & Smith, 2000). For those who want to see Goffman's work extended and applied to new social conditions—such as mobile telecommunication, tourist photography, or mobility—we recommend the edited volume *The Contemporary Goffman* (Jacobsen, 2010a), and for those with a keen interest in Goffman's utility in media and communication studies, see *Erving Goffman—A Critical Introduction to Media and Communication Theory* (Winkin & Leeds-Hurwitz, 2013). A fine, concise, and digestible overview of Goffman's life and work is found in the chapter by Gary Alan Fine and Philip Manning (2003). Finally, several issues of academic journals have been devoted to appreciative or critical analyses and applications of Goffman's perspective, such as volume 2, issue 1 (1983) of *Theory, Culture & Society* and volume 12, issues 1 and 2 (1989) of *Human Studies*. Besides this is also an enormous emporium of articles, theses, and projects scattered in journals and libraries and on the Internet, all testifying to the continuous importance and vitality of Goffman's view of the social world. For those interested in archival information and a variety of available and continually updated material on Goffman, there is a homepage—The Erving Goffman Archives—containing a lot of interesting information, articles, and commentaries. To access this information, visit the website at www.unlv.edu/centers/cdclv/ega/index.html.

Conclusion

Seen in hindsight—and revisiting the chapters of this book—it is indeed difficult not to deem Erving Goffman's endeavor successful, although Robert Erwin once stated that Goffman's "particular phraseology never caught on. . . . Goffman was noticed but not embraced" (Erwin, 1992, p. 338). It is our contention and conviction that this is a gross exaggeration—Goffman was both noticed and embraced. As many of the chapters in this book have shown, Goffman—more than most of his contemporaries, and even more so than most of his successors—managed to coin terminology and provide analyses that were embraced, interpreted, and applied by later generations of students and scholars and that helped in shaping research agendas or increasing awareness within a variety of scientific disciplines and subdisciplines. So although Goffman is no longer—in person—a part of the sociological landscape, he is in a variety of more or less direct and indirect ways still present among us today. This leaves us with a legacy to nurture and a vision and passion to carry forward. As Eliot Friedson contended:

> We are left with Erving Goffman's own self-as-sociologist, not a theory or even the basis for a theory. We are left with his struggle to assert his self as sociologist against the seductive resistance of the conventions of the world. We see him employing with imagination and passion any resources that seem useful to illuminate aspects of human life that most of us overlook and to show us more of humanity than we could otherwise see. (Friedson, 1983, p. 362)

So fortunately, sociology will not have to get along or do without Erving Goffman. His spirit lives on in ever-new generations of newcomers to the discipline who in his work and perspective can glimpse opportunities for making the microworld in which we all participate a bit more tangible and understandable—and perhaps a bit more human as well.

In this final chapter, we have discussed our own reading of Goffman as a sociologist par excellence, we have provided a comprehensive list of references to research—classic and contemporary—using Goffman's ideas within a variety of specific empirical contexts thereby testifying to and exemplifying how Goffman remains a strong source of inspiration for colleagues and students around the world, and finally we have proposed some recommended readings for those interested in digging deeper into Goffman. The last words in this book, however, belong to Erving Goffman himself—in fact, some of his own last published words—as he in his famous posthumously published presidential address sarcastically proclaimed why there is some need for sociology after all:

> I've heard it said that we [the sociologists] should be glad to trade what we've so far produced for a few really good conceptual distinctions and a cold beer. But there's nothing in the world we should trade for what we do have: the bent to sustain in regard to all elements of social life a spirit of unfettered, unsponsored inquiry, and the wisdom not to look elsewhere but ourselves and our discipline for this mandate. That is our inheritance and that so far is what we have to bequeath. If one must have warrant addressed to social needs, let it be for unsponsored analyses of the social arrangements enjoyed by those with institutional authority—priests, psychiatrists, school teachers, police, generals, government leaders, parents, males, whites, nationals, media operators, and all the other well-placed persons who are in a position to give official imprint to versions of reality. (Goffman, 1983a, p. 17)

Questions

- How, where, why, and when can Erving Goffman's ideas and concepts most readily, most importantly, and most creatively be applied in contemporary social research?
- If Erving Goffman had lived for another decade or two, what do you think he would have been writing about?
- What would be the main challenges to Erving Goffman's sociological perspective in contemporary society?
- After reading this book, if you were asked to describe Erving Goffman's work using only three words, what would they be?

Glossary

Abduction A mode of reasoning or logic of inference that borrows insights from, respectively, induction and deduction but that—contrary to their clear-cut theory generation or theory testing—is primarily concerned with a line of reasoning that moves from observation to the proposition of a hypothesis that can account for or explain the observed phenomenon (at times called qualified guessing).

Backstage One of the important regions in Goffman's dramaturgy. "Backstage" describes the activities that take place behind the scenes. Being backstage, actors may relax and feel less restrained by interactional roles although not necessarily behaving authentically (see *frontstage*).

Character contests An interactional sequence involving a confrontation between two individuals both attempting to maintain their face at the other's expense.

Chicago School Descriptive label used to define the researchers—sociologists and social workers—working at the sociology department at the University of Chicago from the late 19th century and onward and who, despite differences in themes and approaches, particularly promoted an interactionist research focus and relied on qualitative research methods.

Civil inattention A minor interaction ritual and type of unfocused interaction by which people acknowledge the presence of others without violating their privacy. By performing civil inattention, people display themselves as nonthreatening interactional parties.

Creative abduction A notion invented by Umberto Eco to describe a type of abduction (see *abduction*) that, in particularly imaginative and creative way, seeks to account for, give meaning to, or explain a given observed phenomenon.

193

Deference   The behaviors or courtesies by which actors demonstrate respect or appreciation of other people's selves. To receive signs of deference, people need to behave in appropriate ways (see *demeanor*).

Definition of the situation   Designating the interactional process involving individuals' cooperation regarding the maintenance or negotiation of a particular way of understanding a social situation. A specific definition of the situation involves specific interactional norms and role requirements.

Demeanor   The appearance and behavior of a person. When presenting himself in good demeanor and thus recognizing interactional norms, a person will receive deference from the social environment (see *deference*).

Dramaturgy   The use of theatrical and dramaturgical concepts to describe aspects of social life. Dramaturgy focuses on the performative and role-playing aspects of social interaction. Goffman used the dramaturgical concepts to describe the elements and processes of the interaction order.

Felicity's condition   Denotes the background assumption or principle underlying all other background assumptions in verbal and nonverbal interaction, which binds social interaction together and makes it safe, recognizable, understandable, and meaningful to participants.

Footing   A notion closely connected to that of *frame* that refers to the ways in which participants in verbal interaction align themselves to others or to the content of what is being said in a given social situation.

Frame   A concept that captures the mental equipment people actively draw on when trying to understand the situations and occurrences taking place around them and that helps them organize their experiences and navigate in social situations.

Frame analysis   The name for the analysis of *frames*, which are those mental maps, matrices of perception, or implicit and underlying understandings that govern our comprehension and definition of situations and guide our actions. Frame analysis involves trying to understand why people act in certain ways and how they organize their experiences according to various specific frames.

Frontstage   An important region in Goffman's dramaturgy. Engaging in a performance on the frontstage, people perceive themselves to be in front of an audience, and thus they attempt to make impressions by playing roles and by giving and giving off information.

Genderism   A term reserved for the gender-based construction of gender roles, which, for example, involve predictable representations of men and women, often stereotypical gender expectations and gender images, a highly organized arrangement between the sexes, different gender identities, and gender-specific practices.

Grounded theory   A methodological approach building on a radical inductivist position that, through specified sampling, coding, and analytical procedures, is primarily concerned with generating concepts and constructing theory based on the collection of data material rather than on testing or verifying existing theories.

Impression management   The acts by which people create impressions of themselves and situations for an audience. This involves the information that people purposely give and information given off unknowingly as well as the monitoring of others in order to detect their impression management.

Interaction order   A social domain regulated by certain norms in which people are physically copresent. According to Goffman, the interaction order is the order that can be observed in people's face-to-face interactions and an order worthy of study in its own right.

Interaction ritual   The defensive or protective acts and procedures used in social interaction to display respect for others and to avoid embarrassment and threats to the course of social interaction. Interaction ritual involves a symbolic aspect as people display respect for individuals' faces and for the underlying social order.

Keying   Concept that means something like "using a key" and refers to the utterances or actions that signal the meaning of interaction to participants, including its laminations, its relation to different frames, and so forth. When using specific keys, we unlock and define or redefine situations in different ways.

Labeling theory   A theoretical perspective on deviance rooted in symbolic interactionism defining labeling as a dynamic and interactive process involving initial acts and societal reaction resulting in the definition of individuals as deviant as a result of their violation of socially constructed rules.

Looping   A source of mortification involving an interactive process by which an individual's attempt to protect himself against mortification is interpreted as resistance and treated as an aspect of his failure.

Maverick   Someone who consciously stands outside of, straddles, or sits astride the barricades between official and well-established paradigms in social research and provides an original perspective.

Metaphor   Textual or literary device used to show or propose the similarity between two—often unconnected—realms of being (for example, everyday life and theatrical performance) that, through their combination, imaginatively helps shed light on overlooked, undiscovered, or hidden aspects of the phenomenon one seeks to understand.

Methodology of violation   An approach to investigating social life that as its point of departure has the study of situations when rules are broken, norms are violated, or crises occur in the normal and smooth functioning or regulated order of everyday life.

Microsociology   A branch of sociology primarily concerned with different aspects of everyday life such as social interaction, identity, and agency in situational or face-to-face settings and often neglecting or less interested in more conventional macrosociological topics such as social inequality, politics, or structural arrangements.

Moral career   A process taking place in institutional arrangements that involves the transformation of a person from a normal human being to a less valued human person stripped of his human dignity and civilian rights.

Mortification of self   A process through which an individual is bereaved of the necessary resources to present himself as a free, self-determined, and competent citizen, resulting in experiences of loss of human dignity and self-respect.

Participant observation   Method of data collection—at times more broadly subsumed under the headings of ethnography or fieldwork—in which the researcher actively participates in the lives and actions of those studied and often subjects him/herself to the same life conditions of his/her research subjects.

Performance   The behavior or activities that a person presents in front of an audience. When engaging in performance, actors create impressions of themselves for an audience in order to facilitate interaction and to establish or maintain identity.

Region   A notion used by Goffman to describe that social interaction takes place within different settings involving different roles and perceptions of audience. The main regions in Goffman's dramaturgy are frontstage, backstage, and outside the stage.

Rituals   Symbolic acts by which someone or something regarded as sacred is treated with appropriate respect.

Role distance   A term describing the acts by which a person displays some level of detachment from the role he is presently performing. By practicing role distance, a person acknowledges playing a certain social role but disassociates himself from the specific type of role available in the situation.

Self   The image of a person that is produced from the impressions and responses in social situations. In Goffman's perspective, the self is thus a product that emerges from the performances of the actor, the actual scene, and the interpretations of the audience.

Sign vehicles   A notion proposed by Goffman to describe the ways that individuals use the particular setting, their manner, and their appearance to convey information about themselves. These vehicles constitute the major parts of a person's front.

Sophisticated irony   A term used to describe how irony or a playful ironic stance toward one's research topic, one's readers, or one's own methodology and findings may serve important analytical purposes such as, for example, creating a sense of familiarity with what is described, teasing or seducing the reader, allowing for sarcastic comments, or providing a bulwark against critique.

Stigma   A social process by which individuals displaying discrediting attributes or behaviors are negatively labeled and sanctioned. Stigma often involves status loss and feelings of shame, anxiety, and embarrassment.

Symbolic interactionism   An approach to or perspective on sociology, often regarded as microsociological or social psychological, concerned with studying how people through processes of social interaction (such as verbal or nonverbal behavior) with others and definitions of the situation develop, rely on, and derive subjective meaning about others, selves, and society.

System requirements Those preconditions or communication-technical demands of interaction (in Goffman's case, primarily verbal interaction or talk) that interaction—as a system of mutual engagement between participants—must abide by if it is to succeed as interaction.

Territories (of the self) Goffman's term for the area around an individual, particular objects to which an individual has priority rights, an individual's temporal turn or place, or information about an individual of which the individual is expected to have control. In Goffman's ethological analysis, these territories that can be encroached on by others constitute the self.

Total institution A type of institution with an encompassing character and with a blocking of inmates' contact with the outside world as well as their possibilities of leaving the establishment.

Bibliography of Goffman's Writings

Goffman, E. (1949). *Some characteristics of response to depicted experience.* Unpublished master's thesis, University of Chicago.

Goffman, E. (1951). Symbols of class status. *British Journal of Sociology, 11,* 294–304.

Goffman, E. (1952). On cooling the mark out: Some aspects of adaptation to failure. *Psychiatry, 15,* 451–463.

Goffman, E. (1953a). *The service station dealer: The man and his work.* Chicago: Social Research Incorporation.

Goffman, E. (1953b). *Communication conduct in an island community.* Unpublished PhD thesis, University of Chicago.

Goffman, E. (1955). On face-work: An analysis of ritual elements in social interaction. *Psychiatry, 18*(3), 213–231.

Goffman, E. (1956a). The nature of deference and demeanor. *American Anthropologist, 58*(3), 473–502.

Goffman, E. (1956b). Embarrassment and social organization. *American Journal of Sociology, 62,* 264–274.

Goffman, E. (1957a). Alienation from interaction. *Human Relations, 10,* 47–59.

Goffman, E. (1957b). On some convergences of sociology and psychiatry. *Psychiatry, 20*(3), 201–203.

Goffman, E. (1957c). Interpersonal persuasion. In B. Schaffner (Ed.), *Group processes.* New York: Josiah Macy Jr. Foundation, pp. 117–193.

Goffman, E. (1957d). Some dimensions of the problem. In D. J. Levinson & R. H. Williams (Eds.), *The patient and the mental hospital.* New York: Free Press, pp. 507–510.

Goffman, E. (1959). *The presentation of self in everyday life.* New York: Overlook Press.

Goffman, E. (1961). *Asylums: Essays on the social situation of mental patients and other inmates.* Harmondsworth: Penguin Books.

Goffman, E. (1963). *Behaviour in public places: Notes on the social organization of gatherings*. New York: Free Press.

Goffman, E. (1964a). *Stigma: Notes on the management of spoiled identity*. Chicago: Aldine.

Goffman, E. (1964b). The neglected situation. *American Anthropologist, 66*(2), special issue: 133–136.

Goffman, E. (1966). Communication and enforcement systems. In K. Archibald (Ed.), *Strategic interaction and conflict*. Berkeley, CA: Institute for International Studies, pp. 198–220.

Goffman, E. (1967). *Interaction ritual: Essays on face-to-face behaviour*. New York: Anchor Books.

Goffman, E. (1969). *Strategic interaction*. Oxford: Basil Blackwell.

Goffman, E. (1971). *Relations in public: Microstudies of the public order*. New York: Basic Books.

Goffman, E. (1972). *Encounters: Two studies in the sociology of interaction*. Harmondsworth: Penguin Books.

Goffman, E. (1974). *Frame analysis: An essay on the organization of experience*. New York: Harper & Row.

Goffman, E. (1976a). Replies and responses. *Language and Society, 5*(3), 257–313.

Goffman, E. (1976b). Gender advertisements: Studies in the anthropology of visual communication. *Society for the Anthropology of Visual Communication, 3*(2), 69–154.

Goffman, E. (1977a). The arrangement between the sexes. *Theory and Society, 4*, 301–331.

Goffman, E. (1977b). Genderisms: An admittedly malicious look at how advertising reinforces sexual role stereotypes. *Psychology Today, 11*(3), 60–63.

Goffman, E. (1977c). La ritualisation de la féminité. *Actes de la recherce en sciences sociales, 14*, 34–50.

Goffman, E. (1979a). *Gender advertisements*. London: Macmillan.

Goffman, E. (1979b). Footing. *Semiotica, 25*(1–2), 1–29.

Goffman, E. (1981a). *Forms of talk*. Oxford: Basil Blackwell.

Goffman, E. (1981b). Reply to Denzin and Keller. *Contemporary Sociology, 10*(1), 60–68.

Goffman, E. (1983a). The interaction order. *American Sociological Review, 48*, 1–17.

Goffman, E. (1983b). Felicity's condition. *American Journal of Sociology, 89*, 1–53.

Goffman, E. (1983c). Microsociologie et historie. In P. Fritsch (Ed.), *Le Sens de L'ordinaire*. Paris: Editions du Centre National de la Recherche Scientifique, pp. 197–202.

Goffman, E. (1989). On fieldwork. *Journal of Contemporary Ethnography, 18*(2), 123–132.

References

Abels, H. (1998). *Interaktion, identität, präsentation*. Wiesbaden: Westdeutsche Verlag.

Abrahams, R. D. (1984). Pros and players. *Raritan, 3*(4), 76–94.

Adler, P., & Adler, P. (1989). The gloried self: The aggrandizement and the constriction of self. *Social Psychology Quarterly, 52*(4), 299–310.

Ainlay, S., Becker, G., & Coleman, L. M. (Eds.). (1986). *The dilemma of difference: A multidisciplinary view of stigma*. New York: Springer.

Alaszewski, A., & Manthorpe, J. (1995). Goffman, the individual, institutions and stigmatization. *Nursing Times, 91*, 38–39.

Albas, D., & Albas, C. (1988). Aces and bombers: The post-exam impression management strategies of students. *Symbolic Interaction, 11*, 289–302.

Album, D. (1995). Hvordan går det med Goffman og Garfinkel? Teorier om samhandling ansikt til ansikt. *Sociologisk Tidsskrift, 4*, 245–262.

Album, D. (1996). *Nære fremmede: Patientkulturen i sykehus [Close strangers: Patient culture in a Norwegian hospital]*. Otta: Tano.

Album, D. (2010). Close strangers: Patient–patient interaction rituals in acute care hospitals. In M. H. Jacobsen (Ed.), *The contemporary Goffman*, pp. 352–371. London: Routledge.

Altheide, D. L. (1997). The news media, the problem frame and the production of fear. *Sociological Quarterly, 38*(4), 647–668.

Anderson, R. J., Hughes, J. A., & Sharrock, W. (1985). Reading sociology: Goffman as example. In R. J. Anderson, J. A. Hughes, & W. Sharrock (Eds.), *The Sociology Game*. London: Longman.

Andreski, S. (1972). *Social sciences as sorcery*. London: Pelican Books.

Atkinson, P. (1989). Goffman's poetics. *Human Studies, 12*(1–2), 59–76.

Attewell, P. (1974). Ethnomethodology since Garfinkel. *Theory and Society, 1*, 179–210.

Baldamus, W. W. (1972). The role of discoveries in social science. In T. Shannin (Ed.), *The rules of the game: Cross-disciplinary essays on models in scholarly thought*, pp. 276–302. London: Tavistock.

Bateson, G. (1972). *Steps to an ecology of mind*. Chicago: University of Chicago Press.

Battershill, C. D. (1990). Erving Goffman as a precursor to post-modern sociology. In S. H. Riggins (Ed.), *Beyond Goffman: Studies on communication, institution and social interaction*, pp. 163–186. Berlin: Mouton de Gruyter.

Bauman, Z. (1967). Image of man in the modern sociology—Some methodological remarks. *Polish Sociological Bulletin, 7*(1), 12–21.

Becker, H. S. (1963). *Outsiders: Studies in the sociology of deviance.* New York: Free Press.

Becker, H. S. (1967). Whose side are we on? *Social Problems, 14*(3), 239–247.

Becker, H. S. (2003). The politics of presentation: Goffman and total institutions. *Symbolic Interaction, 26*, 659–669.

Belknap, P. & Leonard, W. M., II. (1991). A conceptual replication and extension of Erving Goffman's study of gender advertisements. *Sex Roles, 25*(3/4), 103–118.

Bell, P., & Milic, M. (2002). Goffman's *Gender Advertisements* revisited: Combining content analysis with semiotic analysis. *Visual Communication, 1*(2), 203–222.

Berger, B. M. (1973). A fan letter on Erving Goffman. *Dissent, 20*, 353–361.

Berger, P. L. (1963). *Invitation to sociology: A humanistic perspective.* Garden City, NY: Doubleday.

Berger, P. L., & Luckmann, T. (1966). *The social construction of reality.* Harmondsworth: Penguin Books.

Bergesen, A. (1984). Reflections on Erving Goffman. *Quarterly Journal of Sociology, 8*, 51–54.

Berman, M. (1972). Weird but brilliant light on the way we live now: Review of *Relations in public*. In G. A. Fine & G. W. H. Smith (Eds.), *Erving Goffman: A four-volume set*, Vol I., pp. 266–277 (Sage Masters in Modern Social Thought Series). London: Sage Publications.

Birenbaum, A., & Sagarin, E. (Eds.). (1973). *People in places: The sociology of the familiar.* London: Nelson.

Birrell, S. (1981). Sport as ritual: Interpretations from Durkheim to Goffman. *Social Forces, 60*, 354–376.

Birrell, S., & Donnelly, P. (2004). Reclaiming Goffman: Erving Goffman's influence on the sociology of sport. In R. Giulianotti (Ed.), *Sport and modern social theorists*, pp. 49–64. Basingstoke, UK: Palgrave/Macmillan.

Blumer, H. (1969). *Symbolic interactionism: Perspective and method.* Berkeley: University of California Press.

Bock, P. K. (1988). The importance of Erving Goffman to psychological anthropology. *Ethos, 16*, 3–20.

Boeskov, B. (1975). Sindsygdom: en social tilbøjelighed. In Bo Gregersen (Ed.), *Om Goffman—11 artikler*, pp. 142–157. Copenhagen: Hans Reitzels Forlag.

Bonsu, S. K. (2007). The presentation of dead selves in everyday life: Obituaries and impression management. *Symbolic Interaction, 30*(2), 199–219.

Borey, V. (2004). Tenant–landlord conflict: Goffman's interaction ritual applied. *Suite101.com: The Genuine Article.*

Bottomore, T., & Nisbet, R. (Eds.) (1978). *A history of sociological analysis.* New York: Basic Books.

Bouissac, P. (1990). Incidents, accidents, failures: The representation of negative experience in public entertainment. In S. H. Riggins (Ed.), *Beyond Goffman: Studies on communication, institution and social interaction*, pp. 409–442. Berlin: Mouton de Gruyter.

Boulton, M. (2001). "We pray by his mouth": Karl Barth, Erving Goffman and a theology of invocation. *Modern Theology, 17*(1), 67–83.

Bourdieu, P. (1983). Erving Goffman: Discoverer of the infinitely small. *Theory, Culture & Society, 2*(1), 112–113.

Bourdieu, P. (1998). *Masculine domination*. Stanford, CA: Stanford University Press.

Bourdieu, P., & Wacquant, L. J. D. (1992). *An invitation to reflexive sociology:* Chicago: University of Chicago Press.

Bovone, L., & Rovati, G. (Eds.). (1992). *L'ordine dell'interazione: La sociologia di Erving Goffman*. Rome: Armando Editore.

Branaman, A. (1997). Goffman's social theory. In C. Lemert & A. Branaman (Eds.), *The Goffman reader*, pp. xvi–lxxxii. Oxford: Blackwell.

Branaman, A. (2003). Interaction and hierarchy in everyday life. In A. J. Treviño (Ed.), *Goffman's legacy*. New York: Rowman and Littlefield.

Branaman, A. (2010). The protean Goffman: Erving Goffman and the new individualism. In M. H. Jacobsen (Ed.), *The Contemporary Goffman*, pp. 232–255. London: Routledge.

Branco, D. J. (1983). *Dramaturgical rhetoric: Erving Goffman's theory of communication-conduct*. Iowa City: University Library Microfilms.

Brandt, B., & Tatsis, K. (2009). Using Goffman's concepts to explore collaborative interaction processes in elementary school mathematics. *Research in Mathematics Education, 11*(1), 39–55.

Brent, E. E. et al. (1989). Erving: A program to teach sociological reasoning from the dramaturgical perspective. *Teaching Sociology, 17*(1), 38–48.

Brent, J. (1993). *Charles Sanders Peirce: A life*. Bloomington: Indiana University Press.

Brewster, B. H., & Bell, M. M. (2009). The environmental Goffman: Toward an environmental sociology of everyday life. *Society & Natural Resources, 23*(1), 45–57.

Brickell, C. (2005). Masculinities, performativity and subversion: A sociological reappraisal. *Men and Masculinities, 8*(1), 24–43.

Brinkmann, S., Jacobsen, M. H., & Kristiansen, S. (2014). Historical overview of qualitative research in the social sciences. In P. Leavy (Ed.), *The Oxford handbook of qualitative research methods*. Oxford: Oxford University Press.

Brissett, D., & Edgley, C. (Eds.). (1990). *Life as theater* (2nd ed.). Chicago: Aldine de Gruyter.

Brittan, A. (1973). *Meanings and situations*. London: Routledge and Kegan Paul.

Brown, D. K. (2003). Goffman's dramaturgical sociology: Developing a meaningful theoretical context and exercise involving embarrassment and social organization. *Teaching Sociology, 31*, 288–299.

Brown, R. H. (1976). Social theory as metaphor: On the logic of discovery for sciences of conduct. *Theory and Society, 3*, 169–197.

Brown, R. H. (1977). *A poetics for sociology: Toward a logic of discovery for the human sciences*. Cambridge: Cambridge University Press.

Brown, R. E. (2005). Acting presidential: The dramaturgy of Bush versus Kerry. *American Behavioral Scientist, 49*(1), 78–91.

Bulmer, M. (1984). *The Chicago school of sociology: Institutionalization, diversity and the rise of sociological research*. Chicago: University of Chicago Press.

Burke, K. (1936/1984). *Permanence and change*. Indianapolis, IN: Bobbs-Merrill.

Burns, T. (1992). *Erving Goffman*. London: Routledge.

Butler, J. (1993). *Bodies that matter: On the discursive limits of sex*. London: Routledge.

Bynum, J., & Pranter, C. (1984). Goffman: content and method for seminal thought. *Free Inquiry in Creative Sociology, 12*, 95–99.

Cahill, S., Fine, G. A., & Grant, L. (1995). Dimensions in qualitative research. In K. S. Cook, G. A. Fine, & J. S. House (Eds.), *Sociological perspectives on social psychology*, pp. 605–628. Needham Heights, MA: Allyn and Bacon.

Cappetti, C. (1993). *Writing Chicago: Modernism, ethnography and the novel*. New York: Columbia University Press.

Carnevale, F. A. (2007). Revisiting Goffman's *Stigma:* The social experience of families with children requiring mechanical ventilation at home. *Journal of Child Health Care, 11*(1), 7–18.

Carter, A. (1979). Female persons. *The Guardian*, 31 May.

Caudill, W. (1962). Review of Erving Goffman's *Asylums. American Journal of Sociology, 68*, 366–369.

Cavan, R. S. (1983). The Chicago school of sociology, 1918–1933. *Urban Life, 11*, 407–420.

Chayko, M. (1993). What is real in the age of virtual reality? "Reframing" frame analysis for a technological world. *Symbolic Interaction, 16*(2), 171–181.

Chriss, J. J. (1993). Durkheim's cult of the individual as civil religion: Its appropriation by Erving Goffman. *Sociological Spectrum, 13*, 251–275.

Chriss, J. J. (1995a). Some thoughts on recent efforts to further systematize Goffman. *Sociological Forum, 10*(1), 177–186.

Chriss, J. J. (1995b). Habermas, Goffman, and communicative action: Implications for professional practice. *American Sociological Review, 60*, 545–565.

Chriss, J. J. (1999). Role distance and the negational self. In G. Smith (Ed.), *Goffman and social organization: Studies in a sociological legacy*, pp. 64–80. London: Routledge.

Collett, J. L., & Childs, E. (2009). Meaningful performances: Considering the contributions of the dramaturgical approach to studying family. *Sociology Compass, 3–4*, 689–706.

Collins, R. (1981a). The three stages of Goffman. In R. Collins, *Sociology since the midcentury: Essays in theory cumulation*, pp. 219–253. New York: Academic Press.

Collins, R. (1981b). On the microfoundations of macrosociology. *American Journal of Sociology, 86*(5), 984–1014.

Collins, R. (1985). *Three sociological traditions*. New York: Oxford University Press.

Collins, R. (1986). The passing of intellectual generations: Reflections on the death of Erving Goffman. *Sociological Theory, 4*(1), 106–113.

Collins, R. (1988a). *Theoretical sociology*. San Diego: Harcourt Brace.

Collins, R. (1988b). Theoretical continuities in Goffman's Work. In P. Drew. & A. Wootton (Eds.), *Erving Goffman—Exploring the interaction order*, pp. 41–63. Boston: Northeastern University Press.

Collins, R. (1990). Stratification, emotional energy and the transient emotions. In T. D. Kemper (Ed.), *Research agendas in the sociology of emotions*, pp. 27–57. Albany: State University of New York Press.

Collins, R. (1994). *Four sociological traditions*. Oxford: Oxford University Press.

Collins, R. (2004). *Interaction ritual chains*. Princeton, NJ: Princeton University Press.

Collins, R., & Makowsky, M. (1993). *The discovery of society*. New York: McGraw-Hill.

Combs, J., & Mansfield, M. (Eds.). (1976). *Drama in life*. New York: Hastings House.

Cooley, C. H. (1902). *Human nature and the social order*. New York: Scribner's.

Corradi, C. (1990). The metaphoric structure of scientific explanation. *Philosophy and Social Criticism, 16*(3), 161–178.

Corsaro, W. A. (1983). Review of Erving Goffman's *Forms of talk*. *American Journal of Sociology, 89*, 220–222.

Coser, L. (1976). Sociological theory from the Chicago dominance to 1965. *Annual Review of Sociology, 2*, 145–160.

Cosgrave, J. F. (2008). Goffman revisited: Action and character in the era of legalized gambling. *International Journal of Criminology and Sociological Theory, 1*(1), 80–96.

Craib, I. (1978). Erving Goffman: *Frame analysis*. *Philosophy of the Social Sciences, 8*, 79–86.

Crossley, N. (1995). Body techniques, agency and intercorporeality: On Goffman's *Relations in public*. *Sociology, 29*(1), 133–149.

Czyżewski, M. (1987). Erving Goffman on the individual: A reconstruction. *Polish Sociological Bulletin, 17*(3), 31–41.

Dahrendorf, R. (1973). *Homo sociologicus*. London: Routledge and Kegan Paul.

Damari, C. (2012). From Durkheim to Goffman: Collective consciousness and meta-frame. In A. Salvini, D. Altheide, & C. Nuti (Eds.), *The present and future of symbolic interactionism* (Vol. II), pp. 39–46. Milan: Franco Angeli/Sociologia.

David, P. (1980). The reluctant self-presentation of Erving Goffman. *The Times Higher Education Supplement*, September 19, p. 7.

Davis, M. S. (1971). That's interesting—Towards a phenomenology of sociology and a sociology of phenomenology. *Philosophy of the Social Sciences, 1*(4), 309–344.

Davis, M. S. (1975). Review of *Frame analysis*. *Contemporary Sociology, 4*(6), 599–603.

Davis, M. S. (1997). Georg Simmel and Erving Goffman: Legitimators of the socio-logical investigation of human experience. *Qualitative Sociology, 20*(3), 369–388.

Dawe, A. (1973). The underworld-view of Erving Goffman. *British Journal of Sociology, 24,* 246–253.

Dell, P., & Marinova, D. (2002). Erving Goffman and the Internet. *Theory of science (teorie vedy). Journal for Theory of Science, Technology and Communication, 4,* 85–98.

Denzin, N. K. (2002). Much ado about Goffman. *American Sociologist, 33*(2), 105–117.

Denzin, N. K., & Keller, C. (1981). *Frame analysis* reconsidered. *Contemporary Sociology, 10*(1), 52–60.

Dillard, C., Browning, L. D., Sitkin, S. B., & Sutcliffe, K. M. (2000). Impression management and the use of procedures at the Ritz-Carlton: Moral standards and dramaturgical discipline. *Communication Studies, 51*(4), 404–414.

Ditton, J. (Ed.). (1980). *The view from Goffman.* London: Macmillan.

Donnelly, C. M., & Wright, B. R. E. (2013). Goffman goes to church: Face-saving and the maintenance of collective order in religious ceremonies. *Sociological Research Online, 18*(1).

Drake, M. S. (2005). Erving Goffman's political sociology and the politics of disabled people's movement in the UK. In B. Haas (Ed.), *Macht—Performativität, Performanz und Polittheater seit 1990,* pp. 61–73. Würzberg: Königshausen und Neumann.

Drew, P., & Wootton, A. (Eds.). (1988a). *Erving Goffman—Exploring the interaction order.* Boston: Northeastern University Press.

Drew, P., & Wootton, A. (1988b). Introduction. In P. Drew & A. Wootton (Eds.), *Erving Goffman—Exploring the interaction order,* pp. 1–13. Boston: Northeastern University Press.

Durkheim, É. (1912/1943). *The elementary forms of religious life.* New York: Free Press.

Durkheim, É. (1982). *The rules of sociological method.* New York: Free Press.

Eco, U. (1984). *Semiotics and the philosophy of language.* London: Macmillan.

Edmondson, R. (1984). *Rhetoric in sociology.* London: Macmillan.

Elias, N. (1939/1994). *The civilizing process.* Oxford: Blackwell.

Eliasoph, N. (1990). Political culture and the presentation of a political self: A study of the public sphere in the spirit of Erving Goffman. *Theory and Society, 19,* 465–494.

Elkind, D. (1975). Encountering Erving Goffman. *Human Behavior, 4*(3), 25–30.

Elliot, A. (2001). *Concepts of the self.* Cambridge: Polity Press.

Entman, R. M. (1993). Framing: Toward clarification of a fractured paradigm. *Journal of Communication, 43*(4), 51–58.

Erwin, R. (1992). The nature of Goffman. *The Centennial Review, 36,* 327–342.

Ewing, D. W. (2002). Disability and feminism: Goffman revisited. *Journal of Social Work in Disability & Rehabilitation, 1*(2), 73–82.

Farrall, S., & Calverley, A. (2006). *Understanding desistance from crime: Theoretical directions in resettlement and rehabilitation*. Berkshire, UK. Open University Press.

Fine, G. A., (1984). Negotiated orders and organizational cultures. *Annual Review of Sociology, 10*, 239–262.

Fine, G. A., & Manning, P. (2003). Erving Goffman. In G. Ritzer (Ed.), *The Blackwell companion to major contemporary social theorists*. Oxford: Blackwell.

Fine, G. A., & Martin, D. D. (1990). Sarcasm, satire, and irony as voices in Erving Goffman's *Asylums*. *Journal of Contemporary Ethnography, 19*(1), 89–115.

Fine, G. A., & Martin, D. D. (1995). Humour in ethnographic writing: Sarcasm, satire, and irony as voices in Erving Goffman's *Asylums*. In J. van Maanen (Ed.), *Representation in ethnography*, pp. 185–197. London: Sage Publications.

Fine, G. A., & Smith, G. W. H. (Eds.). (2000). *Erving Goffman: A four-volume set* (Sage Masters in Modern Social Thought Series). London: Sage Publications.

Fontana, A. (1980). The mask and beyond: The enigmatic sociology of Erving Goffman. In J. D. Douglas (Ed.), *Introduction to the sociologies of everyday life*, pp. 62–81. Boston: Allyn and Bacon.

Ford, J. (1975). *Paradigms and fairy tales, volume 1–2*. London: Routledge and Kegan Paul.

Fosberg, H., & Vagli, Å. (2006). The social construction of emotions in child protection case-talk. *Qualitative Social Work, 5*(1), 9–31.

Foss, D. C. (1972). Self and the revolt against method. *Philosophy of the Social Sciences, 2*, 291–307.

Foucault, M. (1961/1973). *Madness and civilization: A history of insanity in an age of reason*. New York: Vintage Books.

Foucault, M. (1977). *Discipline and punish: The birth of the prison*. London: Penguin.

Franzese, R. J. (2009). *The sociology of deviance: Difference, tradition and stigma*. Springfield, IL: Charles C. Thomas Publishers.

Friedson, E. (1983). Celebrating Erving Goffman. *Contemporary Sociology, 12*(4), 359–362.

Frisby, D. (1981). *Sociological impressionism: A reassessment of the social theory of Georg Simmel*. London: Heinemann.

Gamson, W. A. (1985). Goffman's legacy to political sociology. *Theory and Society, 14*(5), 605–622.

Gardner, C. B. (1989). Analyzing gender in public places: Rethinking Goffman's vision of everyday life. *American Sociologist, 20*(1), 42–56.

Gardner, C. B., & Gronfein, W. P. (2005). Reflections on varieties of shame induction, shame management and shame avoidance in some works of Erving Goffman. *Symbolic Interaction, 28*(2), 175–182.

Garfinkel, H. (1956). Conditions of successful degradation ceremonies. *American Journal of Sociology, 61*(4), 420–424.

Garfinkel, H. (1967). *Studies in ethnomethodology.* Englewood Cliffs, NJ: Prentice-Hall.

Garfinkel, H. (2002). *Ethnomethodology's program: Working out Durkheim's aphorism* (edited by A. W. Rawls). Lanham, MD: Rowman and Littlefield Publishers.

Gellner, E. (1975). Ethnomethodology: The re-enchanted industry or the Californian way of subjectivity. *Philosophy of the Social Sciences, 5*(4), 431–450.

Gergen, K. J. (1991). *The saturated self: Dilemmas of identity in contemporary life.* New York: Basic Books.

Giddens, A. (1976). *New rules of sociological method.* London: Hutchinson University Library.

Giddens, A. (1984). *The constitution of society.* Cambridge: Polity Press.

Giddens, A. (1987). *Social theory and modern sociology.* Cambridge: Polity Press.

Giddens, A. (1988). Goffman as a systematic social theorist. In P. Drew & A. Wootton (Eds.), *Erving Goffman—Exploring the interaction order,* pp. 260–279. Boston: Northeastern University Press.

Giglioli, P. P. (1984). Una lettura durkheimiana di Goffman. *Rassegna italiana di sociologia, 3,* 401–427.

Gillespie, J. B. (1980). The phenomenon of the public wife: An exercise in Goffman's impression management. *Symbolic Interaction, 3*(2), 109–126.

Glaser, B. G., & Strauss, A. L. (1964). Awareness contexts and social interaction. *American Sociological Review, 29*(5), 669–679.

Glaser, B. G., & Strauss, A. L. (1965). *Awareness of dying.* Chicago: Aldine.

Glaser, B. G., & Strauss, A. L. (1967). *The discovery of grounded theory: Strategies for qualitative research.* Chicago: Aldine de Gruyter.

Goffman, E. (1949). *Some characteristics of response to depicted experience.* Unpublished master's thesis, University of Chicago.

Goffman, E. (1953a). *The service station dealer: The man and his work.* Chicago: Social Research Incorporation.

Goffman, E. (1953b). *Communication conduct in an island community.* Unpublished PhD thesis, University of Chicago.

Goffman, E. (1956). The nature of deference and demeanor. *American Anthropologist, 58*(3), 473–502.

Goffman, E. (1959). *The presentation of self in everyday life.* New York: The Overlook Press.

Goffman, E. (1961). *Asylums: Essays on the social situation of mental patients and other inmates.* Harmondsworth: Penguin Books.

Goffman, E. (1963). *Behavior in public places: Notes on the social organization of gatherings.* New York: Free Press.

Goffman, E. (1964). *Stigma: Notes on the management of spoiled identity.* Chicago: Aldine.

Goffman, E. (1967). *Interaction ritual: Essays on face-to-face behaviour.* New York: Anchor Books.

Goffman, E. (1969). *Strategic interaction.* Oxford: Basil Blackwell.

Goffman, E. (1971). *Relations in public: Microstudies of the public order.* New York: Basic Books.

Goffman, E. (1972). *Encounters: Two studies in the sociology of interaction.* Harmondsworth: Penguin Books.

Goffman, E. (1974). *Frame analysis: An essay on the organization of experience.* New York: Harper & Row.

Goffman, E. (1977a). The arrangement between the sexes. *Theory and Society, 4,* 301–331.

Goffman, E. (1977b). Genderisms: An admittedly malicious look at how advertising reinforces sexual role stereotypes. *Psychology Today, 11*(3), 60–63.

Goffman, E. (1977c). La ritualisation de la féminité. *Actes de la recherce en sciences sociales, 14,* 34–50.

Goffman, E. (1979). *Gender advertisements.* London: Macmillan.

Goffman, E. (1981a). *Forms of talk.* Oxford: Basil Blackwell.

Goffman, E. (1981b). Reply to Denzin and Keller. *Contemporary Sociology, 10*(1), 60–68.

Goffman, E. (1983a). The interaction order. *American Sociological Review, 48,* 1–17.

Goffman, E. (1983b). Felicity's condition. *American Journal of Sociology, 89,* 1–53.

Goffman, E. (1983c). Microsociologie et historie. In P. Fritsch (Ed.), *Le Sens de L'ordinaire.* Paris: Editions du Centre National de la Recherche Scientifique. pp. 197–202

Goffman, E. (1989). On fieldwork. *Journal of Contemporary Ethnography, 18*(2), 123–132.

Gonos, G. (1977). "Situation" versus "frame": The "interactionist" and "structuralist" analyses of everyday life. *American Sociological Review, 42,* 854–867.

Gonzales, P. B. (1993). Shame, peer and oscillating frames in DWI conviction: Extending Goffman's sociological landscape. *Symbolic Interaction, 16*(3), 257–271.

Gouldner, A. W. (1970). *The coming crisis of western sociology.* London: Heinemann.

Gregersen, B. (Ed.). (1975). *Om Goffman—11 artikler.* Copenhagen: Hans Reitzels Forlag.

Grimshaw, A. D. (1983). Erving Goffman: A personal appreciation. *Language in Society, 12*(1), 147–148.

Gusfield, J. R. (1995). Preface: A second Chicago school? In G. A. Fine (Ed.), *A second Chicago school?—The development of a postwar American sociology,* pp. ix–xvi. Chicago: University of Chicago Press.

Habermas, J. (1973/1997). *Legitimation crisis.* Cambridge: Polity Press.

Habermas, J. (1984). *The theory of communicative action vol. 1: Reason and the rationalization of society.* Boston: Beacon Press.

Hacking, I. (2004). Between Michel Foucault and Erving Goffman: Between discourse in the abstract and face-to-face interaction. *Economy and Society, 33*(3), 277–302.

Hall, J. A. (1977). Sincerity and politics: "Existentialists" vs. Goffman and Proust. *Sociological Review, 25*(3), 535–550.

Hancock, J. T., Toma, C., & Ellison, N. (2007). The truth about lying in online dating profiles. *CHI 2007 Proceedings,* April 28–May 3. Available at http://portal.acm.org/citation.cfm?id=1240624.1240697

Handler, R. (2009). Erving Goffman and the gestural dynamics of modern selfhood. *Past & Present, 203*(4), 280–300.

Handler, R. (2012). What's up, Doctor Goffman? Tell us where the action is! *Journal of the Royal Anthropological Institute* (New Series), *18,* 179–190.

Hannerz, U. (1980). The city as theater: Tales of Goffman. In U. Hannerz, *Exploring the city: Inquiries toward an urban anthropology.* New York: Columbia University Press.

Hare, P., & Blumberg, H. (1988). *Dramaturgical analysis of social interaction.* New York: Praeger.

Hargreaves, T. (2011). Pro-environmental interaction: Engaging Goffman on pro-environmental behaviour change. *CSERGE Working Paper,* 2011–04.

Hartland, N. G. (1994). Goffman's attitude and social analysis. *Human Studies, 17,* 251–266.

Hatch, J. A. (1987). Impression management in kindergarten classrooms: An analysis of children's face-work in peer interactions. *Anthropology & Education Quarterly, 18*(2), 100–115.

Hazelrigg, L. (1992). Reading Goffman's framing as provocation of a discipline. *Human Studies, 15,* 239–264.

Heath, C. (1988). Embarrassment and interactional organisation. In P. Drew & A. Wootton (Eds.), *Erving Goffman—Exploring the interaction order,* pp. 136–160. Boston: Northeastern University Press.

Heede, D. (1997). *Det tomme menneske: Introduktion til Michel Foucault* [*The empty man: An introduction to the works of Michel Foucault*]. Copenhagen: Museum Tusculanum Press.

Heilman, S. C. (1979). Communication and interaction: A parallel in the theoretical outlooks of Erving Goffman and Ray Birdwhistell. *Communication, 4*(2), 221–234.

Henslin, J. M., & Biggs, M. A. (1978). Dramaturgical desexualization: The sociology of vaginal examination. In J. M. Henslin & E. Sagarin (Eds.), *The sociology of sex: An introductory reader,* pp. 243–272. New York: Schoken Books.

Hettlage, R., & Karl L. (Eds.). (1991). *Erving Goffman: Ein soziologischer Klassiker der zweiten Generation.* Bern: Haupt.

Hillyard, S. (1999). Responding to text construction: Goffman's reflexive imagination. In A. Massey & G. Walford (Eds.), *Studies in educational ethnography: Explorations in methodology, volume 2,* pp. 57–71. Bingley: Emerald.

Hinshaw, S. P. (2007). *The mark of shame: Stigma of mental illness and agenda for change.* New York: Oxford University Press.

Hochschild, A. R. (1979). Emotion work, feeling rules, and social structure. *American Journal of Sociology, 85,* 551–575.

Hochschild, A. R. (1983). *The managed heart: Commercialization of human feeling.* Berkeley: University of California Press.

Hochschild, A. R. (1990). Gender codes in women's advice books. In S. H. Riggins (Ed.), *Beyond Goffman: Studies on communication, institution and social interaction,* pp. 277–294. Berlin: Mouton de Gruyter.

Hollis, M. (1977). *Models of man: Philosophical thoughts on social action.* Cambridge: Cambridge University Press.

Holstein, J. A., & Gubrium, Jaber F. (2000). *The self we live by: Narrative identity in a postmodern world.* New York: Oxford University Press.

Hopper, M. (1981). Five key concepts of the dramaturgical perspective. *Free Inquiry in Creative Sociology, 9*(1), 47–52.

Hughes, E. C. (1969). Review of Erving Goffman: *Interaction ritual. American Journal of Sociology, 75*(3), 425–426.

Hymes, D. (1984). On Erving Goffman. *Theory and Society, 13,* 621–631.

Isaac, J. (Ed.). (1989). *Le parler frais d'Erving Goffman.* Paris: Éditions de Minuit.

Isaac, J. (2002). *Erving Goffman et al microsociologie* (2nd ed.). Paris: PUF.

Jacobsen, M. H. (Ed.). (2008). *Encountering the everyday—An introduction to the sociologies of the unnoticed.* London: Palgrave/Macmillan.

Jacobsen, M. H. (Ed.). (2010a). *The contemporary Goffman.* London: Routledge.

Jacobsen, M. H. (2010b). Recognition as ritualized reciprocation—The interaction order as a realm of recognition. In M. H. Jacobsen (Ed.), *The contemporary Goffman,* pp. 199–231. London: Routledge.

Jacobsen, M. H. (2014). Den metaforiske fantasi—Kreativ rekontekstualisering og rekonstruktion i kvalitativ metode. In J. E. Møller, S. Bengtsen, & K. P. Munk (Eds.), *Metodefetichisme—Kvalitativ metode på afveje?* Aarhus: Aarhus University Press (forthcoming).

Jacobsen, M. H., Antoft, R., & Jørgensen, A. (2013). Chicago vice and virtue—The poetic imagination meets the sociological imagination. In M. H. Jacobsen, M. S. Drake, K. Keohane, & A. Petersen (Eds.), *Imaginative methodologies in the social sciences—Creativity, poetics and rhetorics in social research,* pp. 23–54. Farnham: Ashgate.

Jacobsen, M. H., & Kristiansen, S. (2002). *Erving Goffman—Sociologien om det elementære livs sociale former.* Copenhagen: Hans Reitzels Forlag.

Jacobsen, M. H., & Kristiansen, S. (2006). Goffmans metaforer—Om den genbeskrivende og rekontekstualiserende metode hos Erving Goffman. *Sosiologi i dag, 36*(1), 5–33.

Jacobsen, M. H., & Kristiansen, S. (2009). Micro-recognition—Erving Goffman as recognition thinker. *Sosiologisk Årbok/Yearbook of Sociology, 14*(3–4), 47–76.

Jacobsen, M. H., & Kristiansen, S. (2010). Labelling Erving Goffman—The presentation and appropriation of Erving Goffman in sociology. In M. H. Jacobsen   (Ed.), *The contemporary Goffman,* pp. 64–97. London: Routledge.

Jacobsen, M. H., & Kristiansen, S. (2012). Micro-social interaction and everyday life. In G. C. Aakvaag, M. H. Jacobsen, & T. Johansson (Eds.), *Introduction to sociology: Scandinavian sensibilities,* pp. 238–255. London: Pearson Education.

James, W. (1950). *Principles of psychology, volume 2.* New York: Dover.

Jameson, F. (1976). On Goffman's frame analysis. *Theory and Society, 3*(1), 119–133.

Jaworski, G. D. (2000). Erving Goffman: The reluctant apprentice. *Symbolic Interaction, 23*(3), 299–308.

Jenkins, R. (2008). Erving Goffman: A major theorist of power? *Journal of Power, 2*(2), 157–168.

Jenkins, R. (2010). The 21st-century interaction order. In M. H. Jacobsen (Ed.), *The contemporary Goffman*, pp. 257–274. London: Routledge.

Jensen, O. B. (2006). "Facework," flow and the city: Simmel, Goffman and mobility in the contemporary city. *Mobilities, 1*(2), 143–165.

Jensen, O. B. (2010). Erving Goffman and everyday life mobility. In M. H. Jacobsen (Ed.), *The contemporary Goffman*, pp. 333–351. London: Routledge.

Johansson, C. (2007). Goffman's sociology: An inspiring source for developing public relations theory. *Public Relations Review, 33*(3), 275–280.

Jørgensen, A., & Smith, D. (2008). The Chicago school of sociology: Survival in the urban jungle. In M. H. Jacobsen (Ed.), *Encountering the everyday—An introduction to the sociologies of the unnoticed*, pp. 45–68. London: Palgrave/ Macmillan.

Kalekin-Fishman, D. (1988). Games, rituals and theater: Elements in Goffman's grammar of social action. *Sociologia Internationalis, 26*(2), 133–146.

Kang, M. E. (1997). The portrayal of women's images in magazine advertisements: Goffman's gender analysis revisited. *Sex Roles, 37*(11–12), 979–996.

Katz, I. (1982). *Stigma: A social psychological analysis.* New York: Lawrence Erlbaum.

Kendon, A. (1988). Goffman's approach to face-to-face interaction. In P. Drew & A. Wootton (Eds.), *Erving Goffman—Exploring the interaction order*, pp. 14–40. Boston: Northeastern University Press.

Kim, K. (2002). *Order and agency in modernity: Talcott Parsons, Erving Goffman and Harold Garfinkel.* New York: State University of New York Press.

Kjørup, S. (1985). *Forskning og samfund [Research and society].* Copenhagen: Gyldendal.

Knorr-Cetina, K. (1981). The micro-sociological challenge of macro-sociology: Towards a reconstruction of social theory and methodology. In K. Knorr-Cetina & A. V. Cicourel (Eds.), *Advances in social theory and methodology: Toward an integration of micro- and macrosociologies*, pp. 1–47. London: Routledge and Kegan Paul.

Kristiansen, S. (2000). *Kreativ sociologi—Om Erving Goffmans sociologiske teori og metode [Creative sociology—On the sociological method and theory of Erving Goffman].* Unpublished PhD thesis, Department of Social Relations and Organisation, Aalborg University.

Kristiansen, S. (2002). Det kvalitative continuum: om data og teoriudvikling i kvalitativ sociologi. In M. H. Jacobsen, S. Kristiansen, & A. Prieur (Eds.), *Liv, fortælling, tekst—Strejftog i kvalitativ sociologi*, pp. 315–340. Aalborg: Aalborg Universitetsforlag.

Kuzmics, H. (1991). Embarrassment and civilization: On some similarities and differences in the work of Goffman and Elias. *Theory, Culture & Society, 8,* 1–30.

Langman, L. (1992). Alienation and everyday life: Goffman meets Marx at the shopping mall. In F. Geyer & W. Heinz (Eds.), *Alienation, society and the individual: Continuity and change in theory and research*, pp. 107–124. New Brunswick, NJ: Transaction.

Lanigan, R. L. (1988). Is Erving Goffman a phenomenologist? *Critical Studies in Mass Communication, 5,* 335–345.

Larsen, J. (2010). Goffman and the tourist gaze: A performative perspective on tourism mobilities. In M. H. Jacobsen (Ed.), *The contemporary Goffman*, pp. 313–332. London: Routledge.

Laursen, E. (1997). Selvet mellem personlighed og rolle [Self between personality and role]. Unpublished paper, Department of Sociology and Social Work, Aalborg University.

Layder, D. (1998). *Sociological practice: Linking theory and social research.* London: Sage Publications.

Ledger, M. (1982). The observer. *Pennsylvania Gazette,* February 28, pp. 36–42.

Leeds-Hurwitz, W. (1986). *Erving Goffman and the concept of social order.* Paper presented at the conference Erving Goffman: An Interdisciplinary Appreciation, University of York, July 8–11.

Lemert, C. (1997). Goffman. In C. Lemert & A. Branaman (Eds.), *The Goffman reader*, pp. ix–xliii. New York: Blackwell.

Lemert, C., & A. Branaman (Eds.). (1997). *The Goffman reader.* New York: Blackwell.

Lindgren, G. (1994). Fenomenologi i praktikken. In B. Starrin & P. Svensson (Eds.), *Kvalitativ metod och vetenskabsteori*, pp. 91–110. Lund: Studentlitteratur.

Ling, R. (2010). The "unboothed" phone: Goffman and the use of mobile communication. In M. H. Jacobsen (Ed.), *The contemporary Goffman*, pp. 257–274. London: Routledge.

Link, B. G., & Phelan, J. C. (2001). Conceptualizing stigma. *Annual Review of Sociology, 27,* 363–385.

Littlejohn, S. W. (1977). Review essay: Frame analysis and communication. *Communication Research, 4,* 485–492.

Lofland, J. (1984). Erving Goffman's sociological legacies. *Urban Life, 13*(1), 7–34.

Lofland, L. H. (1995). Social interaction: Continuities and complexities in the study of nonintimate sociality. In K. Cook, G. A. Fine, & J. S. House (Eds.), *Sociological perspectives on social psychology*, pp. 176–201. Needham Heights, MA: Allyn & Bacon.

Luckmann, T. (1985). On Goffman's last work. *Semiotica, 53,* 175–178.

Luhmann, N. (1973/1979). *Trust and power.* Chichester, UK: John Wiley and Sons.

Luhmann, N. (1984/1995). *Social systems.* Stanford, CA: Stanford University Press.

Lyman, S. M. (1973). Civilization: Contents, discontents, malcontents. *Contemporary Sociology, 2,* 360–366.

Lyman, S. M., & Scott, M. B. (1970). *A sociology of the absurd*. New York: Appleton-Century-Crofts.

Lyman, S. M., & Scott, M. B. (1975). *The drama of social reality*. New York: Oxford University Press.

Lyotard, J.-F. (1984). *The postmodern condition: A report on knowledge*. Manchester, UK: Manchester University Press.

Lysgaard, S. (1976). *Arbeiderkollektivet: En studie i de underordnedes sosiologi [The worker collectivity: A sociology of subordinates]*. Oslo: Oslo University Press.

MacCannell, D. (1990). The descent of the ego. In S. H. Riggins (Ed.), *Beyond Goffman: Studies on communication, institution, and social interaction*, pp. 19–40. New York: Mouton de Gruyter.

MacIntyre, A. (1969). The self as a work of art. *New Statesman*, March 28, 447–448.

Mali, J. (2008). Comparison of the characteristics of homes for older people in Slovenia with Goffman's concept of the total institution. *European Journal of Social Work, 11*(4), 431–443.

Manning, P. K. (1976). The decline of civility: A comment on Erving Goffman's sociology. *Canadian Review of Sociology and Anthropology, 13*(1), 13–25.

Manning, P. K. (1980). Goffman's framing order: Style as structure. In J. Ditton (Ed.), *The view from Goffman*, pp. 252–284. London: Macmillan.

Manning, P. K. (2008). Goffman on organizations. *Organization Studies, 29*(5), 677–699.

Manning, P. K., & Hawkins, K. (1990). Legal decisions: A frame analytic perspective. In S. H. Riggins (Ed.), *Beyond Goffman: Studies on communication, institution and social interaction*, pp. 203–234. New York: Mouton de Gruyter.

Manning, P. (1991). Drama as life: The significance of Goffman's changing use of the theatrical metaphor. *Sociological Theory, 9*(1), 70–86.

Manning, P. (1992). *Erving Goffman and modern sociology*. Stanford, CA: Stanford University Press.

Manning, P. (2005). Reinvigorating the tradition of symbolic interactionism. *Symbolic Interaction, 28*(2), 167–173.

Markowitz, F. E. (1998). The effects of stigma on the psychological well-being and life satisfaction of persons with mental illness. *Journal of Health and Social Behavior, 39*, 335–347.

Marx, G. T. (1984). Role models and role distance: A remembrance of Erving Goffman. *Theory and Society, 13*, 649–662.

Marx, G. T. (2004). Some concepts that may be useful in understanding the myriad forms and contexts of surveillance. *Intelligence and National Security, 19*(2), 226–248.

Mathiesen, T. (1965). *The defences of the weak: A sociological study of a Norwegian correctional institution*. London: Tavistock.

Matthews, F. H. (1977). *Quest for an American sociology: Robert E. Park and the Chicago school*. Montreal: McGill University Press.

Matza, D. (1969). *Becoming deviant*. Englewood Cliffs, NJ: Prentice-Hall.

McDonald, G., Higgins, J., & Shuker, M. J. (2008). Addressing the baseline: Erving Goffman and the ethics in a postgraduate degree for practising teachers. *Teaching in Higher Education, 13*(2), 233–244.

McGregor, G. (1986). A view from the fort: Erving Goffman as Canadian. *Canadian Review of Sociology and Anthropology, 23*(4), 531–543.

McGregor, G. (1995). *Gender advertisements* then and now: Goffman, symbolic interactionism and the problem of history. *Studies in Symbolic Interaction, 17*, 3–42.

McHugh, P. (1968). *Defining the situation: The organization of meaning in social interaction.* Indianapolis, IN: Bobbs-Merrill.

Mead, G. H. (1934/1967). *Mind, self and society.* Chicago: University of Chicago Press.

Messinger, S. L., et al. (1962). Life as theater: Notes on the dramaturgic approach to social reality. *Sociometry, 25*(1), 98–110.

Meyrowitz, J. (1990). Redefining the situation: Extending dramaturgy into a theory of social change and media effects. In S. H. Riggins (Ed.), *Beyond Goffman: Studies on communication, institution and social interaction*, pp. 65–98. New York: Mouton de Gruyter.

Millen, N., & Walker, C. (2002). Overcoming the stigma of chronic illness: Strategies for normalisation of a "spoiled identity." *Health Sociology Review, 10*, 89–97.

Miller, H. (1995). *The presentation of self in electronic life.* Paper presented at a conference on Embodied Knowledge and Virtual Space, at Goldsmith's College, June 1995.

Miller, T. G. (1986). Goffman, positivism and the self. *Philosophy of the Social Sciences, 16*(2), 177–196.

Mills, C. W. (1959). *The sociological imagination.* New York: Oxford University Press.

Morris, M. B. (1977). *An excursion into creative sociology.* Oxford: Blackwell.

Mortensen, N. (2000). Det moderne individs paradokser [The paradoxes of the modern self]. *Distinktion, 1*, 91–104.

Mullins, N. (1973). *Theories and theory groups in contemporary American sociology.* New York: Harper and Row.

Münch, R. (1986). The American creed in sociological theory: Exchange, negotiated order, accommodated individualism, and contingency. *Sociological Theory,* 4: 41–60.

Musil, R. (1953/1995). *The man without qualities, volume I.* London: Minerva.

Nahavandi, F. (1979). *Introduction à la sociologie d'Erving Goffman.* Brussels: Editions de l'université.

Neale, J., Nettleton, S., & Pickering, L. (2011). Recovery from problem drug use: What can we learn from the sociologist Erving Goffman? *Drugs: Education, Prevention and Policy, 18*(1), 3–9.

Nelson, K. B. (2009). Enhancing the attendee's experience through creative design of the event environment: Applying Goffman's dramaturgical perspective. *Journal of Convention & Event Tourism, 10*(2), 120–133.

Neri, G. S. (2002). *Goffman oltre Goffman: Ulteriori sviluppi del modelle drammaturgico*. Rome: Bibliosofica.

Nisbet, R. A. (1970). *The social bond: An introduction to the study of society*. New York: Alfred A. Knopf.

Nisbet, R. (1976/2002). *Sociology as an art form*. New Brunswick: Transaction Books.

Nizet, J., & Rigaux, N. (2005). *La Sociologie de Erving Goffman*. Paris: Éditions La Découverte.

Nunberg, G. (1981). The theatricality of everyday life. *New York Times Book Review*, May 10.

O'Mealy, J. H. (2013). *Alan Bennett: A critical introduction*. London: Routledge.

O'Neill, J. (1981). A preface to *Frame analysis*. *Human Studies, 4*, 359–364.

Oommen, T. K. (1990). Erving Goffman and the study of everyday protest. In S. H. Riggins (Ed.), *Beyond Goffman: Studies on communication, institution and social interaction*, pp. 389–408. New York: Mouton de Gruyter.

Oromaner, M. (1980). Erving Goffman and the academic community. *Philosophy of the Social Sciences, 10*, 287–291.

Park, G. (1990). Making sense of religion by direct observation: An application of frame analysis. In S. H. Riggins (Ed.), *Beyond Goffman: Studies on communication, institution and social interaction*, pp. 235–276. New York: Mouton de Gruyter.

Parsons, T., & Bales, R. F. (1955). *Family socialization and interaction processes*. New York: Routledge.

Partington, M., & Cushion, C. J. (2012). Performance during performance: Using Goffman to understand the behaviours of elite youth football coaches during games. *Sports Coaching Review, 1*(2), 93–105.

Paxton, M. (2004). Gone fishin': A framing analysis of the fight over a small town's city seal. *Journal of Media and Religion, 3*(1), 43–55.

Peirce, C. S. (1979). *Collected papers*. Cambridge, MA: University of Harvard Press.

Peräkylä, A. (1988). Four frames of death in modern hospital. In A. Gilmore & S. Gilmore (Eds.), *A safer death: Multidisciplinary aspects of terminal care*, pp. 41–51. New York: Plenum Press.

Perry, N. (2000). The two cultures of the total institution. In G. A. Fine & G. W. H. Smith (Eds.), *Erving Goffman: A four-volume set*, Vol. III, pp. 173–183 (Sage Masters in Modern Social Thought Series). London: Sage Publications.

Persson, A. (2012). *Ritualisering och sårbarhety—Ansikte mot ansikte med Goffmans perspektiv på social interaction*. Malmö: Liber.

Petrunik, M. (1980). The rise and fall of "labelling theory": The construction and destruction of a sociological strawman. *Canadian Journal of Sociology, 5*(3), 213–233.

Pettit, M. (2011). The con man as model organism: The methodological roots of Erving Goffman's dramaturgical self. *History of the Human Sciences, 24*(2), 138–154.

Philips, A. (2010). On Erving Goffman. *The Threepenny Review*, Fall 2010. Available at http://www.threepennyreview.com/samples/phillips_f10.html

Phillips, J. (1983). Goffman's linguistic turn: A comment on *Forms of talk*. *Theory, Culture & Society, 2*(1), 114–116.

Pinch, T. (2010). The invisible technologies of Goffman's sociology: From the merry-go-round to the Internet. *Technology and Culture, 51*(2), 409–424.

Platt, J. (1995). Research methods and the second Chicago school. In G. A. Fine (Ed.), *A second Chicago school?—The development of a postwar American sociology*, pp. 82–107. Chicago: University of Chicago Press.

Posner, J. (1978). Erving Goffman: His presentation of self. *Philosophy of the Social Sciences, 8*, 67–78.

Psathas, G. (1996). Theoretical perspectives on Goffman: Critique and commentary. *Sociological Perspectives, 39*(3), 383–391.

Puriola, A.-M. (2002). The multiple faces of everyday life: Frame analysis of early childhood practices. *European Early Childhood Education Research Journal, 10*(2), 31–47.

Raab, J. (2008). *Erving Goffman: Klassiker der Wissenssoziologie*. Konstanz: UVK Verlagsgesellschaft.

Rasmussen, S. A. (1975). Stigma [Stima]. In B. Gregersen (Ed.), *Om Goffman—11 artikler* [*On Goffman—11 articles*], pp. 92–102. Copenhagen: Hans Reitzels Forlag.

Rawls, A. W. (1984). Interaction as a resource for epistemological critique. *Sociological Theory, 2*, 222–252.

Rawls, A. W. (1987). The interaction order *sui generis:* Goffman's contribution to social theory. *Theoretical Sociology, 5*, 136–149.

Renfrow, D. G. (2004). A cartography of passing in everyday life. *Symbolic Interaction, 27*(4), 485–506.

Rettie, R. M. (2009). Mobile telephone communication: Extending Goffman to mediated interaction. *Sociology, 43*(3), 421–438.

Richard, M. P. (1986). Goffman revisited: Relatives vs. administrators in nursing homes. *Qualitative Sociology, 9*(4), 321–338.

Richardson, L. (1990). *Writing strategies*. Newbury Park, CA: Sage Publications.

Riesman, D., Glazer, N., & Denney, R. (1953/2001). *The lonely crowd: A study of the changing American character*. New Haven, CT: Yale University Press.

Riggins, S. H. (Ed.). (1990). *Beyond Goffman: Studies on communication, institution and social interaction*. Berlin: Mouton de Gruyter.

Rigney, D. (2001). *The metaphorical society: An invitation to social theory*. Lanham, MD: Rowman and Littlefield Publishers.

Ritsher, J. B., & Phelan, J. C. (2004). Internalized stigma predicts erosion of morale among psychiatric outpatients. *Psychiatry Research, 129*, 257–265.

Ritzer, G. (1992). *Sociological theory* (3rd ed.). New York: McGraw-Hill.

Rogoff, B., & Lave, J. (Eds.). (1984). *Everyday cognition: Its development in social contexts*. Cambridge, MA: Harvard University Press.

Rosch, E. (1978). Principles of categorization. In E. Rosch & B. B. Lloyd (Eds.), *Cognition and categorization*, pp. 27–48. Hillsdale, NJ: Lawrence Erlbaum Associates.

Rosenfeld, S. (1997). Labeling mental illness: The effects of services and perceived stigma on life satisfaction. *American Sociological Review, 62*, 660–672.

Ross, D. A. R. (2007). Backstage with the knowledge boys and girls: Goffman and distributed agency in an organic online community. *Organization Studies, 28*(3), 307–325.

Rutledge, S. E., Abell, N., Padmore, J., & McCann, T. J. (2008). AIDS stigma in health services in the eastern Caribbean. *Sociology of Health and Illness, 31*, 17–34.

Ryle, G. (1949). *The concept of mind.* Chicago: University of Chicago Press.

Sannicolas, N. (1997). *Erving Goffman, dramaturgy, and on-line relationships.* Available at www.members.aol.com/Cybersoc.

Sarbin, T. R. (2003). The dramaturgical approach to social psychology: The influence of Erving Goffman. In R. J. Sternberg (Ed.), *The anatomy of impact—What makes the great works of social psychology great*, pp. 125–136. Washington, DC: American Psychological Association.

Sarmicanic, L. (2004). Goffman, pets and people: An analysis of humans and their companion animals. *ReVision, 27*(2), 42–47.

Scambler, G. (2006). Jigsaws, models and the sociology of stigma. *Journal of Critical Realism, 5*(2), 273–289.

Scheff, T. J. (1990). *Microsociology: Discourse, emotion and social structure.* Chicago: University of Chicago Press.

Scheff, T. J. (2003). The Goffman legacy—Deconstructing/reconstructing social science. In A. J. Treviño (Ed.), *Goffman's legacy*, pp. 50–70. New York: Rowman and Littlefield.

Scheff, T. J. (2005). Looking-glass self: Goffman as symbolic interactionist. *Symbolic Interaction, 28*, 147–166.

Scheff, T. J. (2006). *Goffman unbound!—A new paradigm for social science.* Boulder, CO: Paradigm Publishers.

Scheff, T. J. (2010). A new Goffman: Robert W. Fuller's politics of dignity. In M. H. Jacobsen (Ed.), *The contemporary Goffman*, pp. 185–198. London: Routledge.

Scheibe, K. E. (2002). *The drama of everyday life.* Cambridge, MA: Harvard University Press.

Schimmelfennig, F. (2002). Goffman meets IR: Dramaturgical action in international community. *International Review of Sociology, 12*(3), 417–437.

Schutz, A. (1945). On multiple realities. *Philosophy and Phenomenological Research, 5*(4), 533–576.

Schutz, A. (1970). Concept and theory formation in the social sciences. In D. Emmet & A. MacIntyre (Eds.), *Sociological theory and philosophical analysis*, pp. 1–19. New York: Macmillan.

Schwalbe, M. L. (1993). Goffman against postmodernism: Emotion and the reality of the self. *Symbolic Interaction, 16*(4), 333–350.

Schwartz, H., & Jacobs, J. (1979). *Qualitative methods: A method to the madness.* New York: Free Press.

Shalin, D. N. (2010). Erving Goffman's self-ethnographies: Interfacing biography, theory and history. Available at http://doingmodernity.blogspot.dk/2012/04/goffmans-self-ethnographies-by-dmitri.html

Sharrock, W. (1999). The omnipotence of the actor: Erving Goffman and "the definition of the situation." In G. Smith (Ed.), *Goffman and social organization: Studies in a sociological legacy*, pp. 119–137. London: Routledge.

Sharron, A. (2000). Frame paralysis: When time stands still. In G. A. Fine & G. W. H. Smith (Eds.), *Erving Goffman: A four-volume set*, Vol. III, pp. 212–238 (Sage Masters in Modern Social Thought Series). London: Sage Publications.

Sijuwade, P. O. (1995). Counterfeit intimacy: A dramaturgical analysis of an erotic performance. *Social Behavior and Personality, 23*(4), 369–376.

Simmel, G. (1909). The problem of sociology. *American Journal of Sociology, 15*(3), 289–320.

Simmel, G. (1971). The problem of sociology. In *Georg Simmel: On individuality and social forms* (selected writings edited and translated by D. N. Levine), pp. 23–35. Chicago: University of Chicago Press.

Simmel, G. (1992). *Soziologie: Untersuchungen über die Formen der Vergesellschaftung* (Gesamtausgab, Vol. II). Frankfurt am Main: Suhrkamp.

Simmel, G. (1998). *Hvordan er samfundet muligt? [How is society possible?]* Copenhagen: Gyldendal.

Smith, G. (1988). The sociology of Erving Goffman. *Social Studies Review, 3*, 118–122.

Smith, G. (Ed.). (1999a). *Goffman and social organization: Studies of a sociological legacy.* London: Routledge.

Smith, G. (1999b). Introduction: Interpreting Goffman's sociological legacy. In G. Smith (Ed.), *Goffman and social organization: Studies in a sociological legacy*, pp. 1–18. London: Routledge.

Smith, G. (2003). Chrysalid Goffman: A note on "Some Characteristics of Response to Depicted Experience." *Symbolic Interaction, 26*(4), 645–658.

Smith, G. (2006). *Erving Goffman.* London: Taylor and Francis.

Smith, G. (2010). Reconsidering *Gender advertisements:* Performativity, framing and display. In M. H. Jacobsen (Ed.), *The contemporary Goffman*, pp. 165–184. London: Routledge.

Smith, G., & Jacobsen, M. H. (2010). Goffman's textuality—Literary sensibilities and sociological rhetorics. In M. H. Jacobsen (Ed.), *The contemporary Goffman*, pp. 119–146. London: Routledge.

Snell, P. (2010). From Durkheim to the Chicago school: Against the "variables sociology" paradigm. *Journal of Classical Sociology, 10*(1), 51–67.

Stein, M. (1991). Sociology and the prosaic. *Sociological Inquiry, 61*(4), 421–433.

Strong, P. M. (1983). The importance of being Erving. *Sociology of Health and Illness, 5*(3), 345–355.

Stubbs, M. (1983). Dimensions of sociolinguistics. *Language in Society, 12*, 77–82.

Summers-Effler, E. (2007). Ritual theory. In J. E. Stets & J. H. Turner (Eds.), *Handbook of the sociology of emotions*, pp. 135–154. New York: Springer.

Sylvest, N. (1975). Interaktionsregler. In B. Gregersen (Ed.), *Om Goffman—11 artikler*, pp. 123–141. Copenhagen: Hans Reitzels Forlag.

Tannen, D. (1979). What's in a frame? Surface evidence for underlying expectations. In R. O. Freedle (Ed.), *New directions in discourse processing*, pp. 14–56. Norwood, NJ: Ablex.

Thomas, W. I. (1923). *The unadjusted girl*. Boston: Little, Brown.

Time Magazine. (1969). Exploring a shadow world. *Time Magazine*, January 10, 50–51.

Tiryakian, E. A. (1962). *Sociologism and existentialism—Two perspectives on the individual and society*. Englewood Cliffs, NJ: Prentice-Hall.

Treviño, A. J., (Ed.). (2003a). *Goffman's legacy*. New York: Rowman and Littlefield.

Treviño, A. J., (2003b). Erving Goffman and the interaction order. In A. J. Treviño (Ed.), *Goffman's legacy*, pp. 1–49. New York: Rowman and Littlefield.

Tseëlon, E. (1992a). Is the presented self sincere? *Theory, Culture & Society, 9*(2), 115–128.

Tseëlon, E. (1992b). Self presentation through appearance: A manipulative vs. a dramaturgical approach. *Symbolic Interaction, 15*(4), 501–513.

Turner, J. H. (2002). *Face to face: Toward a sociological theory of interpersonal behavior*. Stanford, CA: Stanford University Press.

Turner, R. E., & Edgley, C. (1976). Death as theater: A dramaturgical analysis of the American funeral. *Sociology and Social Research, 60*(4), 377–392.

Turner, R. (2010). Remembering Erving Goffman. Available at http://cdclv.unlv .edu/archives/interactionism/goffman/turner_roy_10.html

van Krieken, R. (1998). *Norbert Elias*. London: Routledge.

Verhoeven, J. C. (1993). An Interview with Erving Goffman, 1980. *Research on Language and Social Interaction, 26*(3), 317–348.

Waksler, F. C. (1989). Erving Goffman's sociology: An introductory essay. *Human Studies, 12*, 1–18.

Waksler, F., & Psathas, G. (1989). Selected books and articles about Erving Goffman and of related interest. *Human Studies, 12*, 177–181.

Wallace, R. A., & Wolf, A. (1999). *Contemporary sociological theory: Expanding the classical tradition*. Englewood-Cliffs, CA: Prentice Hall.

Wanenchak, S. (2010). Tags, threads and frames: Toward a synthesis of interaction ritual and Livejournal roleplaying. *Game Studies, 10*(1). Available at http:// gamestudies.org/1001/articles/wanenchak.

Watson, R. (1983). Goffman, talk and interaction: Some modulated responses. *Theory, Culture & Society, 2*(1), 103–108.

Weber, M. (1972). Georg Simmel as sociologist. *Social Research, 39*, 155–163.

Wedel, J. M. (1978). Ladies, we've been framed! Observations on Erving Goffman's *The arrangement between the sexes. Theory & Society, 5*(1), 113–125.

Weigert, A. J. (1981). *Sociology of everyday life*. London: Longman.

Weigert, A. J. (2003). Terrorism, identity and public order: A perspective from Goffman. *Identity: An International Journal of Theory and Research, 3*(2), 93–113.

West, C., & Zimmerman, D. (1987). Doing gender. *Gender and Society*, 1(2), 121–151.

Wexler, M. N. (1984). The enigma of Goffman's sociology. *Quarterly Journal of Ideology*, 8, 40–50.

White, R., & Hanson, D. (2002). Corporate self, corporate reputation and corporate annual reports: Re-enrolling Goffman. *Scandinavian Journal of Management*, 18, 285–301.

Wiley, N. (1979). The rise and fall of dominating theories in American sociology. In W. Snizek et al. (Eds.), *Contemporary issues in theory and research*, pp. 49–79. Westport, CT: Greenwood Press.

Williams, P., & Weninger, C. (2012). Applying Goffman's assumptions to a new media environment. In A. Salvini, D. Altheide, & C. Nuti (Eds.), *The present and future of symbolic interactionism* (volume II), pp. 47–60. Milan: Franco Angeli/Sociologia.

Williams, R. (1983). Sociological tropes: A tribute to Erving Goffman. *Theory, Culture & Society*, 2, 99–102.

Williams, R. (1988). Understanding Goffman's methods. In P. Drew & A. Wootton (Eds.), *Erving Goffman—Exploring the interaction order*, pp. 64–88. Boston: Northeastern University Press.

Williams, R. (1998). Erving Goffman. In R. Stones (Ed.), *Key sociological thinkers*. New York: New York University Press.

Williams, S. J. (2000). Goffman, interactionism, and the management of stigma in everyday life. In G. A. Fine & G. W. H. Smith (Eds.), *Erving Goffman: A four-volume set* (Sage Masters in Modern Social Thought Series). London: Sage Publications.

Winkin, Y. (1983). The French (re)presentation of Goffman's presentation and other books. *Theory, Culture & Society*, 2(1), 109–111.

Winkin, Y. (1988). *Erving Goffman: Les moments et leurs hommes*. Paris: Seuil.

Winkin, Y. (1999). Erving Goffman: What a life?—The uneasy making of an intellectual biography. In G. Smith (Ed.), *Goffman and social organization: Studies in a sociological legacy*, pp. 19–41. London: Routledge.

Winkin, Y. (2000). Baltasound as the symbolic capital of social interaction. In G. A. Fine & G. W. H. Smith (Eds.), *Erving Goffman: A four-volume set* (Sage Masters in Modern Social Thought Series), Vol. I, pp. 193–212. London: Sage Publications.

Winkin, Y. (2010). Goffman's greenings. In M. H. Jacobsen (Ed.), *The contemporary Goffman*, pp. 51–63. London: Routledge.

Winkin, Y., & Leeds-Hurwitz, W. (2013). *Erving Goffman—A critical introduction to media and communication theory*. New York: Peter Lang.

Young, T. R. (1971). The politics of sociology: Gouldner, Goffman and Garfinkel. *American Sociologist*, 6(4), 276–281.

Ytreberg, E. (2002). Erving Goffman as the theorist of mass media. *Critical Studies in Media Studies*, 19(4), 481–497.

Ytreberg, E. (2010). The question of calculation: Erving Goffman and the pervasive planning of communication. In M. H. Jacobsen (Ed.), *The contemporary Goffman*, pp. 293–312. London: Routledge.

Zeitlin, I. M. (1973). The social psychology of Erving Goffman. In I. M. Zeitlin, *Rethinking sociology: A critique of contemporary theory*, pp. 191–214. New York: Appleton-Century-Crofts.

Zussman, R. (2001). Review: Still lonely after all these years. *Sociological Forum*, 16(1), 157–166.

Ølgaard, B. (1975). Når mennesker mødes [Human encounters]. In B. Gregersen (Ed.), *Om Goffman—11 artikler [On Goffman—11 Articles]*, pp. 42–65. Copenhagen: Hans Reitzels Forlag.

Østerberg, D. (1993). *Fortolkende sociologi, volume 1: Almene emner ogmetodologi.* Oslo: Universitetsforlaget.

Index

About the Authors

Michael Hviid Jacobsen (born 1971) is a professor of sociology at Aalborg University, Denmark. He has published many titles as author or editor, including *The Transformation of Modernity* (Ashgate, 2001), *Erving Goffman* (Hans Reitzels Forlag, 2002), *The Sociology of Zygmunt Bauman* (Ashgate 2008), *Public Sociology* (Aalborg University Press, 2009), *Encountering the Everyday* (Palgrave/Macmillan, 2009), *The Contemporary Goffman* (Routledge, 2010), *Utopia: Social Theory and the Future* (Ashgate, 2013), *Imaginative Methodologies in the Social Sciences* (Ashgate, 2013), *Deconstructing Death* (University Press of Southern Denmark, 2013), and *The Poetics of Crime* (Ashgate, 2014).

Søren Kristiansen (born 1971) is a professor of sociology at Aalborg University, Denmark. He has, as author or editor, published several titles on the work of Erving Goffman, including *Kreativ sociologi* (Aalborg University, 2000), *Erving Goffman* (Hans Reitzels Forlag, 2002), and *Mikrosociologi og social samhandling* (Hans Reitzels Forlag, 2004) and numerous articles in Danish and international journals. In recent years, he has turned his attention toward the sociology of gambling.

ⓈSAGE research**methods**

The essential online tool for researchers from the world's leading methods publisher

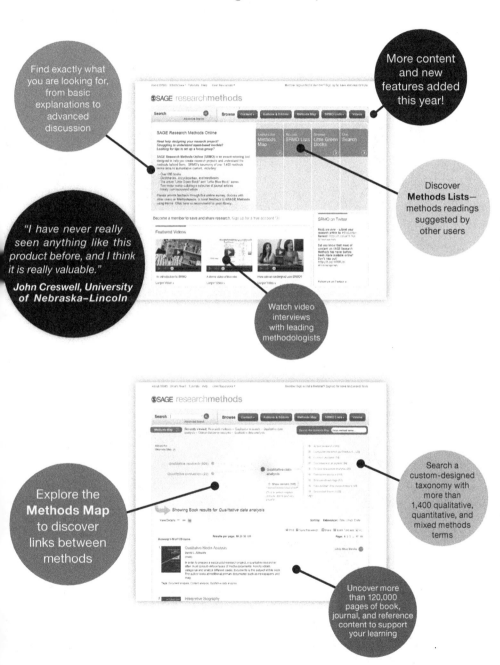

Find exactly what you are looking for, from basic explanations to advanced discussion

More content and new features added this year!

"I have never really seen anything like this product before, and I think it is really valuable."
John Creswell, University of Nebraska–Lincoln

Discover **Methods Lists**— methods readings suggested by other users

Watch video interviews with leading methodologists

Explore the **Methods Map** to discover links between methods

Search a custom-designed taxonomy with more than 1,400 qualitative, quantitative, and mixed methods terms

Uncover more than 120,000 pages of book, journal, and reference content to support your learning

Find out more at
www.sageresearchmethods.com